REAL ESTATE
SALES EXAM

REAL ESTATE SALES EXAM

2nd Edition

LearningExpress®

NEW YORK

Library of Congress Cataloging-in-Publication Data:
Real estate sales exam—2nd ed.
  p. cm
  ISBN-13: 978-1-57685-599-7
1. Real estate agents—Licenses—United States—Examinations, questions, etc.
2. Real estate business—Licenses—United States—Examinations, questions, etc.
3. Real property—United States—Examinations, questions, etc.
I. LearningExpress (Organization)
HD278.R433 2007
333.33076—dc22

                                     2007017106

Printed in the United States of America

9 8 7 6 5 4 3 2 1

Second Edition

For more information or to place an order, contact LearningExpress at:
  55 Broadway
  8th Floor
  New York, NY 10006

Or visit us at:
  www.learnatest.com

Contents

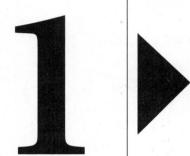

The Real Estate Sales Exam

CHAPTER SUMMARY

Congratulations! You are about to take a step that could mark your entrance to an exciting new career—real estate. This chapter provides an overview of the four major national exams, as well as how this book can help you succeed on whatever exam you take!

F YOU ARE planning to take a real estate licensing exam, this book can help you to get a top score on your exam. It will show you how to put all the pieces of test preparation together. Not only that, this book includes four complete practice exams covering the topics from most real estate sales exams. It also has a real estate math review, a real estate glossary, and a CD-ROM to practice for your exam on the computer!

▶ Your Upcoming Real Estate Exam

In most states, you will be required to pass an exam to become licensed as a real estate salesperson. However, the specific exam you will be required to take depends on the state in which you want to become licensed. If you aren't sure which real estate exam you need to take, contact the real estate commission in the state in which you wish to be licensed for detailed information on specific licensing requirements.

Some states, such as California, administer their own examination for prospective real estate licensees. Other states use the services of an independent testing company. Here are four of the most commonly used independent testing companies, along with their contact information.

Applied Measurement Professionals (AMP), Inc.
8310 Neiman Road
Lenexa, KS 66214-1579
800-345-6559 or 913-541-0400
www.goamp.com

Promissor, Inc. (a Pearson VUE business)
3 Bala Plaza West, Suite 300
Bala Cynwood, PA 19004-3481
610-617-9300
www.promissor.com

Thomson Prometric (formerly Experior)
Canton Crossing
1501 South Clinton Street
Baltimore, MD 21224
866-PROMETRIC (776-6387)
443-455-8000
www.prometric.com
Note: Type "real estate exam" in the Advanced Search
    and click **GO**.

Psychological Services, Inc. (PSI)
3210 East Tropicana
Las Vegas, NV 89121
800-733-9267
www.psiexams.com

The real estate exams used by these independent testing companies to examine prospective real estate professionals are in a multiple-choice question format and are often administered on the computer. Here's a sample list of the typical topics and *approximate* number of multiple-choice questions in each topic for the real estate written exams administered by these four testing companies. Keep in mind that some states vary the total number of questions asked in each topic, and will also have state-specific questions added to the national exam for use in their state. For example, in Texas, an additional 30 questions that relate specifically to Texas laws and rules are included on the real estate licensing exam administered by PSI.

AMP

Topics	Number of Questions
Listing Property	34
Selling Property	22
Property Management	12
Settlement/Transfer of Ownership	17
Financing	12
Professional Responsibilities/Fair Practice/Administration	3
Total Questions	**104**

Note: At least 10% of the questions on this exam will require the use of mathematics.

Thomson Prometric

Topics	Number of Questions
Business Practices and Ethics	17
Agency and Listing	12
Property Characteristics, Descriptions, Ownership, Interests, and Restrictions	14
Property Valuation and the Appraisal Process	5
Real Estate Sales Contracts	14
Financing Sources	8
Property Management	4
Closing/Settlement and Transferring Title	6
Total Questions	**80**

Promissor

Topics	Number of Questions
Real Property Characteristics, Definitions, Ownership, Restrictions, and Transfer	16
Property Valuation and the Appraisal Process	12
Contracts/Agency Relationships with Buyers and Sellers	20
Financing the Transaction and Settlement	20
Leases, Rents, and Property Management	12
Total Questions	**75**

Note: Approximately 10% of the questions on this exam will require the use of mathematics.

PSI

Topics	Number of Questions
Property Ownership	7
Land Use Controls and Regulations	7
Valuation and Market Analysis	7
Financing	8
Laws of Agency	10
Mandated Disclosures	6
Contracts	10
Transfer of Property	7
Practice of Real Estate	10
Real Estate Calculations	5
Specialty Areas	3
Total Questions	**78**

Regardless of whether you take a state-administered real estate exam or one administered by AMP, Thomson Prometric, Promissor, or PSI, you will need to know the same basic real estate information. That is why this book can help you no matter which state you want to become licensed in. The topics on the practice exams in this book reflect most of the same topics on different national exams. The study skills, glossary, and math review also contain invaluable information regardless of which exam you take. In this book, the practice exams will have the following topics and number of questions.

LearningExpress Real Estate Sales Exams

Topics	Number of Questions
Financing	13
Settlement/Transfer of Property	13
Property Management	13
Property Valuations/Appraisal	13
Property Characteristics	13
Business Practices	12
Contracts/Agency Relationships	13
Mathematics	10
Total Questions	**100**

About Licensing Requirements and Exams

By now, you have realized that different states use different exams. However, even if two states use the same testing company, the exams may cover different topics, cost different amounts, or have different passing scores. You should check out your state's education and application procedures. Usually, the most accurate and up-to-date information is available through your state's licensing agency. That is why it is essential to contact your state's real estate licensing department or commission before your exam. For your convenience, here's a list of the contact information for each state's real estate licensing agency.

At the time of publication, the following information was correct. Please understand that websites or other contact information may have changed.

State Licensing Agencies

ALABAMA
Real Estate Commission
1201 Carmichael Way
Montgomery, AL 36106
334-242-5544
www.arec.state.al.us

ALASKA
Real Estate Commission
Robert B. Atwood Building
550 West 7th Avenue, Suite 1500
Anchorage, AK 99501
907-269-8162
www.dced.state.ak.us/occ/prec.htm

ARIZONA
Department of Real Estate
2910 North 44th Street, Suite 100
Phoenix, AZ 85018
602-468-1414
www.re.state.az.us

ARKANSAS
Real Estate Commission
612 South Summit Street
Little Rock, AR 772201-4740
501-683-8010
www.state.ar.us/arec/arecweb.html

CALIFORNIA
Department of Real Estate
2201 Broadway
Sacramento, CA 95818-2500
916-227-0931
www.dre.cahwnet.gov

COLORADO
Department of Regulatory Agencies
Division of Real Estate
1560 Broadway, Suite 925
Denver, CO 80202
303-894-2166
www.dora.state.co.us/Real-Estate

CONNECTICUT
The Connecticut Licensing Center
Real Estate Division
165 Capital Avenue, Room 110
Hartford, CT 06106
860-713-6150
www.ct-clic.com

DELAWARE
Real Estate Commission
Cannon Building
861 Silver Lake Boulevard, Suite 203
Dover, DE 19904-2467
302-739-4522, ext. 219
www.dpr.delaware.gov

FLORIDA
Department of Business and Professional Regulation
1940 North Monroe Street
Tallahassee, FL 32399
850-487-1395
www.MyFloridaLicense.com

GEORGIA
Real Estate Commission
229 Peachtree Street NE
International Tower, Suite 1000
Atlanta, GA 30303-1605
404-656-3916
www.grec.state.ga.us

HAWAII
Real Estate Commission
King Kalahaua Building
335 Merchant Street, Room 333
Honolulu, HI 96813
P.O. Box 3469
Honolulu, HI 96801
808-586-2643
www.state.hi.us/hirec

IDAHO
Real Estate Commission
633 North Fourth Street
P.O. Box 83720
Boise, ID 83720-0077
208-334-3285
www.idahorealestatecommission.com

ILLINOIS
Department of Financial and Professional Regulation
Attention: Real Estate Division
500 East Monroe, Suite 200
Springfield, IL 62701
217-782-3414
www.idfpr.com/DPR/RE/realmain.asp

INDIANA
Professional Licensing Agency
Attention: Real Estate Commission
402 West Washington Street, Room WO72
Indianapolis, IN 46204
317-234-3009
www.in.gov/pla/bandc/estate

IOWA
Professional Licensing and Regulation Division
Real Estate Division
1918 SE Hulsizer Avenue
Ankeny, IA 50021
515-281-7393
www.state.ia.us/government/com/prof/sales/home.htm

KANSAS
Real Estate Commission
Three Townsite Plaza
120 SE Sixth Avenue, Suite 200
Topeka, KS 66603-3511
785-296-3411
www.ink.org/public/krec

KENTUCKY
Real Estate Commission
10200 Linn Station Road, Suite 201
Louisville, KY 40223
502-429-7250 or 888-373-3300
www.krec.ky.gov

LOUISIANA
Real Estate Commission
P.O. Box 14785
Baton Rouge, LA 70898-4785
800-821-4529, in state 255-765-0191
www.lrec.state.la.us

MAINE
Department of Professional and Financial Regulation
Office of Licensing and Registration
35 State House Station
Augusta, ME 04333
207-624-8521
www.state.me.us/pfr.olr

MARYLAND
Real Estate Commission
500 North Calvert Street
Baltimore, MD 21202-3651
410-230-6200
www.dllr.state.md.us/license/occprof/recomm.html

MASSACHUSETTS
Real Estate Board
239 Causeway Street, Suite 500
Boston, MA 02114
617-727-2373
www.mass.gov/dpl/boards/re/index.htm

MICHIGAN
Department of Commerce
BOPR–Office of Commercial Services
P.O. Box 30243
Lansing, MI 48909
517-241-1781 or 517-241-9233
www.michigan.gov/cis

MINNESOTA
Department of Commerce
85 Seventh Place East
St. Paul, MN 55101
651-296-6319
www.commerce.state.mn.us

MISSISSIPPI
Real Estate Commission
2506 Lakeland Drive, Suite 300
Flowood, MS 39232
P.O. Box 12685
Jackson, MS 39236-2685
601-932-9191
www.mrec.state.ms.us

MISSOURI
Real Estate Commission
3605 Missouri Boulevard
P.O. Box 1339
Jefferson City, MO 65102-1339
573-751-2628
http://pr.mo.gov/realestate.asp

MONTANA
Board of Realty Regulation
301 South Park Avenue, Fourth Floor
P.O. Box 200513
Helena, MT 59620-0513
406-444-2961
www.realestate.mt.gov

NEBRASKA
Real Estate Commission
1200 N Street, Suite 402
Lincoln, NE 68505
P.O. Box 94667
Lincoln, NE 68509-4667
402-471-2004
www.nrec.state.ne.us

NEVADA
Nevada Department of Business and Industry
Real Estate Division
788 Fairview Drive, Suite 200
Carson City, NV 89701-5453
775-687-4280
www.red.state.nv.us

NEW HAMPSHIRE
Real Estate Commission
State House Annex, Fourth Floor
25 Capital Street
Concord, NH 03301
603-271-2701
www.nh.gov/nhrec.license.html

NEW JERSEY
Real Estate Commission
20 West State Street
Trenton, NJ 08625
P.O. Box 328
Trenton, NJ 08625-0328
609-292-8300
www.nj.gov/dobi/remnu.shtml

NEW MEXICO
Real Estate Commission
5200 Oakland Avenue NE, Suite B
Albuquerque, NM 87113
505-222-9810 or 800-801-7505
http://rld.state.nm.us/b&c.recom/index.htm

NEW YORK
Department of State
Division of Licensing Services
P.O. Box 22001
Albany, NY 12201-2001
Alfred E. Smith Building
80 South Swan Street, Tenth Floor
Albany, NY 12201
518-474-2651
www.dos.state.ny.us/lcns/realest.html

NORTH CAROLINA
Real Estate Commission
1313 Navaho Drive
P.O. Box 17100
Raleigh, NC 27619-7100
919-875-3700
www.ncrec.state.nc.us

NORTH DAKOTA
Real Estate Commission
200 East Main Avenue, Suite 204
Bismark, ND 58502-0727
701-328-9749
www.governor.state.nd.us/boards

OHIO
Department of Commerce
Division of Real Estate and Professional Licensing
77 South High Street, 20th Floor
Columbus, OH 43215-6133
614-466-4100
www.com.state.oh.us/real

OKLAHOMA
Real Estate Commission
Shepherd Mall
2401 NW 23rd Street, Suite 18
Oklahoma City, OK 73107
405-521-3387 or 866-521-3389
www.orec.ok.gov

OREGON
Real Estate Agency
1177 Center Street NE
Salem, OR 97301-2505
503-378-4170
www.rea.state.or.us

PENNSYLVANIA
Real Estate Commission
P.O. Box 2649
Harrisburg, PA 17105-2649
717-783-3658
www.dos.state.pa.us/estate

RHODE ISLAND
Department of Business Regulation
Division of Commercial Licensing and Regulation
Real Estate
233 Richmond Street, Suite 230
Providence, RI 02903-4230
401-222-2255
www.dbr.state.ri.us

SOUTH CAROLINA
Department of Labor Licensing and Regulation
Real Estate Commission
Synergy Business Park
Kingstree Building
110 Centerview Drive, Suite 201
Columbia, SC 29210
P.O. Box 11847
Columbia, SC 29211-1847
803-896-4400
www.llr.state.sc.us/POL/RealEstateCommission

SOUTH DAKOTA
Real Estate Commission
221 West Capitol, Suite 101
Pierre, SD 57501
605-773-3600
www.state.sd.us/dcr/realestate

TENNESSEE
Real Estate Commission
500 James Robertson Parkway
Volunteer Plaza, Suite 180
Nashville, TN 37243-1151
800-342-4031
www.state.tn.us/commerce/boards/trec

TEXAS
Real Estate Commission
1101 Camino La Costa
Austin, TX 78752
P.O. Box 12188
Austin, TX 78711-2188
512-459-6544 or 800-250-TREC (8732)
www.trec.state.tx.us

UTAH
Division of Real Estate
Heber M. Wells Building
160 East 300 South, Second Floor
Salt Lake City, UT 84111
P.O. Box 146711
Salt Lake City, UT 84114-6711
801-530-6747
www.commerce.utah.bov/dre

VERMONT
Real Estate Commission
81 River Street
Montpelier, VT 05609-1106
802-828-3228
http://professionals.org/opr1/real_estate

VIRGINIA
Department of Professional and
    Occupational Regulation
3600 West Broad Street
Richmond, VA 23230-4917
804-367-8526
www.dpor.virginia.gov/dporweb/reb_main.cfm

WASHINGTON
Department of Licensing
Real Estate Program
P.O. Box 9048
Olympia, WA 98507-9048
360-664-6488 or 360-664-6500
www.dol.wa.gov/business/realestate

WEST VIRGINIA
Real Estate Commission
300 Capitol Street, Suite 400
Charleston, WV 25301
304-558-3555
www.wvrec.org

WISCONSIN

Bureau of Direct Licensing and Real Estate

Department of Regulation and Licensing

1400 East Washington Avenue, Room 112

P.O. Box 8935

Madison, WI 53708-8935

608-266-2112

http://drl.wi.gov

WYOMING

Real Estate Commission

2020 Carey Avenue, Suite 702

Cheyenne, WY 82002-0180

307-777-7141

http://realestate.state.wy.us

▶ The Right Questions

Once you've found your state's agency, it's important to know the right questions to ask. To find out everything you need to know about your exam, use the following checklist of questions.

- Which exam is given in my state?
- What are the topics covered on this exam?
- How many questions are there?
- What are the state-specific real estate topics covered on this exam?
- Is the exam multiple choice?
- Is the exam handwritten, or is it given on the computer?
- How do I register?
- How much does the exam cost?
- How long will the exam take to complete?
- Can I use a calculator on the exam?
- If I can use a calculator, what kind of calculators are permitted?
- Where is the exam given?
- What day is the exam given?
- Can I reschedule my exam?
- What time is the exam?
- What do I have to bring to the exam?
- What is not allowed at the test centers?
- If the exam is given on the computer, will I be allowed to practice on a computer before the exam begins?
- How is the exam scored?
- What is the passing score?
- Are there separate passing scores for different parts of the exam?
- When will I receive my score report?
- What happens if I do not pass the exam?
- Can I retake my exam?
- If I have special needs, how do I arrange for them?

▶ How This Book Can Help You

The process of preparing for a real estate exam does not have to be an overwhelming task. This book guides you through several manageable steps. The first step is to finish this chapter. Then, move on to Chapter 2, which explains how to set up an individualized study plan and presents specific study strategies you can use during your study sessions. You will find the steps to take in order to maximize your chances for scoring high on your exam. You will also find when to take sample exams so you can check your scores and still have enough time to focus on the areas in which you need more work. In addition, you will increase your understanding and retention of the real estate material you are studying by using many different study strategies, not just one or two.

While you are reading Chapter 2, take the time to create an individualized study plan that will fit your needs and schedule. This is a crucial step in the test-preparation process. After you finish reading Chapter 2, spend some time using each different study strategy explained in that chapter.

Chapter 3 contains the first of four practice exams. You should take this practice exam before you begin studying. That way, you will be able to find your strengths and weaknesses, and you will be able to focus your studying on exactly the topics that are giving you the most trouble.

After you finish your first practice exam, you will find a real estate refresher course. This review covers several real estate topics that will be on a real estate sales exam. Because you already know which topics on the first exam gave you trouble, you can focus on those topics.

After the real estate refresher course comes the real estate math review. This contains a basic review of arithmetic, algebra, geometry, and word problems. It also covers the types of real estate calculations you will face on a real estate sales exam.

Need help with real estate terms? Chapter 6 has a real estate glossary with the most commonly tested and used real estate terms. This glossary will help you prepare for not only your exam, but also your career.

Once you have reviewed the course, the math, and the glossary, it's time for more practice exams. There are three more practice exams in this book. After every exam, you should review topics that still give you the most trouble and study accordingly. For more study tips, start reading Chapter 2.

The LearningExpress Test Preparation System

CHAPTER SUMMARY

Taking the real estate sales exam can be tough. It demands a lot of preparation if you want to achieve a top score. Your career depends on your passing the exam. The LearningExpress Test Preparation System, developed exclusively for LearningExpress by leading test experts, gives you the discipline and attitude you need to be a winner.

FACT: TAKING A real estate licensing exam is not easy, and neither is getting ready for it. Your future career as a real estate salesperson depends on your getting a passing score, but all sorts of pitfalls can keep you from doing your best on this exam. Here are some of the obstacles that can stand in the way of your success:

- being unfamiliar with the format of the exam
- being paralyzed by test anxiety
- leaving your preparation to the last minute
- not preparing at all!
- not knowing vital test-taking skills: how to pace yourself through the exam, how to use the process of elimination, and when to guess
- not being in tip-top mental and physical shape
- arriving late at the test site, having to work on an empty stomach, or being uncomfortable during the exam because the room is too hot or cold

What's the common denominator in all these test-taking pitfalls? One word: control. Who's in control, you or the exam?

Here's some good news: The LearningExpress Test Preparation System puts you in control. In nine easy-to-follow steps, you will learn everything you need to know to make sure that you are in charge of your preparation and your performance on the exam. Other test takers may let the test get the better of them or may be unprepared or out of shape, but not you. You will have taken all the steps you need to take to get a high score on your real estate licensing exam.

Here's how the LearningExpress Test Preparation System works: Nine easy steps lead you through everything you need to know and do to get ready to master your exam. Each of the steps includes both reading about the step and one or more activities. It's important that you do the activities along with the reading, or you won't be getting the full benefit of the system. Each step tells you approximately how much time that step will take you to complete.

Step 1: Get Information	50 minutes
Step 2: Conquer Test Anxiety	20 minutes
Step 3: Make a Plan	30 minutes
Step 4: Learn to Manage Your Time	10 minutes
Step 5: Learn to Use the Process of Elimination	20 minutes
Step 6: Know When to Guess	20 minutes
Step 7: Reach Your Peak Performance Zone	10 minutes
Step 8: Get Your Act Together	10 minutes
Step 9: Do It!	10 minutes
Total	**3 hours**

We estimate that working through the entire system will take you approximately three hours, although it's perfectly okay if you work faster or slower. If you take an afternoon or evening, you can work through the whole LearningExpress Test Preparation System in one sitting. Otherwise, you can break it up and do just one or two steps a day for the next several days. It's up to you—remember, you are in control.

▶ Step 1: Get Information

Time to complete: 50 minutes
Activity: Read Chapter 1, "The Real Estate Sales Exam"

Knowledge is power. The first step in the LearningExpress Test Preparation System is finding out everything you can about the real estate sales exam given in your state. Once you have your information, the other steps in the LearningExpress Test Preparation System will show you what to do about it.

Part A: Straight Talk about the Real Estate Sales Exam

Why do you have to take this exam, anyway? You have already been through your pre-license course; why should you have to go through a rigorous exam? It's simply an attempt on the part of your state to be sure you have the knowledge and skills necessary for a licensed real estate agent. Every profession that requires practitioners to exercise financial and fiduciary responsibility to clients also requires practitioners to be licensed—and licensure requires an exam. Real estate is no exception.

It's important for you to remember that your score on the real estate sales exam does not determine how smart you are or even whether you will make a good real estate agent. There are all kinds of things an exam like this can't test: whether you have the drive and determination to be a top salesperson, whether you will faithfully exercise your responsibilities to your clients, whether you can be trusted with confidential information about people's finances, etc. Those kinds of things are hard to evaluate, while a computer-based test is easy to evaluate.

This is not to say that the exam is not important! The knowledge tested on the exam is knowledge you will need to do your job. And your ability to enter the profession you've trained for depends on your passing this exam. And that's why you are here—using the LearningExpress Test Preparation System to achieve control over the exam.

Part B: What's on the Test

If you haven't already done so, stop here and read Chapter 1 of this book, which gives you an overview of the four major exams. Then, go online and read the most up-to-date information about your state's exam directly from the test developers.

▶ Step 2: Conquer Test Anxiety

Time to complete: 20 minutes
Activity: Take the Test Stress Quiz

Having complete information about the exam is the first step in getting control of the exam. Next, you have to overcome one of the biggest obstacles to test success: test anxiety. Test anxiety not only impairs your performance on the exam itself, but also keeps you from preparing! In Step 2, you will learn stress management techniques that will help you succeed on your exam. Learn these strategies now, and practice them as you work through the exams in this book, so they will be second nature to you by exam day.

Combating Test Anxiety

The first thing you need to know is that a little test anxiety is a good thing. Everyone gets nervous before a big exam—and if that nervousness motivates you to prepare thoroughly, so much the better. Many actors, actresses, and musicians feel anxious before their performances. Their stage fright doesn't impair their performances; in fact, it probably gives them a little extra edge—just the kind of edge you need to do well, whether on a stage or in an examination room.

Above is the Test Stress Quiz. Stop and answer the questions to find out whether your level of test anxiety is something you should worry about.

Stress Management before the Test

If you feel your level of anxiety getting the best of you in the weeks before the test, here is what you need to do to bring the level down again:

- **Get prepared.** There's nothing like knowing what to expect and being prepared for it to put you in control of test anxiety. That's why you are reading this book. Use it faithfully, and remind yourself that you are better prepared than most of the people taking the test.

- **Practice self-confidence.** A positive attitude is a great way to combat test anxiety. This is no time to be humble or shy. Stand in front of the mirror and say to your reflection, "I am prepared. I am full of self-confidence. I am going to ace this test. I know I can do it." Say it into a tape recorder and play it back once a day. If you hear it often enough, you will believe it.

- **Fight negative messages.** Every time someone starts telling you how hard the exam is or how it's almost impossible to get a high score, start saying your self-confidence messages. Don't listen to the negative messages. Turn on your tape recorder and listen to your self-confidence messages.
- **Visualize.** Imagine yourself reporting for duty on your first day as a real estate salesperson. Think of yourself talking with clients, showing homes, and best of all, making your first sale. Visualizing success can help make it happen—and it reminds you of why you are going to all this work in preparing for the exam.
- **Exercise.** Physical activity helps calm your body down and focus your mind. Besides, being in good physical shape can actually help you do well on the exam. Go for a run, lift weights, go swimming—and do it regularly.

Stress Management on Test Day

There are several ways you can bring down your level of test anxiety on test day. They will work best if you practice them in the weeks before the test, so you know which ones work best for you.

- **Deep breathing.** Take a deep breath while you count to five. Hold it for a count of one, and then let it out for a count of five. Repeat several times.
- **Move your body.** Try rolling your head in a circle. Rotate your shoulders. Shake your hands from the wrist. Many people find these movements very relaxing.
- **Visualize again.** Think of the place where you are most relaxed: lying on the beach in the sun, walking through the park, or whatever. Now close your eyes and imagine you are actually there. If you practice in advance, you will find that you need only a few seconds of this exercise to experience a significant increase in your sense of well-being.

When anxiety threatens to overwhelm you right there during the exam, there are still things you can do to manage the stress level:

- **Repeat your self-confidence messages.** You should have them memorized by now. Say them silently to yourself, and believe them!
- **Visualize one more time.** This time, visualize yourself moving smoothly and quickly through the test, answering every question right and finishing just before time is up. Like most visualization techniques, this one works best if you have practiced it ahead of time.
- **Find an easy question.** Find an easy question, and answer it. Getting even one question finished gets you into the test-taking groove.
- **Take a mental break.** Everyone loses concentration once in a while during a long test. It's normal, so you shouldn't worry about it. Instead, accept what has happened. Say to yourself, "Hey, I lost it there for a minute. My brain is taking a break." Put down your pencil, close your eyes, and do some deep breathing for a few seconds. Then you will be ready to go back to work.

Try these techniques ahead of time, and determine which ones work best for you!

▶ Step 3: Make a Plan

Time to complete: 30 minutes
Activity: Construct a study plan

Maybe the most important things you can do to get control of yourself and your exam is to make a study plan. Too many people fail to prepare simply because they fail to plan. Spending hours on the day before the exam poring over sample test questions raises your level of test anxiety and is simply no substitute for careful preparation and practice over time.

Don't fall into the cram trap. Take control of your preparation time by mapping out a study schedule. On the following pages are two sample schedules, based on the amount of time you have before you take the real estate sales exam. If you are the kind of person who needs deadlines and assignments to motivate you for a project, here they are. If you are the kind of person who doesn't like to follow other people's plans, you can use the suggested schedules here to construct your own.

Even more important than making a plan is making a commitment. You can't review everything you learned in your real estate courses in one night. You have to set aside some time every day for study and practice. Try for at least 20 minutes a day. Twenty minutes daily will do you much more good than two hours once a week.

Don't put off your study until the day before the exam. Start now. A few minutes a day, with half an hour or more on weekends, can make a big difference in your score.

Schedule A: The 30-Day Plan

If you have at least a month before you take the real estate sales exam, you have plenty of time to prepare—as long as you don't waste it! If you have less than a month, turn to Schedule B.

Time	Preparation
Days 1–4	Skim over the written materials from your training program, particularly noting areas you expect to be emphasized on the exam and areas you don't remember well. On Day 4, concentrate on those areas.
Day 5	Take the first practice practice exam in Chapter 3.
Day 6	Score the first practice exam. Use the "Exam 1 for Review" on page 54 to see which topics you need to review most. Identify two areas that you will concentrate on before you take the second practice exam.
Days 7–10	Study the two areas you identified as your weak points. Don't forget, there is the real estate refresher course in Chapter 4, the real estate math review in Chapter 5, and the real estate glossary in Chapter 6. Use these chapters to improve your score on the next practice test.
Day 11	Take your second practice exam.
Day 12	Score the second practice exam. Identify one area to concentrate on if you want take a third practice exam different from the one you're studying for.
Days 13–18	Study the one area you identified for review. Again, use the refresher course, math review, and glossary for help.
Day 19	Take the third practice exam. in Chapter 8.
Day 20–21	Once again, identify one area to review, based on your score on the third practice exam. Study the one area you identified for review. Use the refresher course, math review, and glossary for help.
Days 22–25	Take an overview of all your training materials, consolidating your strengths and improving on your weaknesses.
Days 26–27	Review all the areas that have given you the most trouble in the three practice exams you have taken so far.
Day 28	Take the fourth practice exam in Chapter 9. Note how much you have improved!
Day 29	Review one or two weak areas by studying the refresher course, math review, and glossary.
Day before the exam	Relax. Do something unrelated to the exam and go to bed at a reasonable hour.

Schedule B: The Ten-Day Plan

If you have two weeks or less before you take the exam, use this ten-day schedule to help you make the most of your time.

Time	Preparation
Day 1	Take your first practice exam in Chapter 3 and score it using the answer key at the end of the chapter. Use the "Exam 1 for Review" on page 54 to see which topics you need to review most.
Day 2	Review one area that gave you trouble on the first practice exam. Use the real estate refresher course in Chapter 4, the real estate math review in Chapter 5, and the real estate glossary in Chapter 6 for extra practice in these areas.
Day 3	Review another area that gave you trouble on the first practice exam. Again, use the refresher course, math review, and glossary for extra practice.
Day 4	Take the second practice exam in Chapter 7 and score it.
Day 5	If your score on the second practice exam doesn't show improvement on the two areas you studied, review them. If you did improve in those areas, choose a new weak area to study today.
Day 6	Take the third practice exam in Chapter 8 and score it.
Day 7	Choose your weakest area from the third practice exam to review. Use the refresher course, math review, and glossary for extra practice.
Day 8	Review any areas that you have not yet reviewed in this schedule.
Day 9	Take a fourth practice exam in Chapter 9 and score it.
Day 10	Use your last study day to brush up on any areas that are still giving you trouble. Use the refresher course, math review, and glossary.
Day before the exam	Relax. Do something unrelated to the exam and go to bed at a reasonable hour.

▶ Step 4: Learn to Manage Your Time

Time to complete: 10 minutes to read, many hours of practice!
Activity: Practice these strategies as you take the sample tests in this book

Steps 4, 5, and 6 of the LearningExpress Test Preparation System put you in charge of your exam by showing you test-taking strategies that work. Practice these strategies as you take the sample tests in this book, and then you will be ready to use them on test day.

First, you will take control of your time on the exam. It's a terrible feeling to find that there are five minutes left when you are only three-quarters of the way through the test. Here are some tips to keep that from happening to *you*.

- **Follow directions.** Some real estate sales exams are given on the computer. If a tutorial is offered before the exam, you should take your time going through the tutorial before the exam. Read the directions carefully and ask questions before the exam begins if there's anything you don't understand.
- **Pace yourself.** If there is a timer on the screen as you take the exam, keep an eye on it. This will help you pace yourself. For example, when one-quarter of the time has elapsed, you should be one-quarter of the way through the test. If you are falling behind, pick up the pace a bit. If you do not take your exam on a computer, use your watch or the clock in the testing room to keep track of the time you have left.
- **Keep moving.** Don't waste time on one question. If you don't know the answer, skip the question and move on. You can always go back to it later.
- **Don't rush.** Though you should keep moving, rushing won't help. Try to keep calm and work methodically and quickly.

▶ Step 5: Learn to Use the Process of Elimination

Time to complete: 20 minutes
Activity: Complete the Using the Process of Elimination worksheet

After time management, your next most important tool for taking control of your exam is using the process of elimination wisely. It's standard test-taking wisdom that you should always read all the answer choices before choosing your answer. This helps you find the right answer by eliminating wrong answer choices. Sure enough, that standard wisdom applies to your exam, too.

Let's say you are facing a question that goes like this:

Alicia died, leaving her residence in town and a separate parcel of undeveloped rural land to her brother Brian and her sister Carrie, with Brian owning one-quarter interest and Carrie owning three-quarters interest. How do Brian and Carrie hold title?
  a. as tenants in survivorship
  b. as tenants in common
  c. as joint tenants
  d. as tenants by the entirety

You should always use the process of elimination on a question like this, even if the correct answer jumps out at you. Sometimes, the answer that jumps out isn't correct after all. Let's assume, for the purpose of this exercise, that you are a little rusty on property ownership terminology, so you need to use a little intuition to make up for what you don't remember. Proceed through the answer choices in order.

So you start with choice **a**. This one is pretty easy to eliminate; this tenancy doesn't have to do with survivorship. Because the real estate sales exam is given on a computer, you won't be able to cross out answer choices; instead, make a mental note that choice **a** is incorrect.

Choice **b** seems reasonable; it's a kind of ownership that two people can share. Even if you don't remember much about tenancy in common, you could tell it's about having something "in common." Make a mental note, "Good answer. I might use this one."

Choice **c** is also a possibility. Joint tenants also share something in common. If you happen to remember that joint tenancy always involves equal ownership rights, you mentally eliminate this choice. If you don't, make a mental note, "Good answer" or "Well, maybe," depending on how attractive this answer looks to you.

Choice **d** strikes you as a little less likely. Tenancy by the entirety doesn't necessarily have to do with two people sharing ownership. This doesn't sound right, and you have already got a better answer picked out in choice **b**. If you are feeling sure of yourself, you can mentally eliminate this choice.

If you're pressed for time, you should choose choice **b**. If you have the time to be extra careful, you could compare your answer choices again. Then, choose one and move on.

If you are taking a test on paper, like the practice exams in this book, it's good to have a system for marking good, bad, and maybe answers. We're recommending this one:

X = bad
✓ = good
? = maybe

If you don't like these marks, devise your own system. Just make sure you do it long before test day—while you're working through the practice exams in this book—so you won't have to worry about it during the exam.

Even when you think you are absolutely clueless about a question, you can often use the process of elimination to get rid of one answer choice. If so, you are better prepared to make an educated guess, as you will see in Step 6. More often, the process of elimination allows you to get down to only two possibly right answers. Then you are in a strong position to guess. And sometimes, even though you don't know the right answer, you find it simply by getting rid of the wrong ones, as you did in the previous example.

Try using your powers of elimination on the questions in the following worksheet, Using the Process of Elimination. The questions aren't about real estate work; they're just designed to show you how the process of elimination works. The answer explanations for this worksheet show one possible way you might use the process to arrive at the correct answer.

The process of elimination is your tool for the next step, which is knowing when to guess.

Use the process of elimination to answer the following questions.

1. Ilsa is as old as Meghan will be in five years. The difference between Ed's age and Meghan's age is twice the difference between Ilsa's age and Meghan's age. Ed is 29. How old is Ilsa?
   a. 4
   b. 10
   c. 19
   d. 24

2. "All drivers of commercial vehicles must carry a valid commercial driver's license whenever operating a commercial vehicle." According to this sentence, which of the following people need NOT carry a commercial driver's license?
   a. a truck driver idling his engine while waiting to be directed to a loading dock
   b. a bus operator backing her bus out of the way of another bus in the bus lot
   c. a taxi driver driving his personal car to the grocery store
   d. a limousine driver taking the limousine to her home after dropping off her last passenger of the evening

3. Smoking tobacco has been linked to
   a. increased risk of stroke and heart attack.
   b. all forms of respiratory disease.
   c. increasing mortality rates over the past ten years.
   d. juvenile delinquency.

4. Which of the following words is spelled correctly?
   a. incorrigible
   b. outragous
   c. domestickated
   d. understandible

Answers

Here are the answers, as well as some suggestions as to how you might have used the process of elimination to find them.

1. **d.** You should have eliminated choice **a** right away. Ilsa can't be four years old if Meghan is going to be Ilsa's age in five years. The best way to eliminate other answer choices is to try plugging them in to the information given in the problem. For instance, for choice **b**, if Ilsa is 10, then Meghan must be 5. The difference in their ages is 5. The difference between Ed's age, 29, and Meghan's age, 5, is 24. Does 24 equal 2 times 5? No. Therefore, choice **b** is incorrect. You could eliminate choice **c** in the same way and be left with choice **d**.

2. **c.** Note the word *not* in the question, and go through the choice one by one. Is the truck driver in choice **a** "operating a commericial vehicle"? Yes, idling counts as "operating," so he needs to have a commercial driver's license. Likewise, the bus operator in choice **b** is operating a commercial vehicle; the question doesn't say the operator has to be on the street. The limo driver in choice **d** is operating a commercial vehicle, even if it doesn't have a passenger in it. However, the cabbie in choice **c** is *not* operating a commercial vehicle, but his own private car.

3. **a.** You could eliminate choice **b** simply because of the presence of the word *all*. Such absolutes hardly ever appear in correct answer choices. Choice **c** looks attractive until you think a little about what you know—aren't *fewer* people smoking these days, rather than more? So how could smoking be responsible for a higher mortality rate? (If you didn't know that *mortality rate* means the rate at which people die, you might keep this choice as a possibility, but you would still be able to eliminate two answers and have only two to choose from.) And choice **d** is not logical, so you could eliminate that one, too. And you are left with the correct choice, **a**.

4. **a.** How you used the process of elimination here depends on which words you recognized as being spelled incorrectly. If you knew that the correct spellings were *outrageous*, *domesticated*, and *understandable*, then you were home free. You probably knew that at least one of those words was wrong!

▶ Step 6: Know When to Guess

Time to complete: 20 minutes
Activity: Complete Your Guessing Ability worksheet

Armed with the process of elimination, you are ready to take control of one of the big questions in test taking: Should I guess? The short answer is *yes*. Some exams have what's called a guessing penalty, in which a fraction of your wrong answers is subtracted from your right answers—not all real estate sales exams work like that. Usually, the number of questions you answer correctly yields your raw score. So you have nothing to lose and everything to gain by guessing.

The more complicated answer to the question "Should I guess?" depends on you—your personality and your guessing intuition. There are two things you need to know about yourself before you go into the exam:

- Are you a risk taker?
- Are you a good guesser?

You will have to decide about your risk-taking quotient on your own. To find out if you are a good guesser, complete the following worksheet, Your Guessing Ability. Frankly, even if you are a play-it-safe person with lousy intuition, you're still safe in guessing every time. The best thing would be if you could overcome your anxieties and go ahead and mark an answer. But you may want to have a sense of how good your intuition is before you go into the exam.

Your Guessing Ability

The following are ten really hard questions. You are not supposed to know the answers. Rather, this is an assessment of your ability to guess when you don't have a clue. Read each question carefully, just as if you did expect to answer it. If you have any knowledge at all of the subject of the question, use that knowledge to help you eliminate wrong answer choices.

1. September 7 is Independence Day in
  a. India.
  b. Costa Rica.
  c. Brazil.
  d. Australia.

2. Which of the following is the formula for determining the momentum of an object?
  a. $p = mv$
  b. $F = ma$
  c. $P = IV$
  d. $E = mc^2$

3. Because of the expansion of the universe, the stars and other celestial bodies are all moving away from each other. This phenomenon is known as
  a. Newton's first law.
  b. the big bang.
  c. gravitational collapse.
  d. Hubble flow.

4. American author Gertrude Stein was born in
  a. 1713
  b. 1830
  c. 1874
  d. 1901

5. Which of the following is NOT one of the Five Classics attributed to Confucius?
  a. *I Ching*
  b. *Book of Holiness*
  c. *Spring and Autumn Annals*
  d. *Book of History*

6. The religious and philosophical doctrine that holds that the universe is constantly in a struggle between good and evil is known as
  a. Pelagianism.
  b. Manichaeanism.
  c. neo-Hegelianism.
  d. Epicureanism.

7. The third chief justice of the U.S. Supreme Court was
  a. John Blair.
  b. William Cushing.
  c. James Wilson.
  d. John Jay.

8. Which of the following is the poisonous portion of a daffodil?
  a. the bulb
  b. the leaves
  c. the stem
  d. the flowers

9. The winner of the Masters golf tournament in 1953 was
   a. Sam Snead.
   b. Cary Middlecoff.
   c. Arnold Palmer.
   d. Ben Hogan.

10. The state with the highest per capita personal income in 1980 was
   a. Alaska.
   b. Connecticut.
   c. New York.
   d. Texas.

Answers

Check your answers against the following correct answers.

1. c.
2. a.
3. d.
4. c.
5. b.
6. b.
7. b.
8. a.
9. d.
10. a.

▶ How Did You Do?

You may have simply gotten lucky and actually known the answers to one or two questions. In addition, your guessing was more successful if you were able to use the process of elimination on any of the questions. Maybe you didn't know who the third chief justice was (question 7), but you knew that John Jay was the first. In that case, you would have eliminated choice **d** and, therefore, improved your odds of guessing correctly from one in four to one in three.

According to probability, you should get $2\frac{1}{2}$ answers correct, so getting either two or three right would be average. If you got four or more correct, you may be a really terrific guesser. If you got one or none correct, you may be a really bad guesser.

Keep in mind, though, that this is only a small sample. You should continue to keep track of your guessing ability as you work through the sample questions in this book. Circle the numbers of questions you guess on as you make your guesses; or, if you don't have time while you take the practice exams, go back afterward and try to remember which questions you guessed on. Remember, on an exam with four answer choices, your chance of getting a correct answer is one in four. So keep a separate "guessing" score for each exam. How many questions did you guess on? How many did you get right? If the number you got right is at least one-fourth of the number of questions you guessed on, you are at least an average guesser, maybe better—and you should always go ahead and guess on the real exam. If the number you got right is significantly lower than one-fourth of the number you guessed on, you would, frankly, be safe in guessing anyway, but maybe you would feel more comfortable if you guessed only selectively, when you can eliminate an incorrect answer or at least have a good feeling about one of the answer choices.

► Step 7: Reach Your Peak Performance Zone

Time to complete: 10 minutes to read; weeks to complete!
Activity: Complete the Physical Preparation Checklist

To get ready for a challenge like a big exam, you have to take control of your physical, as well as your mental, state. Exercise, proper diet, and rest will ensure that your body works with, rather than against, your mind on test day, as well as during your preparation.

Exercise

If you don't already have a regular exercise program going, the time during which you are preparing for an exam is actually an excellent time to start one. And if you are already keeping fit—or trying to get that way—don't let the pressure of preparing for an exam fool you into quitting now. Exercise helps reduce stress by pumping wonderful good-feeling hormones called endorphins into your system. It also increases the oxygen supply throughout your body, including your brain, so you will be at peak performance on test day.

Thirty minutes of vigorous activity—enough to raise a sweat—every day should be your aim. If you are really pressed for time, every other day is okay. Choose an activity you like, and get out there and do it. Jogging with a friend always makes the time go faster, or take your MP3 player.

But don't overdo it; you don't want to exhaust yourself. Moderation is the key.

Diet

First, cut out the junk. Go easy on caffeine and nicotine, and eliminate alcohol and any other drugs from your system at least two weeks before the exam. Promise yourself a special treat the night after the exam, if need be.

What your body needs for peak performance is simply a balanced diet. Eat plenty of fruits and vegetables, along with protein and carbohydrates. Foods high in lecithin (an amino acid), such as fish and beans, are especially good "brain foods."

The night before the exam, you might "carbo-load" the way athletes do before a contest. Eat a big plate of spaghetti, rice and beans, or your favorite carbohydrate.

Rest

You probably know how much sleep you need every night to be at your best, even if you don't always get it. Make sure you do get that much sleep, though, for at least a week before the exam. Moderation is important here, too. Extra sleep will just make you groggy.

If you are not a morning person and your exam will be given in the morning, you should reset your internal clock so that your body doesn't think you are taking an exam at 3:00 A.M. You have to start this process well before the exam. The way it works is to get up half an hour earlier each morning, and then go to bed half an hour earlier that night. Don't try it the other way around; you will just toss and turn if you go to bed early without having gotten up early. The next morning, get up another half an hour earlier, and so on. How long you will have to do this depends on how late you are used to getting up. Use the Physical Preparation Checklist on page 29 to make sure you are in tip-top form.

▶ Step 8: Get Your Act Together

Time to complete: 10 minutes to read; time to complete will vary
Activity: Complete Final Preparations worksheet

You are in control of your mind and body; you are in charge of test anxiety, your preparation, and your test-taking strategies. Now it's time to take charge of external factors, such as the testing site and the materials you need to take the exam.

Find Out Where the Exam Is and Make a Trial Run

Do you know how to get to the testing site? Do you know how long it will take to get there? If not, make a trial run, preferably on the same day of the week at the same time of day. Make note, on the Final Preparations worksheet on page 30, of the amount of time it will take you to get to the exam site. Plan on arriving 30–45 minutes early so you can get the lay of the land, use the bathroom, and calm down. Then, figure out how early you will have to get up that morning, and make sure you get up that early every day for a week before the exam.

Gather Your Materials

The night before the exam, lay out the clothes you will wear and the materials you have to bring with you to the exam. Plan on dressing in layers; you won't have any control over the temperature of the examination room. Have a sweater or jacket you can take off if it's warm. Use the checklist on the Final Preparations worksheet to help you pull together what you will need.

Don't Skip Breakfast

Even if you don't usually eat breakfast, do so the morning of the exam. A cup of coffee doesn't count. Don't eat doughnuts or other sweet foods, either. A sugar high will leave you with a sugar low in the middle of the exam. A mix of protein and carbohydrates is best: Cereal with milk, or eggs with toast, will do your body a world of good.

Physical Preparation Checklist

For the week before the exam, write down what physical exercise you engaged in and for how long, as well as what you ate for each meal. Remember, you are trying for at least 30 minutes of exercise every other day (preferably every day) and a balanced diet that's light on junk food.

Exam minus 7 days

Exercise: _____ for _____ minutes
Breakfast: _____
Lunch: _____
Dinner: _____
Snacks: _____

Exam minus 6 days

Exercise: _____ for _____ minutes
Breakfast: _____
Lunch: _____
Dinner: _____
Snacks: _____

Exam minus 5 days

Exercise: _____ for _____ minutes
Breakfast: _____
Lunch: _____
Dinner: _____
Snacks: _____

Exam minus 4 days

Exercise: _____ for _____ minutes
Breakfast: _____
Lunch: _____
Dinner: _____
Snacks: _____

Exam minus 3 days

Exercise: _____ for _____ minutes
Breakfast: _____
Lunch: _____
Dinner: _____
Snacks: _____

Exam minus 2 days

Exercise: _____ for _____ minutes
Breakfast: _____
Lunch: _____
Dinner: _____
Snacks: _____

Exam minus 1 day

Exercise: _____ for _____ minutes
Breakfast: _____
Lunch: _____
Dinner: _____
Snacks: _____

Final Preparations

Getting to the Exam Site

Location of exam: _____

Date: _____

Departure time: _____

Do I know how to get to the exam site? Yes _____ No _____
If no, make a trial run.

Time it will take to get to exam site: _____

Things to Lay Out the Night Before

Clothes I will wear   _____

Sweater/jacket   _____

Watch   _____

Photo ID   _____

No. 2 pencils   _____

Calculator   _____

_____   _____

_____   _____

▶ Step 9: Do It!

Time to complete: 10 minutes, plus test-taking time
Activity: Ace your real estate sales exam!

Fast-forward to exam day. You are ready. You made a study plan and followed through. You practiced your test-taking strategies while working through this book. You are in control of your physical, mental, and emotional state. You know when and where to show up and what to bring with you. In other words, you are better prepared than most of the other people taking the exam with you. You are psyched.

Just one more thing. When you are done with the exam, you will have earned a reward. Plan a celebration. Call up your friends and plan a party, or have a nice dinner for two—whatever your heart desires. Give yourself something to look forward to.

And then do it. Go into the exam, full of confidence, armed with test-taking strategies you have practiced until they're second nature. You are in control of yourself, your environment, and your performance on the exam. You are ready to succeed. So do it. Go in there and ace the exam. And look forward to your future career as a real estate salesperson!

3 ▶ Real Estate Sales Exam 1

CHAPTER SUMMARY

This is the first of four practice exams in this book. Take this exam to see how you would do if you took the exam today and to find out what your strengths and weaknesses are.

I F YOU PREFER to take a practice exam on a computer, use the CD-ROM included at the back of this book. Taking the exams on a computer is good practice for the real exam. On the other hand, if using a computer isn't convenient for you, taking the exams on paper will accomplish the same goal—letting you know the areas in which you are strong and the areas in which you need more work.

Take this exam in as relaxed a manner as possible, without worrying about timing. You can time yourself on the other three exams. You should, however, make sure that you have enough time to take the entire exam in one sitting. Find a quiet place where you can work without interruptions.

The answer sheet is on the following page, and then comes the exam. After you have finished, use the answer key and explanations to learn your strengths and your weakness. Then use the scoring section at the end of this chapter to see how you did overall.

▶ Real Estate Sales Exam 1 Answer Sheet

	a	b	c	d			a	b	c	d			a	b	c	d
1.	a	b	c	d		36.	a	b	c	d		71.	a	b	c	d
2.	a	b	c	d		37.	a	b	c	d		72.	a	b	c	d
3.	a	b	c	d		38.	a	b	c	d		73.	a	b	c	d
4.	a	b	c	d		39.	a	b	c	d		74.	a	b	c	d
5.	a	b	c	d		40.	a	b	c	d		75.	a	b	c	d
6.	a	b	c	d		41.	a	b	c	d		76.	a	b	c	d
7.	a	b	c	d		42.	a	b	c	d		77.	a	b	c	d
8.	a	b	c	d		43.	a	b	c	d		78.	a	b	c	d
9.	a	b	c	d		44.	a	b	c	d		79.	a	b	c	d
10.	a	b	c	d		45.	a	b	c	d		80.	a	b	c	d
11.	a	b	c	d		46.	a	b	c	d		81.	a	b	c	d
12.	a	b	c	d		47.	a	b	c	d		82.	a	b	c	d
13.	a	b	c	d		48.	a	b	c	d		83.	a	b	c	d
14.	a	b	c	d		49.	a	b	c	d		84.	a	b	c	d
15.	a	b	c	d		50.	a	b	c	d		85.	a	b	c	d
16.	a	b	c	d		51.	a	b	c	d		86.	a	b	c	d
17.	a	b	c	d		52.	a	b	c	d		87.	a	b	c	d
18.	a	b	c	d		53.	a	b	c	d		88.	a	b	c	d
19.	a	b	c	d		54.	a	b	c	d		89.	a	b	c	d
20.	a	b	c	d		55.	a	b	c	d		90.	a	b	c	d
21.	a	b	c	d		56.	a	b	c	d		91.	a	b	c	d
22.	a	b	c	d		57.	a	b	c	d		92.	a	b	c	d
23.	a	b	c	d		58.	a	b	c	d		93.	a	b	c	d
24.	a	b	c	d		59.	a	b	c	d		94.	a	b	c	d
25.	a	b	c	d		60.	a	b	c	d		95.	a	b	c	d
26.	a	b	c	d		61.	a	b	c	d		96.	a	b	c	d
27.	a	b	c	d		62.	a	b	c	d		97.	a	b	c	d
28.	a	b	c	d		63.	a	b	c	d		98.	a	b	c	d
29.	a	b	c	d		64.	a	b	c	d		99.	a	b	c	d
30.	a	b	c	d		65.	a	b	c	d		100.	a	b	c	d
31.	a	b	c	d		66.	a	b	c	d						
32.	a	b	c	d		67.	a	b	c	d						
33.	a	b	c	d		68.	a	b	c	d						
34.	a	b	c	d		69.	a	b	c	d						
35.	a	b	c	d		70.	a	b	c	d						

▶ Real Estate Sales Exam 1

1. A developer includes restrictive covenants in the deeds for all properties within a subdivision. These covenants may dictate all of the following EXCEPT the
   a. owner's use of the property.
   b. style of architecture.
   c. appearance of outbuildings and fences.
   d. ethnic character of future owners.

2. Broker Bryant deposited a tenant's security deposit into his own bank account and later transferred the money to his owner client's trust account. Broker Miller deposited a tenant's security deposit into her own bank account and used the money to pay personal obligations. Which of the following statements is true?
   a. Both Bryant and Miller are only guilty of commingling funds.
   b. Both Bryant and Miller are guilty of conversion of funds.
   c. Bryant is guilty of commingling, and Miller is guilty of both commingling and conversion of funds.
   d. Bryant is guilty of nothing, and Miller is guilty of commingling funds.

3. Frances is buying a home for $200,000 and getting a 95% loan-to-value conventional loan. She will be paying an annual PMI premium of 0.45%. How much is the monthly premium payment?
   a. $75
   b. $900
   c. $71.25
   d. $855

4. Pamela Jones, a single woman, deeded a life estate in one of her rental houses to her aunt Martha. The deed included a provision that the property is to be returned to her ownership upon the death of her aunt. Pamela has what type of interest in the property?
   a. a remainder interest
   b. an interest in severalty
   c. a reversionary interest
   d. a partition interest

5. Karl installed special ovens, ranges, walk-in coolers, and other equipment in the space he leased for his restaurant. The lease expires soon, and he is planning to move to a new location. Can Karl remove and take these fixtures to his new location?
   a. No, the installed fixtures become the property of the landlord.
   b. Yes, these are trade fixtures and may be removed prior to vacating, and Karl must leave the premises in the same condition as when he leased.
   c. Yes, fixtures are always the property of the person who installed them.
   d. not unless he purchases them back from the building owner

6. What will the amount of taxes payable be if the property's assessed value is $85,000 and the tax rate is 50 mills in a community where the equalization factor is 120%?
   a. $10,200
   b. $5,100
   c. $3,460
   d. $4,250

7. In inflationary times, a property manager would NOT want a long-term lease based on
   a. graduated payments.
   b. the consumer price index.
   c. a fixed rate.
   d. a cost-of-living index.

8. The buyer of a cooperative apartment receives shares in the cooperative and a
   a. proprietary lease.
   b. bargain and sale deed.
   c. joint tenancy.
   d. limited partnership.

9. A lender is providing 90% of the financing for a new house. If the house appraises for $75,000, what is the buyer's down payment?
   a. $7,500
   b. $67,500
   c. $9,000
   d. $750

10. A broker tells residents in a particular neighborhood that certain minorities are moving into the area and that property values may be affected as a result. He encourages owners to list and sell before values drop. What is this called under fair housing law?
   a. profiling
   b. redlining
   c. steering
   d. blockbusting

11. What is 75% of $250,000?
   a. $187,500
   b. $182,500
   c. $62,500
   d. none of the above

12. Which of the following statements best describes a real estate agent's liabilities concerning environmental hazards?
   a. Residential real estate agents do not need to know about environmental conditions.
   b. A real estate licensee could be liable if he or she should have known about a condition, even if the seller neglected to disclose it.
   c. Disclosure of environmental hazards is the responsibility of the seller.
   d. Unless the buyer asks, the real estate agent doesn't have to worry about it.

13. A purchase in which the seller holds title until a specified number of payments have been made is known as a
   a. contract for deed.
   b. deferred transfer mortgage.
   c. future delivery purchase.
   d. land sales mortgage.

14. In a loan closing, proper signatures on the promissory note create
   a. the indebtedness of the borrower.
   b. the lien on the property.
   c. the transfer of ownership to a trustee.
   d. recordation of the lien on the land records.

15. The Civil Rights Act of 1866 prohibits discrimination in real estate based on
   a. race.
   b. race and gender.
   c. handicap and country of origin.
   d. gender and religion.

16. A buyer is obtaining a conventional loan that requires 29/33 ratios. He earns $75,000 a year, and has a $450 car payment. What is his maximum principal, interest, taxes, and insurance (PITI) payment?
a. $1,612.50
b. $1,812.50
c. $21,750
d. $2,475

17. The federal ban on discrimination based on familial status is intended to provide equal access to rentals for
a. unmarried couples.
b. people with children.
c. single tenants.
d. the elderly.

18. The legal right to pass over your neighbor's land is an
a. encroachment.
b. estate in land.
c. easement.
d. example of eminent domain.

19. A heating and cooling engineer is drawing up the specifications for the HVAC system in a new building. The floor space measures 200' × 150' and the ceiling is 12' high. How much airspace does the engineer have to heat and cool?
a. 33,333 square yards
b. 300,000 square feet
c. 13,333 cubic yards
d. 36,000 cubic feet

20. The holder of a life estate may do all of the following EXCEPT
a. pay the property taxes and special assessments.
b. maintain the property.
c. mortgage the life interest.
d. direct the disposition of the property at the end of the measuring life.

21. Ken Laughton's house is "for sale by owner." Robert Hall falls in love with it during an open house, tells Ken he'll pay the full asking price, and promises to send Ken an earnest money check for $5,000. Ken accepts the offer. The contract between them is
a. enforceable by court action if either tries to back out.
b. invalid because it lacks consideration.
c. valid only if there were witnesses.
d. unenforceable.

22. When the appraiser estimates the value of an investment property, the potential gross income includes all of the following EXCEPT
a. payment of full rental prices by all tenants with full occupancy.
b. licensing fees by vendors and concessionaires.
c. parking and storage fees.
d. settlement by the state for the loss of land by eminent domain.

23. Charles Chow is buying a new home and will be leasing his current house. He does not want to rent to a family with children. Can he legally do so?

    a. yes

    b. no

    c. yes, but only if city ordinances allow it

    d. yes, but only if the tenants are age 55 or older

24. An owner is planning to build on newly purchased property. Zoning laws state that no improvement may exceed 50 feet in height, architectural guidelines limit improvements to 45 feet in height, and the deed restriction states the maximum height is 30 feet. What is the tallest building the owner can legally construct?

    a. 50 feet

    b. 45 feet

    c. 30 feet

    d. The new building can be any size the owner wants.

25. When determining reproduction cost, the appraiser may use any of the following EXCEPT

    a. price-per-square-foot method.

    b. cubic-foot method.

    c. unit-in-place method.

    d. consumer-price-index method.

26. Tenancy by the entirety is a special form of ownership available only to

    a. sole owners.

    b. corporations.

    c. married couples.

    d. limited partners.

27. Agent Converse has just returned from a closing for a property that sold for $125,000. The property was listed by Sporty's Real Estate Company. Converse received 2.5% of the sale price total commission for the transaction from the closing agent. Converse is on a 55/45 split with his company. About how much commission will Converse receive?

    a. $6,250

    b. $3,750

    c. $1,719

    d. $1,406

28. Charlie's Cheeseburgers is located in a small building in an area that is now zoned for office development. Charlie was allowed to remain because he has a

    a. delicious product that will appeal to nearby office workers.

    b. non-conforming use.

    c. variance.

    d. special use permit.

29. A seller principal asks a salesperson to do something in a particular way. The broker disagrees with the seller and instructs the salesperson to handle the matter differently. Whose instruction should the salesperson follow?

    a. the seller

    b. the broker

    c. the buyer

    d. none of the above

30. What is the definition of an appraisal?
- **a.** a definite market price at a certain point in time
- **b.** an estimate of value at a certain point in time
- **c.** a mathematical analysis of a property's use and value
- **d.** a property's average value determined by comparable sold properties

31. Jason's Landscape Services, Inc. owns a 42-acre tree farm. What is the form of ownership of this property?
- **a.** joint tenancy
- **b.** tenants in common
- **c.** joint and several estate
- **d.** severalty

32. To increase the effective yield on a $250,000 loan by $\frac{1}{4}$% when one discount point is equivalent to an increase in the APR of $\frac{1}{8}$%, how much would the lender collect at settlement in loan discount?
- **a.** $2,500
- **b.** $3,125
- **c.** $5,000
- **d.** $6,250

33. The formula for determining the value of investment property is
- **a.** net operating income ÷ capitalization rate = value.
- **b.** potential gross income ÷ capitalization rate = value.
- **c.** effective gross income × capitalization rate = value.
- **d.** cost of replacing the property × capitalization rate = value.

34. IRS Form 8300 must be filed at what point in a real estate transaction?
- **a.** at time of closing
- **b.** when monies are deposited in broker's escrow account
- **c.** when a buyer brings more than $10,000 in cash to the closing or as earnest money
- **d.** never

35. Which of the following terms best describes the parties to a purchase and sales contract?
- **a.** mortgagee/mortgagor
- **b.** vendor/vendee
- **c.** grantor/grantee
- **d.** optioner/optionee

36. What kind of contract conveys the covenant of quiet enjoyment and right to use the property but does not convey ownership title to the property?
- **a.** quitclaim deed
- **b.** possession deed
- **c.** lease
- **d.** license

37. Agent Loc Nguyen represented Daniel Pham in the purchase of a tract of land owned by Perry Miller. Perry did not have his property listed with a broker but agreed to pay Loc's broker a commission fee. What is the proper description of the agency relationships that exist in this transaction?
- **a.** Daniel is Loc's client, and Perry is his customer.
- **b.** Daniel is Loc's customer, and Perry is his client.
- **c.** Loc is a dual agent and must function as a facilitator.
- **d.** Loc's broker is an undisclosed dual agent, which is illegal.

38. Amy Reed, a salesperson for ABC Realty, is required by contract to attend meetings, dress in a uniform, and prospect for four hours per day. She receives a biweekly paycheck, less withholdings for taxes and Social Security. Amy's relationship with the firm is that of
   a. an employee.
   b. an independent contractor.
   c. a manager.
   d. a consultant.

39. At a general meeting of a brokers' trade association, several members begin talking about fees and business practices. This sort of activity could be considered
   a. a violation of the Sherman Anti-Trust Act.
   b. activity prohibited by the Better Business Bureau.
   c. an appropriate activity within the association.
   d. a good way for brokers to learn about the different practices nationwide.

40. Real estate agent Jared referred his friend Jackson to Laura, a commercial agent in his firm. Laura represented Jackson in leasing office space for his company. How should the 25% referral fee from Laura to Jared be paid?
   a. Laura should pay Jared directly when she receives her commission from the landlord.
   b. Laura should request the landlord to pay Jared his portion of the commission.
   c. The entire commission must be paid to their broker by the owner, and the broker pays both Laura and Jared.
   d. Laura should pay Jared directly when she receives her commission from their broker.

41. The correct formula for estimating value using the cost approach is
   a. cost to reproduce + depreciation – value of land = value.
   b. depreciation + value of land – cost to reproduce = value.
   c. cost to reproduce – depreciation + value of land = value.
   d. value of land + cost to reproduce + depreciation = value.

42. Rita Morgan has $86,576 left on her 8.5% mortgage. Her monthly payment is set at $852.56 for principal and interest (she pays her own taxes and insurance). How much of her next payment will go to reduce the principal?
   a. $116.76
   b. $239.31
   c. $613.25
   d. $735.80

43. Westover Timber Company purchased several hundred acres of timberland. What type of property are the trees?
   a. The trees are personal property.
   b. The trees are real property.
   c. The trees are real property while growing on the land and personal property after being harvested.
   d. Vegetation cannot be considered property.

44. A single-family property located in an industrial area has minimum value because of the principle of
   a. diminishing returns.
   b. contribution.
   c. competition.
   d. conformity.

45. The lender's underwriting criteria would accept a housing expense to income ratio of 33% and a ratio of total debt service of up to a maximum of 38% of monthly gross income. The applicant has an outstanding college loan payable at the rate of $250 per month and a car payment of $450 monthly. Gross annual income is established at $100,000 per annum. What is the maximum PITI the lender will approve?
  a. $2,750
  b. $2,566.67
  c. $2,666.67
  d. $2,716.54

46. A tenant in a strip mall pays a monthly rental that includes all property maintenance charges, utilities, and cleaning services. This is known as a
  a. net lease.
  b. percentage lease.
  c. ground lease.
  d. gross lease.

47. The cost approach is best suited for estimating the value of
  a. a large tract of land.
  b. the income generated by a commercial property.
  c. a historic building.
  d. a condominium apartment.

48. While the objective in the cost approach is generally to estimate the value of both land and improvements, the land typically is appraised using the
  a. income approach.
  b. gross rent multiplier approach.
  c. market data approach.
  d. option approach.

49. A borrower obtains a $100,000 mortgage at 7.5%. If the monthly payment of $902.77 is credited first to interest and then to principal, what will the balance of the principal (rounded to the nearest dollar) be after the borrower makes the first payment?
  a. $99,772
  b. $99,722
  c. $99,097
  d. $99,375

50. If a homeowner has a first mortgage loan balance of $63,250, a second mortgage balance of $12,000, and unpaid taxes of $3,015, how much equity does he have in his $100,000 home?
  a. $25,000
  b. $21,735
  c. $100,000
  d. $24,750

51. After John Rawlings bought his apartment, he started receiving his own property tax bills. This indicates that he has bought into a
  a. condominium.
  b. cooperative.
  c. leasehold.
  d. syndicate.

52. The party most likely to sue for specific performance in the purchase of real estate is the
  a. buyer.
  b. seller.
  c. broker.
  d. mortgage insurance company.

53. A property was listed for $360,000 and sold for 98% of the list price. The seller agreed to pay the listing broker 5% of the sales price as commission. What was the amount paid to a cooperative broker who produced the buyer for 50% of the total commission?
a. $9,000
b. $8,280
c. $8,820
d. $9,280

54. Mills are often used in calculating
a. mortgage interest.
b. property tax rates.
c. real estate commissions.
d. fire insurance premiums.

55. The difference between the market value of a property and the sum of the liens against it is called
a. equity.
b. leverage.
c. cash asset.
d. pledge.

56. A buyer needs an interest rate of 6.25% to qualify for the loan. He is buying a house for $237,500 and getting a 95% loan. His will pay two discount points to get the desired interest rate and also pay other closing costs of $2,929. Including the down payment, what is the buyer's total move-in cost?
a. $19,316.50
b. $14,804
c. $7,441.50
d. $19,613

57. What are the three approaches to property appraisal?
a. cost, income, and economic
b. sales comparison, cost, and income
c. construction, income, and market data
d. economic, capitalization, and sales comparison

58. If a jurisdiction requires private property for public use, the first step begins with
a. an amicable negotiation.
b. seeking an injunction against transfer of the property to a third party.
c. obtaining a writ of attachment.
d. beginning condemnation proceedings.

59. The annual real estate taxes on a property are $2,400. The seller pays taxes in arrears in two installments, on June 1 and October 1. If the closing is scheduled for August 28, what taxes will be due and how will the information appear on the HUD 1?
a. Credit seller $1,596 and debit buyer $1,596.
b. Credit buyer $2,400 and debit seller $2,400.
c. Debit seller $804 and credit buyer $804.
d. Credit buyer $2,796 and debit seller $2,796.

60. The obligation of protecting any deposits entrusted to an agent is an example of the fiduciary duty of
a. competence.
b. disclosure.
c. accounting.
d. obedience.

61. A sales contract contains a clause stating that the buyer's property in another county must sell, close, and fund by a certain date or the buyer may terminate the contract and receive his or her earnest money back. What is this clause?
   a. right of first refusal
   b. constructive notice
   c. contingency
   d. inchoate

62. Which of the following would most likely be considered incurable depreciation?
   a. a broken window
   b. a roof with curled and cracked shingles
   c. improvements beyond those of other homes in the area
   d. rotted fencing

63. The penalty for a first violation of federal fair housing laws can be as much as
   a. $1,000
   b. $5,000
   c. $10,000
   d. $100,000

64. Escrow monies can be defined as, and include,
   a. promissory notes.
   b. earnest money.
   c. security deposits.
   d. all of the above

65. The seller offers to pay three points on the buyer's 80% loan. If the house sells for $250,000, what is the expense to the seller?
   a. $2,400
   b. $6,000
   c. $3,000
   d. $2,000

66. A house sold for $82,000 and was assessed at 90%. If property taxes are $4.30 per $100 of value, what are the annual taxes?
   a. $3,773.40
   b. $4,300
   c. $3,526
   d. $3,173.40

67. If a commercial building producing an annual gross income of $136,000 is sold for $888,000, what is its gross income multiplier?
   a. 0.153
   b. 15.3
   c. 12.07
   d. 6.53

68. A buyer paid $5,000 for an option to purchase a property within 180 days for $200,000. Within a month, the buyer made an offer to buy the property immediately for $180,000. Which of the following is true in this situation?
   a. The option money is forfeited.
   b. The owner may accept the offer for $180,000.
   c. The buyer is in default of the option agreement.
   d. Both parties are in violation of contract law.

69. Bernie Ray is confined to a wheelchair and has applied to rent a house from Larry Sabar. He must have certain modifications made to the property to accommodate his handicapped status. Who is financially responsible for these modifications?
   a. Neither is responsible; it is negotiable.
   b. Bernie, the tenant, is responsible.
   c. Larry, the landlord, is responsible.
   d. Larry, the landlord, is not required to rent to Bernie under these circumstances.

70. Net operating income is found by
   a. multiplying effective gross income by the cap rate.
   b. dividing effective gross income by the cap rate.
   c. subtracting market income from the appraiser's estimate of potential gross income.
   d. subtracting yearly operating expenses from effective gross income.

71. Zoning regulations establish the permitted uses of land as well as
   a. building heights, setbacks, and density.
   b. the price of improvements, appurtenances, and amenities.
   c. restrictions on ownership.
   d. property rights.

72. How many cubic yards of space are there in a room 27 feet long, 18 feet wide, and 9 feet high?
   a. 4,374 cubic meters
   b. 162 cubic yards
   c. 4,374 cubic feet
   d. 162 cubic feet

73. The Real Estate Settlement Procedures Act applies to which of the following?
   a. all one- to four-family residential closings
   b. all residential government mortgage loans
   c. all one- to four-family residential transactions financed by a federally related mortgage loan
   d. all federally related lending

74. Which of the following effects, if any, does zoning have on property values?
   a. Values are unchanged because owners have the freedom to develop land as they wish.
   b. Value is enhanced because of the principle of conformity.
   c. Value is diminished because of the lack of creative use of land.
   d. Value is not related to zoning; it is a product of supply and demand.

75. How many square miles are in 12.5 sections of a township?
   a. 12.5
   b. 50
   c. 18
   d. 80

76. Charlie has the right to cross Tommy's property to get to his property. What is the right called?
   a. a license
   b. an easement by prescription
   c. an appurtenant easement
   d. an easement in gross

77. Consideration to bind a contract may be in the form of
   a. cash or cash equivalent only.
   b. anything that the parties agree upon as long as it has monetary value.
   c. money, promises, or services.
   d. thoughtful treatment of the other party's feelings.

78. The federal government requires a leaflet about possible lead paint contamination to be given to any potential purchaser or tenant of a residence built before
   a. 1995
   b. 1987
   c. 1981
   d. 1978

79. Which of the following would be included in a spot survey of a single lot?
   a. the location of any improvements
   b. identification of any public transit services
   c. directions to shopping areas
   d. the zoning classifications of adjacent properties

80. Broker Murphy has finalized the negotiation on his listing at 1000 Cash Avenue. He received earnest money of $5,000 for the deal. He must
   a. put the check in the deal file and turn it over to the closing agency when it closes.
   b. put the check in his company's escrow account.
   c. put the check in his company's operating account.
   d. put the check in his personal account.

81. Real estate agent Gonzalez is listing a property for sale. To determine a range of value for an asking price, the agent will use which of the following procedures?
   a. an appraisal of the property
   b. a broker's price opinion
   c. a cost estimate
   d. a competitive market analysis

82. A broker obtains an exclusive listing. Until the broker fulfills that contract, it is best described as
   a. executory.
   b. partial performance.
   c. having been executed.
   d. a unilateral agreement.

83. The contract sales price on a house is $257,000, and it appraised for $260,000. If the buyer is getting a 90% loan-to-value loan, what is the amount financed?
   a. $231,300
   b. $250,700
   c. $234,000
   d. $234,300

84. When may a broker functioning as an intermediary appoint one licensee to communicate with the seller and another licensee to communicate with the buyer?
   a. when in the judgment of the broker it is best to make such appointments
   b. when written permission to do so has been obtained from the parties
   c. when the parties have given verbal approval to make such appointments
   d. when the seller has given written consent for the broker to do so

85. When representing a buyer in a real estate transaction, the agent must disclose to the seller all of the following EXCEPT
   a. the buyer's motivating circumstances.
   b. the agent's relationship with the buyer.
   c. any agreement to compensate the agent out of the listing broker's commission.
   d. any potential for the agent to benefit from referring the parties to a subsidiary of the agent's firm for transaction-related services.

86. Pledging property for a loan without giving up possession of the property itself is referred to as
   a. hypothecation.
   b. alienation.
   c. defeasance.
   d. novation.

87. Which of the following statements is NOT true?
   a. A deed of trust or trust deed is an alternative to a two-party mortgage document.
   b. A deed of trust is an alternative form of financing.
   c. In some states, a deed of trust includes a power of sale clause that allows for nonjudicial foreclosure.
   d. The borrower is the trustor or grantor in a trust deed.

88. Herman has a poor credit score but still qualifies for a conventional mortgage loan at an interest rate that is higher than the current market interest rate. Which of the following describes Herman's loan?
   a. conforming
   b. buydown
   c. non-conforming
   d. variable

89. Judson rents retail space for his hunting and fishing supply firm. He pays the landlord a base rent and is responsible for paying the property taxes, insurance, and maintenance. What type of lease is this?
   a. gross lease
   b. percentage lease
   c. net lease
   d. participation lease

90. A prospect for the lease of a commercial property feels the need for adversarial representation and hires a broker to negotiate the lease on his behalf. The contract entered into between the prospect and the broker is called
   a. an authorization to negotiate.
   b. a buyer-broker agreement.
   c. a property management agreement.
   d. a cooperative brokerage agreement.

91. Of the following, which lien has the lowest priority?
   a. property taxes
   b. a mortgage or trust deed
   c. unsecured judgment
   d. a special assessment

92. A salesperson negotiates a sale and obtains a written contract signed by all parties. The sale closes, but the seller refuses to pay the broker a commission. The broker is not willing to sue the seller for the commission because the seller is her favorite brother-in-law. The salesperson may
   a. sue the seller.
   b. sue the broker only.
   c. force the broker to sue the seller.
   d. place a lien against the seller's property for the amount of the commission.

93. A developer received a loan that covers several parcels of real estate and provides for the release of the mortgage lien on each parcel when it is sold and an agreed-upon amount of the original loan is paid. This type of loan arrangement is called a
   a. package loan.
   b. wraparound loan.
   c. blanket loan.
   d. purchase-money loan.

94. A warehouse has outside dimensions of 75 feet by 125 feet. What is the square footage of interior floor space if all four walls are 9 inches thick?
  a. 90,772.50 square feet
  b. 9,225 square feet
  c. 9,077.25 square feet
  d. 9,375 square feet

95. ABC Realty has just listed the property at 3545 Jayhawk Drive. ABC Realty just received a *lis pendens* concerning the property. What does ABC Realty have?
  a. a preliminary title policy
  b. a bill for services from the seller's attorney
  c. a notice that a legal action has been filed that could affect the subject property
  d. a revised tax assessment

96. When property is appraised as part of the loan application process, a copy of the appraisal
  a. belongs to the buyer who paid for it.
  b. is confidential and for the lender's use only.
  c. is furnished to the seller only upon written request.
  d. must be shared with all the parties.

97. A property or neighborhood's life cycle will include the stages of
  a. development, use, stability, and termination.
  b. growth, deterioration, and rebuilding.
  c. growth, equilibrium, and decline.
  d. purchase, resale, and condemnation.

98. Attorney Sam gave Agent Molly $100 to shows his appreciation for the referral of Molly's client. This type of transaction is
  a. legal and a good business practice for future business.
  b. illegal, because it's considered a kickback under RESPA.
  c. illegal; the monies should have been given to Molly's broker.
  d. legal; this program had been worked out by Molly's broker and the attorney.

99. When an owner sells a principal residence, the capital gain is calculated by
  a. subtracting selling expenses from the sales price.
  b. subtracting the sales price from the original purchase price.
  c. reducing the net sales price by the property's adjusted cost basis.
  d. subtracting the selling expenses from the original purchase price.

100. RESPA requires all of the following EXCEPT that the
  a. buyer receives the HUD information booklet from the lender.
  b. lender makes a good-faith estimate of closing costs for the buyer.
  c. buyer is offered a loan that is $\frac{1}{4}$% below market rate.
  d. closing will be conducted using the HUD-1 Uniform Settlement Statement.

► Answers

1. **d.** Restrictive covenants that would be in violation of the law are illegal.

2. **c.** To deposit client funds in the broker's own account is a breach of law known as *commingling*. To use the funds for personal use is known as *conversion*.

3. **c.** $200,000 × .95 = $190,000 loan amount; $190,000 × 0.45 = $855 annual premium; $855 ÷ 12 = $71.25 monthly premium.

4. **c.** A remainder interest would pass ownership to a third person, while a reversionary interest reverts the ownership to the grantor of the deed granting ownership of the life estate.

5. **b.** Fixtures installed by a tenant in the regular course of doing business are called trade fixtures and remain the property of the tenant. The tenant must remove them before the expiration of the lease and repair any damages to the property.

6. **b.** Calculate the tax by multiplying the assessed value times the equalization factor divided by 1,000 multiplied by the mill rate: $85,000 × 1.20 = $102,000 ÷ 1,000 = 102 × 50 = $5,100.

7. **c.** With a fixed-rate lease, the property manager would not have the ability to raise the rent as the market dictates.

8. **a.** A co-op apartment is personal property, not real estate, and no deed is involved. The owners become shareholders in the overall organization and have a proprietary lease to their apartments.

9. **a.** The down payment is the difference between the sales price and the loan amount: 100% − 90% = 10% down payment. Convert 10% to a decimal and multiply: $75,000 × .10 = $7,500.

10. **d.** Blockbusting, also called *panic peddling* or *panic selling*, happens when someone seeks to get listings by predicting negative results as minorities buy homes and move into a neighborhood.

11. **a.** Convert 75% to a decimal and multiply: $250,000 × .75 = $187,500.

12. **b.** A real estate agent should always disclose any possible environmental conditions that would have any effect on the property or on the buyer's intended use.

13. **a.** Property purchased on the installment plan with the seller holding title for at least one year after the date of sale is a contract for deed.

14. **a.** It is the note that creates the debt in an agreement between the borrower and lender.

15. **a.** The law that followed the close of the Civil War extended equal rights in real property to members of all races.

16. **a.** $75,000 ÷ 12 = $6,250 monthly income. $6,250 × .29 = $1,812.50 front-end qualifier. $6,250 × .33 = 2,062.50 − $450 debt = $1,612.50 back-end qualifier.
    The maximum PITI (principal, interest, taxes, and insurance) is the lower of these two qualifiers.

17. **b.** Familial status refers to a parent or guardian who lives with one or more children under the age of 18.

18. **c.** An easement is the right to use the land of another for a specific purpose such as a right-of-way.

19. c. Airspace is three-dimensional and is measured length × width × height = cubic feet. The number of cubic feet is divided by 27 to arrive at cubic yards.

20. d. Within the terms of the life estate, the holder's interest ends at the death of the person (typically, the holder) against whose life the life estate is measured.

21. d. According to the statute of frauds, all contracts for the sale of real estate must be in writing to be enforceable.

22. d. Income from all accounts is considered. Settlements or sale of land are not figured into the calculation.

23. a. The rental of single-family homes is not covered by fair housing law if owned by a private individual who owns three or fewer such houses, if a broker is not used, there was no discriminatory advertising, and the owner sells no more than one house he or she did not live in during the past year.

24. c. When there is a conflict in limitations on the development of property, the most restrictive applies.

25. d. Reliable methods of determining reproduction costs are the square-foot method (most common), cubic-foot method, unit-in-place method, and quantity-survey method.

26. c. Tenancy by the entirety, available in most noncommunity property states, is automatically assumed when a married couple purchases real estate together unless they specify some other form of ownership.

27. c. The company received 2.5% of the sale price, and Converse receives 55% of the company's dollars: $125,000 × .025 = $3,125 × .55 = $1,718.75.

28. b. Despite the change in zoning, Charlie will be allowed to maintain his business as a nonconforming use. He will not be allowed to expand it, however.

29. b. The broker is a single agent of the seller, and the salesperson is a subagent of the seller.

30. b. An appraiser gives an estimate or opinion of value on a certain date based on verifiable data obtained within a certain period of time.

31. d. Forms of co-ownership include joint tenancy and tenants in common. A single entity, such as an individual person, or a legal entity, such as a corporation, own property in severalty, meaning severed from all others.

32. c. $0.25 ÷ 0.125 = 2$ points; $\$250,000 × 2\% = \$5,000$

33. a. Net operating income is divided by the appropriate capitalization rate to arrive at the value of the property.

34. c. The IRS requires that IRS Form 8300 be filed on all cash payments more than $10,000.

35. b. Choice **a** refers to lender/borrower parties, choice **c** defines parties in a transfer of property, and choice **d** refers to parties in a unilateral contract.

36. c. The owner (lessor) retains title and a reversionary interest in the property, and the tenant (lessee) is granted possession of property in a lease.

37. a. Representation by the agent means that Daniel is Loc's client to whom he owes fiduciary duties. Perry is not represented and is a customer to Loc and his broker, even though he is paying the commission. Loc owes Perry honesty and fairness but not fiduciary duties.

38. a. This is a description of the typical characteristics of employee status.

39. a. Any discussion of fees between competitors could be viewed as an attempt to conspire to set the cost of real estate brokerage services, a violation of antitrust law.

40. c. All commission fees must be paid to the primary broker of the firm, who then disburses commissions and/or fees to agents.

41. c. The formula is cost to reproduce – depreciation + value of land = value.

42. b. A year's interest on the present debt would be $7,358.96 ($86,576 × 0.085). A month's interest is $613.25 ($7,358.96 ÷ 12). The principal portion of her payment is $239.31 ($852.56 – $613.25).

43. c. Real property includes the surface land, subsurface, and airspace above, and includes all natural vegetation. When trees are cut, minerals extracted, or other crops harvested, they are severed from the real property and become personal property.

44. d. The principle of conformity states that to retain value, the property should be located within an area of similar properties.

45. b. ($100,000 ÷ 12) × 0.38 is $3,166.67 – ($150 + $450) = $2,566.67

46. a. A net lease is one that includes rent plus operating expenses within the rental price.

47. c. The cost approach is preferable when appraising unique properties.

48. c. Land is appraised by comparing the subject property to recent sales of comparable parcels of land.

49. b. You must determine the monthly interest by multiplying the loan amount by the annual interest rate. Then divide the annual interest amount by 12 to get the monthly amount. Then subtract the monthly interest amount from the monthly payment amount to determine the amount to be applied to the principal. Subtract the amount to be applied to the principal from the beginning balance to determine the remaining loan amount: $100,000 × .075 = $7,500 ÷ 12 = $625; $902.77 – $625.00 = $277.77; $100,000 – $277.77 = $99,722.23

50. d. $63,250 loan balance + $12,000 loan balance = $75,250 total debt; $100,000 value of home – $75,250 debt = $24,750 equity. Taxes are an expense prorated at closing and are not considered a debt.

51. a. A condominium is owned in fee simple just as a single house would be. By contrast, the owner of a cooperative apartment receives shares in a corporation that owns the whole building and pays property taxes on it.

52. a. While a seller's problems may be solved with money damages, a buyer might prefer forcing the seller to sell, because each parcel of real estate is unique.

53. c. 98% = 0.98; $360,000 list price × .98 = $352,800 sales price; 5% = 0.05; $352,800 × 0.05 = $17,640 total commission paid to listing broker; 50% = 0.50; $17,640 × 0.50 = $8,820 commission paid by the listing broker to the selling broker.

54. b. Mills, each one-tenth of a cent, are sometimes used to express the tax rate per dollar of assessed value.

55. a. The difference between market value and debt is equity.

56. a. 95% = .95; $237,500 sales price × .95 = $225,625 loan amount; 2 discount points = 2% = 0.02; $225,625 loan amount × 0.02 = $4,512.50 discount points; $237,500 sales price – $225,625 loan amount = $11,875 down payment; $2,929 closing costs + $4,512.50 points + $11,875 down = $19,316.50 total move-in cost.

57. b. The sales comparison approach estimates value of the subject property based on the most recent sales of comparable properties. The cost approach estimates the value of the land by the sales comparison approach and the actual cost to replace or reproduce the improvements. The income approach estimates value based on the net operating income in relation to comparable capitalization rates of comparable recently sold properties.

58. a. The jurisdiction attempts to purchase the property.

59. d. $2,400 ÷ 2 = $1,200; $2,400 ÷ 12 = $200; $2,400 ÷ 36 = $7; half year at $1,200 plus 7 months at $200 equals $1,400; 28 days at $7 equals $196 for a total $2,796 to be credited to buyer and debited to seller on the HUD 1.

60. c. The agent must be able to account for and produce anything of value entrusted to his or her care. This includes advances of marketing fees, earnest money deposits, and escrows.

61. c. A clause in a contract that requires a certain act to be accomplished or a particular event to take place within a given time before the contract is binding is a contingency.

62. c. This is an example of regression, an external factor, caused by the lower priced homes in the area. External factors are always incurable.

63. c. HUD's penalty for a first offense can be $10,000. The Justice Department may fine for a pattern of repeat violations up to $100,000.

64. d. All of the items are examples of escrow monies.

65. b. Convert 80% to a decimal and multiply: $250,000 × .80 = $200,000 loan amount; Convert 3% to a decimal and multiply: $200,000 × .03 = $6,000 cost of points.

66. d. Convert 90% to a decimal and multiply: $82,000 × .90 = $73,800 loan amount; $4.30 ÷ 100 = $.0430; $73,800 × $.0430 = $3,173.40 annual taxes.

67. d. The gross income multiplier (GIM) is found by dividing the sales price by the gross annual income: $888,000 ÷ $136,000 = 6.529, rounded to 6.53.

68. b. Either party is permitted to attempt to renegotiate the terms of the transaction.

69. b. The handicapped are protected under fair housing law. The handicapped tenant may make reasonable modifications to the property at his or her expense and return the property to its original condition when vacating.

70. d. A property's net operating income is derived by first estimating its potential gross income, then deducting estimated vacancy and collection losses to derive effective gross income, and finally subtracting yearly operating expenses from effective gross income.

71. a. Under the police powers given by the state, local jurisdictions regulate and control the use of the land through enacting and enforcing zoning laws. These laws also address issues such as building heights and setbacks.

72. b. Convert feet to yards (3 feet = 1 yard), and then multiply: 27 ft. × 18 ft. × 9 ft. = 4,374 ft.³. 4,374 ft.³ ÷ 27 = 162 yds.³. The question asks for an answer in terms of cubic yards rather than cubic feet, so the conversion completes the answer.

73. **c.** RESPA covers federally related loans, which include loans made through Federal Housing Administration (FHA) or Veterans Administration (VA), loans intended to be sold to Fannie Mae or Freddie Mac, or any other type of loan regulated by the federal government.

74. **b.** Careful zoning will increase property appreciation.

75. **a.** A section of a township is one square mile.

76. **c.** Charlie has an appurtenant easement from Tommy. This allows Charlie to get to his property. Charlie is said to be the dominant parcel and Tommy is the servient parcel.

77. **c.** If the parties agree, consideration need not be valuable in order to be considered "good" enough.

78. **d.** Lead-based paint has not been used since 1977.

79. **a.** A spot survey discloses any improvements on a property, as well as any encroachments or easements.

80. **b.** All earnest monies held for others must be held in an escrow account, not in anyone's personal account, deal file, or company operating account.

81. **d.** A competitive market analysis is used by real estate agents to give sellers a range of value from which to determine the list price. It is based on comparable properties currently for sale, expired listings, and properties that have recently sold.

82. **a.** A contract that is not yet completely performed is described as executory. When all of its terms and conditions have been met, it is then referred to as executed.

83. **a.** The loan-to-value is based on the sales price or the appraised value, whichever is less: $257,000 \times 90\% = \$231,300$ loan amount.

84. **b.** The broker (intermediary) who wishes to make appointments must obtain written permission from the parties to do so and must give them written notice of who is being appointed to the seller and who is being appointed to the buyer.

85. **a.** The duty of confidentiality extends to buyer clients.

86. **a.** Hypothecation is the pledging of something as collateral or security for payment of a loan.

87. **b.** A trust deed or deed of trust is a three-party security instrument used in many states to create a lien on a property that secures a promissory note.

88. **c.** Conventional loans are either conforming or non-conforming. Conforming loans must meet the Fannie Mae/Freddie Mac uniform standards. Borrowers with low credit scores often qualify for non-conforming loans.

89. **c.** A net lease is net to the landlord because the tenant pays the property expenses. In a gross lease, the tenant pays rent and the landlord pays the property expenses.

90. **b.** A contract wherein the broker represents a buyer or tenant is called a buyer broker agreement or an exclusive right to represent agreement.

91. **c.** Property taxes, special assessments, and secured liens have priority over all others.

92. **b.** Only the broker may sue the principal.

93. **c.** This type of loan is normally used to finance developments, in that it has a partial release clause, thus allowing the take-out of individual properties as they are sold off.

94. **c.** Nine inches for each wall for the length and nine inches for each wall for the width must be subtracted from the building dimensions. 9 inches + 9 inches = 18 inches; 18 inches ÷ 12 inches in a foot = 1.5 feet to be subtracted from each dimension; 75 feet − 1.5 feet = 73.5 feet inside width; 125 feet − 1.5 feet = 123.5 feet inside length; 73.5 feet × 123.5 feet = 9,077.25 square feet of interior floor space.

95. c. A *lis pendens* is a legal notice that a legal suit has been filed or is being filed that could have an affect on the property, but the case hasn't been heard; therefore, the effect on the property cannot be determined.

96. a. The Equal Credit Opportunity Act provides that the borrower is entitled to a copy of the appraisal if the buyer paid for it; in Michigan, the buyer must get the lender's permission to get a copy of the appraisal.

97. c. A building or neighborhood will undergo a period of growth in which it is first developed, followed by a period of relatively little change before the effects of deterioration result in its decline.

98. b. This type of transaction is in violation of the Real Estate Settlement Procedures Act (RESPA).

99. c. Taxable capital gain from the sale of a principal residence is calculated by subtracting the adjusted cost basis from the net proceeds of sale.

100. c. The RESPA regulations have nothing to do with rates.

▶ Scoring

Remember that this practice exam is not correlated exactly to your state's real estate sales exam. In general, to evaluate how you did on this practice exam, find the number of questions you got right, and divide by 100 (the number of questions on this exam). This will give you your score as a percentage. You should hope to score at least 70% on this practice exam.

For now, what's much more important than your overall score is how you did on each of the areas tested by the exam. You need to diagnose your strengths and weaknesses so that you can concentrate your efforts as you prepare. The question types are mixed in the practice exam, so in order to tell where your strengths and weaknesses lie, you will need to compare your answer

sheet with Exam 1 for Review, which shows which of the categories each question falls into.

Use your score in conjunction with the Learning-Express Test Preparation System in Chapter 2 of this book to help you devise a study plan using the real estate refresher course in Chapter 4, the real estate math review in Chapter 5, and the real estate glossary in Chapter 6. You should plan to spend more time on the sections that correspond to the questions you found hardest and less time on the lessons that correspond to areas in which you did well.

Once you have spent some time reviewing, take the second practice exam in Chapter 7 to see how much you've improved.

EXAM 1 FOR REVIEW

Topic	Question Numbers
Financing	3, 14, 32, 42, 45, 49, 55, 83, 86, 87, 88, 93, 96
Settlement/Transfer of Property	4, 20, 26, 31, 51, 58, 59, 73, 79, 85, 95, 99, 100
Property Management	7, 15, 17, 23, 28, 46, 63, 67, 69, 70, 89, 90, 97
Property Valuations/Appraisal	6, 22, 25, 30, 33, 41, 44, 47, 48, 54, 57, 62, 81
Property Characteristics	1, 5, 8, 18, 19, 24, 43, 71, 74, 75, 76, 78, 91
Business Practices	2, 10, 12, 13, 27, 34, 38, 40, 60, 64, 80, 98
Contracts/Agency Relationships	21, 29, 35, 36, 37, 39, 52, 61, 68, 77, 82, 84, 92
Mathematics	9, 11, 16, 50, 53, 56, 65, 66, 72, 94

CHAPTER

4 ▶ Real Estate Refresher Course

CHAPTER SUMMARY

If you want to review real estate concepts for your exam, this is the chapter you need. Using this chapter, you can review just what you need to know for the test.

HOW YOU USE this chapter is up to you. You may want to proceed through the entire course in order, or perhaps, after taking the first practice exam, you know that you need to brush up on just one or two areas. In that case, you can concentrate only on those areas. Following are the major sections of the real estate refresher course.

▶ Real Estate Principles and Practices

Property Characteristics
- Classes of Property
- Land Characteristics
- Encumbrances
- Types of Ownership
- Descriptions of Property

- Government Rights in Land
- Federal Income Tax (Capital Gains and Depreciation)
- Public Controls
- Environmental Hazards and Regulations
- Private Controls
- Water Rights
- Property Condition Disclosure Forms
- Need for Inspection
- Material Facts

Property Valuation/Appraisal
- Value
- Characteristics of Property Value
- Market Value, Market Price, and Cost
- Real Estate Value Cycle
- Principles of Value
- Methods of Estimating Value: Appraisal Process
- Sales Comparison Approach (Market Data Approach)
- Cost Approach
- Income Approach
- Purpose and Use of Appraisal
- Role of the Appraiser
- Competitive or Comparative Market Analysis (CMA)

Financing
- The Loan Documents
- Primary and Secondary Mortgage Markets
- Government and Conventional
- Types of Loan Payment Plans
- Types of Mortgages
- Finance/Credit Laws

Contracts/Agency Relationships
- General
- Offers/Purchase Agreements
- Counteroffers/Multiple Counteroffers

- Leases as Contracts
- Options
- Rescission and Cancellation Agreements
- Broker-Salesperson Agreements
- Law, Definition, and Nature of Agency Relationships
- Creations of Agency and Agency Agreements
- Listing Agreements
- Listing Procedures
- Buyer-Broker Agreements
- Cooperative Transactions
- Responsibilities of the Agent to the Seller/Buyer as Principal
- Termination of Agency
- Commission and Fees

Settlement/Transfer of Property
- Title Insurance
- Deeds
- Settlement Procedures
- Tax Aspects
- Special Processes (Probate and Foreclosure)

Business Practices
- Fair Housing and Anti-Discrimination Laws
- Advertising

Property Management
- Property Management and Landlord/Tenant and Commercial/Income Property
- Common Interest Ownership Properties
- Subdivisions

Note: Mathematics will be covered in Chapter 5.

▶ Property Characteristics

Classes of Property

All property, both real and personal, that can be owned and subsequently inherited is legally known as a **hereditament**. **Land** is the earth's surface including all vegetation (**surface rights**) and going down to the center of the earth including the water, minerals (**subsurface rights**). It also goes upward (**air rights**) to infinity above. Land plus all human-made improvements permanently attached to the land, such as fences, wells, buildings, etc., is known as **real estate**. Land plus improvement plus ownership rights are **real property**. Often, *real estate* and *real property* are used interchangeably.

When an item of personal property or a chattel is permanently attached to real estate, it becomes real property and is identified as a **fixture**. Fixtures become **appurtenances** and remain with the property when ownership transfers to a new owner. Appurtenances also include such things as easements, rights-of-way, or water rights. An exception regarding fixtures occurs when a commercial tenant installs a business fixture to be used in the business for which the space has been leased. **Trade fixtures** remain the property of the tenant and may be removed by the tenant prior to the termination of the lease. The tenant is obligated to repair any damage caused by the removal of a trade fixture.

The determination of a fixture is made by asking and answering the following questions.

1. How is the item attached?
2. Have the improvements been modified to accommodate the item?
3. What was the intent of the attachor?
4. Is there a contractual agreement that defines the item as a fixture or as a chattel?

Land Characteristics

Land, or real estate, has both physical and economic characteristics.

Physical Characteristics

1. **Immobility**—From a physical standpoint, each parcel of land is unique. It cannot be moved because it occupies a fixed geographic location on the earth.
2. **Indestructibility**—Although its features can be modified by human and by the forces of nature, it is indestructible.
3. **Nonhomogeneity**—Each parcel is unique and unlike any other. One parcel may be similar to another, but each occupies a different geographic location on the earth.

Economic Characteristics

1. **Scarcity**—There is a limited amount of the earth's surface. Value comes to land when people want to live on it, work on it, or develop it for recreational purposes.
2. **Improvements**—The value of land is increased or decreased by the modifications made to it, such as buildings, fences, and other human-made improvements. Changes made to surrounding parcels or the construction of roadways nearby may also impact the property's economic value.
3. **Permanence of Investment**—Also called **fixity**, it is created by the fact that land and improvements require long periods of time to pay for themselves.
4. **Situs**—Location preference is the single most important economic characteristic that influences the value of any given parcel of land.

Encumbrances

Anything that obstructs or impairs the use of a property is known as an **encumbrance** and creates a **cloud on title** of the fee simple holder's rights in the property. Common encumbrances include but are not limited to **encroachments**, **easements**, or **liens**.

Encroachments are unauthorized intrusions of the improvements of one property on the surface or in the airspace of an adjoining parcel.

Easements grant a right to use a portion of a property owner's land for a specific purpose. An **easement appurtenant** may grant ingress and egress to an adjoining parcel of land thus creating a **dominant estate** (the parcel that benefits from the easement) and a **servient estate** (the parcel across which the easement passes).

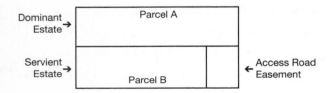

An **easement in gross** does not benefit any one parcel of real estate but rather benefits a number of parcels to bring such things as utilities.

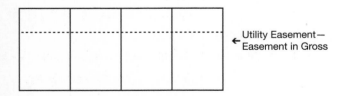

Liens are claims against property that secure payment of a financial obligation owed by the property or the property owner. They come in many varieties.

Liens may be created voluntarily or by operation of law. A lien on real property is **voluntary** if it is imposed with the consent of the property owner. It is **involuntary** if it can be imposed without the consent of the property owner.

A **mechanic's lien** is an example of an involuntary lien. State law specifies the requirements for creating and enforcing a mechanic's lien. In general, a mechanic's lien is available to anyone who provides material or labor for an improvement to real estate, including design services. Sometimes referred to as **mechanic's** and **materialman's liens**, an architect, surveyor, contractor, carpenter, plumber, electrician, landscaper, and many other participants in the construction process are all entitled to a lien on the property if they have not been paid for their services or materials.

There are statutory time periods for:

- providing notice to the property owner of the right to file a **mechanic's** or **materialman's lien**
- filing the lien
- foreclosing on the lien in the event that the underlying debt is not repaid

In some states, a properly filed mechanic's lien may take priority over all other subsequent liens, except for property tax liens.

Foreclosure (sale) of the real estate may be postponed by the property owner during a court hearing on the merits of the case, provided the property owner posts a bond to ensure payment to the claimant. Foreclosure will also be covered in the Financing section.

A **judgment** is a determination of a court that may impose an obligation for payment on a property owner. If the judgment is unpaid, a **writ of attachment** specifies the property that the sheriff will be ordered to sell by a **writ of execution**.

Tax liens are available to federal, state, and local taxing authorities. Enforcement is usually by tax sale. The purchaser receives a tax deed.

- **Property tax or special assessment tax lien** is imposed for nonpayment of state or local property taxes. These taxes take precedence over all other liens.
- A **federal tax lien** is imposed by the IRS for nonpayment of federal income tax, gift tax, or other taxes.
- A **state tax lien** is imposed for nonpayment of state income tax, sales tax, use tax, or other tax.

Other encumbrances might include:

- marital rights
- rights of parties in possession
- outstanding option to purchase
- judgments against the owner
- unpaid tax liens

Types of Ownership

The primary responsibility of a property seller is to convey **marketable title**, an ownership interest that a well-informed buyer can reasonably be expected to accept and that the buyer can transfer in a future transaction. There are several ways in which the buyer can be assured of acceptable title.

A **title search** will reveal the **chain of title**, the history of conveyances and encumbrances that can be found in the public records. The title search begins with the name of the present owner and the instrument that establishes title in that owner as the grantee. Working back through what is called the **grantee index**, the name of the grantor to the present owner is found on the deed in which that owner is the grantee. In this way, the person examining the title can go back to the first recorded document of the property. Then, as a method of checking the validity of the search through the grantee index, the searcher moves forward through the **grantor index** from the first recorded document, verifying that the chain is complete and accurate.

There are many different entities that can acquire ownership in real property: an individual, a group of individuals, a large corporation, a government entity (at any level of government), and more. In addition, there are many different forms of ownership. **Estate in severalty (sole ownership)** occurs when property is held by one person or a single legal entity. The individual's interest is *severed* from everyone else's. **Tenancy in common** involves two or more individuals who own an undivided interest in real property without rights to survivorship (the right of a surviving joint tenant to receive a co-owner's share of interest upon the death of the co-owner). *Undivided* means that each tenant has an interest in the entire property.

The interest in the estate can vary among the tenants. One party can have 40%, another 25%, and another 35%. If a deed conveying property is made out to two people but does not stipulate their relationship, they are presumed (as in many states) to be tenants in common with equal interest. A party can freely dispose of his or her interest by sale, gift, devise, or descent.

Joint tenancy also involves two or more people but includes a right of survivorship. Four unities must exist to create a valid joint tenancy.

1. **Unity of time**. All tenants must acquire their interest at the same moment. Thus, no new tenants can be added at a later time.
2. **Unity of title**. All tenants must acquire their interest from the same source—the same deed, will, or other conveyance.
3. **Unity of interest**. Each tenant has an equal percentage ownership.
4. **Unity of possession**. Each tenant enjoys the same undivided interest in the whole property and right to occupy the property.

Joint tenancy also includes the **right of survivorship**. On the death of a joint tenant, the tenant's interest in the property is extinguished and is absorbed by the remaining joint tenant(s). The last survivor becomes the sole owner.

Tenancy by the entirety is a form of joint tenancy specifically for married couple in noncommunity property states. Tenancy by the entirety requires the aforementioned four unities and one more: **unity of person**. The legal premise is that a husband and wife are an indivisible legal unit. Thus, neither can dispose of the property independently; both must sign the deed in order to transfer the property. Tenancy by the entirety, like joint tenancy, provides the right of survivorship for the remaining spouse.

Community property is based on the premise that each spouse in a marriage is a partner with an equal interest in the property and requires the signature of both spouses to transfer the property. A spouse may also own separate property outside the community property.

Partnerships are very popular forms of ownership, especially for properties held as investments. There are two main types of partnerships.

In a **general partnership** (or **regular partnership**), all the partners have joint and severable liability for any and all debts of the partnership.

In a **limited partnership**, the limited partners are not liable for the obligations of the partnership. However, there must be one or more general partners who carry the personal liability for the financial obligations of the partnership. In both types of partnerships, the partners may have differing interests depending on their contribution to the partnership.

A partnership is different from a **joint venture**. In a joint venture, two or more entities join together to develop a real estate project. For example, a landowner, a developer, a lender, and a major tenant participate in a joint venture to develop an office building or a shopping center. A joint venture is created to accomplish a single business venture. Partnerships are created to pool resources and conduct business for profit on an ongoing basis.

Corporations can hold title to real estate, but a corporation is not a popular vehicle for holding investment property because the income is effectively taxed twice. The corporation pays taxes on any income from the property, and then the stockholders pay taxes again when the after-tax income is distributed to them in the form of dividends. Partnerships, on the other hand, do not pay income taxes. They simply file an information return and distribute all of the pretax income to the partners. The partners then pay taxes according to their individual tax brackets.

To avoid double taxation but retain some of the benefits of a corporation, investors may use a **real estate investment trust (REIT)**. Passive investors—those who do not participate in the management of their properties—are likely to use REITs. A REIT will typically hold a wide variety of investment properties: office buildings, shopping centers, apartments, warehouses, and even raw land.

There are other important types of trusts. For instance, an ***inter vivos* trust** is created during the lifetime of one individual for the benefit of another. (*Inter vivos* means "during the lifetime" in Latin.)

A **land trust** is often created to conceal the identity of the owner(s). Land is the only asset of the trust; the title is conveyed to the trustee. A land trust is usually used when investors want to speculate on land but would prefer that their identity not be revealed.

When you acquire real estate, you get a **bundle of rights** that constitute your interest in real property. The highest and best form of ownership in real property is called a **fee simple estate**. The owner of a fee simple estate has the right to:

- occupy, rent, or mortgage the property
- sell, dispose of, or transfer ownership of the property

- build on the property (or destroy buildings already part of the property)
- mine or extract oil, gas, and minerals
- restrict or allow the use of the property to others

A **leasehold estate** gives the holder of the estate a right to occupy the property until the end of the lease when the right will revert to the fee simple holder.

Descriptions of Property

In order to convey real property, the deed must include an unmistakable description of the property. To satisfy the requirement for legal description in the deed, one of four methods may be used.

1. Metes and bounds. A **metes and bounds** land description identifies a parcel by specifying its shape and boundaries. Typically, a convenient natural or artificial object is identified to locate the beginning corner of the subject tract, and a compass direction is specified. The surveyor, moving in a clockwise direction from the point of beginning, sets the center of a circle compass on each corner of the parcel to find the direction of travel to each successive corner of the subject tract.

A legal description of a property using the metes and bounds method might read something like: "From the pecan tree ten inches in diameter on the west bank of Salado Creek N4° 11' 18"E, 139.58' to a point of beginning." This description would instruct the surveyor on how to begin the metes and bounds survey.

A reference like the pecan tree is seldom used any more. Surveyors now use permanent monuments. At the corner where the survey begins, a monument in the form of an iron pipe or bar one or two inches in diameter is driven into the ground. Concrete or stone monuments may also be used.

To guard against the possibility that the monument might later be destroyed or removed, it is referenced by means of a connection line to a nearby permanent reference mark established by a government survey agency.

2. Rectangular survey system. The **rectangular survey system** (also known as the **government survey system** or **U.S. public lands survey system**) was authorized by Congress in order to systematically divide the land north and west of the Ohio River into six-mile squares, now called **congressional townships**.

This method is based on the system of mapping lines first imagined by ancient geographers and navigators: the east-west latitude lines and the north-south longitude lines that encircle the earth.

Certain longitude lines were selected to act as **principal meridians**. For each of these, an intercepting latitude line was selected as a **baseline**. Land is referenced to a principal meridian and a baseline. Every six miles east and west of each principal meridian, parallel survey lines are drawn. The resulting six-mile wide columns are called **ranges** and are numbered consecutively east and west of the principal meridian.

Every six miles north and south of a baseline, township lines are drawn. They intersect with the range lines and produce six-mile-by-six-mile mapped squares called **townships**. Each tier or row of townships thus created is numbered with respect to the baseline. Each 36-square mile township is divided into 36 one-square-mile units called **sections**, which are numbered 1 through 36, starting in the upper-right corner of the township. Any two sections with consecutive numbers share a common boundary.

Each square mile section contains 640 acres (43,560 square feet). Any parcel of land smaller than a full 640-acre section is identified by its position in the section. This is done by dividing the section into quarters and halves.

This is an example of a legal description using the rectangular survey system method: "The E $\frac{1}{2}$ of the SE $\frac{1}{4}$ of the NE $\frac{1}{4}$ of Section 28."

3. Recorded plat. Reference by **recorded plat** provides the simplest and most convenient method of land description. The vast majority of residential properties are described by this method. When a tract of land is ready for subdividing into lots for homes and businesses, a **plat**, or map, that shows the location and boundaries of individual building lots is filed in the map records at the county court house of the county in which the property is located.

When the surveyor's plat is filed in the public recorder's office, it becomes notice that a metes and bounds survey has been made and a map has been prepared to show in detail the boundaries of each parcel of land. Each parcel is then assigned a lot number. Each block in the tract is given a block number, and the tract itself is given a name or number. A large subdivision may be further divided into sections.

The following diagram is an example of a legal description using the recorded plat method: "Lot 13, Blk. 4, Sec 3 of Briargrove Hills Subdivision."

Numbered sections of the township that is located at Tier 1 North, Range 1 East

Land can also be described by reference to documents other than maps. For instance, if a tract of land was conveyed by deed some years ago and the deed was recorded, the reference can be made to that recorded deed when the property is to be conveyed again. Here's an example of this kind of legal description: "All the land described in the deed from Abraham Jacobs to Regina Murrow recorded in Book 5106, page 146, county of Kent, state of Oregon, at the public recorder's office for said county and state."

4. Assessor's parcel number. In some states, the **assessor's parcel number**, also known as the **appraisal district's account number**, is used to describe land. An appraisal district is responsible for determining the appraised (or market) value of every parcel of real estate in a county. The appraisal district assigns a parcel number to each parcel of land in the county to aid in the assessment of property for tax purposes. These parcel numbers are public information, so real estate brokers, appraisers, and investors can and do use them extensively to assist in identifying real properties.

Although the appraiser's maps are public records, they should not be relied upon as the final authority. The appraisal district's parcel number is never used as a legal description in a deed.

Government Rights in Land

Escheat
When a person dies and leaves no heirs and no instructions as to how to dispose of his or her real and personal property, or when property is abandoned, the ownership of the property reverts to the state. This reversion to the state is called **escheat** from the Anglo-French word meaning "to fall back."

Taxation

The government has the right to collect **property taxes** from property owners to provide funds for services such as schools, fire and police protection, parks, and libraries. The federal government does not tax property, relying on income taxes for operating revenues, but cities, counties, and in some cases the state levy taxes on real property. These taxes are levied according to the value of the property and are called *ad valorem* taxes.

To encourage property owners to pay their taxes in full and on time, the government retains the right to seize ownership of real estate upon which taxes are delinquent and to sell the property to recover the unpaid taxes. The taxing authority must depend upon a judicial foreclosure to collect delinquent taxes.

Property taxes are calculated as:

$$\text{Taxes} = \text{Assessed value} \div \$100 \times \text{Tax rate}$$

In some states, tax rates are established as an amount per $100 of assessed valuation. The assessed value is established by the **County Appraisal District (CAD)**.

Federal Income Tax

The federal government (and in some cases, state governments and even city governments) raises money through income taxes. Real property is affected by these taxes in several ways:

- taxation of cash flows from investment properties (passive activity income)
- taxation of profits from the sale of real properties (capital gains income)
- depreciation deductions on investment properties

Capital Gains

Capital gains from the sale of a principal residence are treated differently from profits on the sale of investment property. The first $250,000 ($500,000 for a married couple filing jointly) of capital gain on the sale of a principal residence is tax exempt. The owner must occupy the home two out of five years preceding the date of sale to qualify. A homeowner could sell a residence every two years, and, as long as no sale produced more than the amount allowed in profits, no capital gains tax would be due.

Capital gains from the sale of other property is taxed at the same rate as any other profit from the sale of a capital asset depending on how long the asset was held and the income of the taxpayer.

Depreciation

Depreciation, a loss in the estimated value of a property, is another factor that affects federal taxes. If you own an investment property, you deduct all operating expenses and interest on any mortgage from the income produced by the property. Depreciation, now called **cost recovery** in the tax code, is based on the premise that the real property's improvements are deteriorating and losing value.

If a property is an apartment or residential property, you can deduct the value of the structure over a life of 27.5 years. Only the building and other improvements can be depreciated. Land cannot be depreciated because the land does not deteriorate physically. Assuming the building is valued at $850,000, one year's depreciation would be $850,000 divided by 27.5 years, or $30,909 per year. Suppose the property produced an income (minus expenses and interest) of $20,000 last year. The investment lost value in the amount of $30,909 and netted only $20,000. $30,909 − $20,000 = $10,909 negative income. No tax is due. In fact, one can carry over the negative amount into subsequent years. To review your math skills, see Chapter 5.

When the property is sold, the owner must recapture cost recovery deductions taken. The recapture will be subtracted from the adjusted basis and affect the capital gains calculation.

The cost recovery deduction is allowed on investment properties, but not on a person's primary residence. However, if you changed your residence and rented your old house, you could then consider it an investment property.

Public Controls

Police Power

The government's right to control the owner's use of private property is called **police power**. The government may enact laws and enforce them to protect the safety, health, morals, and general welfare of the public. Examples of the government's exercise of police power applied to real estate include:

- planning and zoning laws
- building, health, and fire codes
- rent controls

These laws restrict the property owner's use of their land but do not constitute a **taking** (see Eminent Domain). Consequently, there is no payment to the property owner who suffers a loss of value through the exercise of police power.

Eminent Domain

The right of government to take ownership of privately held land is called **eminent domain**. Typically, land is taken for schools, freeways, parks, public housing, urban renewal, and other social and public purposes. Certain nongovernment entities, such as public utilities, may also take ownership of private property for public benefit.

When direct negotiations with the property owner are unsuccessful, the legal proceeding involved in exercising the right of eminent domain is called **condemnation**. The property owner must be paid the fair market value of the property taken.

When only a portion of a parcel of land is being taken, **severance damages** may be awarded in addition to payment for land actually being taken.

An **inverse condemnation** is a proceeding brought about by a property owner demanding that a government entity purchase his land. A property owner might choose this proceeding if his or her land has been adversely affected by the taking of neighboring land. For instance, homeowners at the ends of airport runways may try to force airport authorities to buy their homes because of the noise of aircraft during takeoffs.

Damage awards may also be made when land is not taken but its usefulness is reduced because of a nearby **condemnation**. The award would be considered **consequential damages**. An example of this would be when land is taken for a sewage treatment plant. Privately owned land downwind suffers a loss in value owing to the prevalence of foul odors, so the property owner might be awarded consequential damages.

Environmental Hazards and Regulations

Environmental regulations exist at both federal and state levels. Some of the most important federal laws in this area include:

- the Clean Air Act
- the Clean Water Act
- National Environmental Policy Act
- Comprehensive Environmental Response, Compensation, and Liability Act (CERCLA, or Superfund)
- the Endangered Species Act
- the Safe Drinking Water Act

- the Toxic Substances Control Act
- Residential Lead-Based Paint Hazard Reduction Act

Private Controls

The government is not the only entity that can control land. Developers often create **restrictive covenants** or **deed restrictions** to control everything from the type and size of the homes built in a subdivision to landscaping requirements. Developers can also control what can be parked in a driveway, how high a fence can be built, and whether or not a property owner can run a home-based business on the premises.

Homeowner associations may be created that require every homeowner to maintain membership. Homeowners can be required to pay assessments to the association and may be subject to foreclosure if they become delinquent.

Private restrictions are designed to preserve a quality of life and to enhance the value of residential properties. Many of the issues addressed in zoning laws, such as building lines and single-family occupancy versus multifamily occupancy may be addressed by the Deed Restrictions or Restrictive Covenants placed on the property by the developer. **Restrictions** are also termed **conditions, covenants,** and **restrictions** (CC&Rs). In practice, the term restriction can refer to any a condition, covenant, or restriction.

- A **condition** stipulates an action that a property owner must perform or refrain from performing.
- A **covenant** is a promise of a property owner.
- A **restriction** stipulates a forbidden activity or property use.

Water Rights

Water rights are defined by state law and depend on the water source and use. On a navigable body of water, the property owner's boundary will extend to the water's edge, (average high water line) or the mean vegetation line. On a non-navigable body of water, the property owner's boundary will extend to the center of the body of water.

Littoral rights are defined as the rights of a landowner whose property borders on a non-flowing body of water, such as a lake, ocean, or other body of still water. Owners of riparian land (property bordering a flowing stream) may have **riparian rights**, the rights to use the flowing water.

According to the **natural flow doctrine**, the owner of riparian land is entitled to the ordinary flow of water but may not impede the use of the ordinary flow by a downstream owner.

According to the **doctrine of reasonable use**, individual owners of riparian land have the right to reasonable use of the water that does not prevent use by other owners. States following this principle usually assign a higher priority to some uses, such as the domestic use of water on a residential property.

The **doctrine of prior appropriation** is based on the legal doctrine that the first person to use water had the first rights to the water. A modified form of the doctrine is part of the statutory laws of most western states and water resources are help by the state in trust and allocated by permit.

The **doctrine of beneficial use** allows the first users of a body of water to retain their priority, but imposes the limitation that the water be used for beneficial purpose within a reasonable time.

Water permits issued by the state are used to ration scarce water resources in areas of growing population, particularly in western states.

Use of **underground (subterranean) water** is vital in many states that have insufficient water from surface sources for residential, agricultural, and commercial uses.

Percolating water drains from the surface to underground strata. The states have modified the traditional English rule that there was no limitation on the amount of water a landowner could remove.

The **doctrine of correlative rights** limits the amount of water that can be taken to a proportionate share based on each owner's share of the surface area.

Underground streams confined to well-defined channels can be difficult to establish. If the location of an **underground stream** can be determined by a noninvasive method, the type of distribution applied to surface water will be followed.

Property Condition Disclosure Forms

Many states have adopted various property disclosure forms that real estate sellers are required to furnish to prospective buyers either prior to signing a purchase agreement or at some point prior to closing. Some states may require the real estate licensee to sign a statement disclosing any known information regarding the condition of the property. Failure to provide the required disclosure may result in a voidable or unenforceable purchase contract.

Licensees should always remember to refrain from making any representations about the physical condition of the property and should always recommend that purchasers have the property evaluated by professional inspectors selected and hired by the purchaser.

Need for Inspection

Many conditions (latent structural defects) can exist and may go undetected by the untrained eye. At a minimum, a purchaser should have a professional evaluation done to determine the condition of the structure and the mechanical systems of the property. Failure to do so could result in a buyer facing expensive unexpected repairs soon after closing and a seller and the real estate agents facing legal action brought by an unhappy buyer.

Material Facts

In every jurisdiction, agents have a duty to disclose all know material facts about a property being offered for sale. A **material fact** is any bit of information that a reasonable purchaser would take into consideration when making a decision to purchase or not to purchase, or when making decisions about how much to pay.

▶ Property Valuation/Appraisal

Value

Value is ever-changing, and its movement up and down is influenced by basic economic principles. The actions of buyers and sellers dictate values.

Characteristics of Property Value

Value is typically expressed in monetary worth and must have certain characteristics to be desirable by a person for some purpose. Real estate must have the following four characteristics to be valuable.

- **Utility**—The property must be useful for some need or desire of the owner or buyer.
- **Transferability**—The real estate must have ownership rights that can be transferred from the owner to a person desiring to own or possess those rights.
- **Scarcity**—There is a definite finite supply of real estate.
- **Demand**—Someone must have the means and desire to own the property.

Market Value, Market Price, and Cost

Appraisals are most often used to estimate a property's market value.

Market value can be defined as the price that a buyer will be likely to pay and that a seller will be likely to accept. Market value is an estimate only and not necessarily what a property will actually sell for. The market value is based on the fact that:

- both parties are aware of the condition of the property
- neither party is acting under duress
- financing for the transaction is typical of available rates and terms
- the property is exposed on the market for a reasonable period of time

Market price, or **sales price**, is what the property actually sells for. The sales price can be less than the cost of the land and improvements. This may occur when a property owner over-improves a property, failing to take into account the likely needs of a prospective purchaser.

Cost is the actual cost to construct improvements to the land. Actual cost to build and the cost of the land are usually considered separately. Cost may be more or less that the market value of the real estate.

There are a number of other types of property value, including the following ones.

- **Assessed value:** determined by a County Appraisal District (CAD) or other property taxing entity for property tax purposes
- **Book value:** depreciated cost basis used for accounting and tax purposes
- **Insurance value:** the maximum amount that an insurer will be willing to pay for an insured loss
- **Investment value:** the amount that an investor is willing to pay for the right to receive the cash flow produced by the property or the capitalization rate (rate of return) used to determine market value
- **Loan value:** the maximum loan that can be secured by the property

- **Salvage value:** what the component parts of a building or other improvements will be worth following demolition or removal of the improvements

Real Estate Value Cycle

The **value cycle**, or **life cycle**, of a property also determines worth. The term *life cycle* applies both to individual properties and to neighborhoods.

The initial period of **development (growth or integration)** becomes a period of **equilibrium (when properties are at the highest and best use)**. Equilibrium is followed by **decline (disintegration)**, when property values go down as maintenance requirements increase and are not met. In areas that undergo the substantial expense of building renovation, a period of **revitalization** may occur and the cycle is reestablished.

Principles of Value

Many principles of value underlie the appraisal process, including the following:

- **Anticipation:** the expectation that property value will rise or decline because of some future event.
- **Assemblage (plottage):** bringing a group of adjoining parcels under the same ownership, which may make them more valuable for a particular purpose, such as construction of a residential or commercial development.
- **Change:** forces to which all property is subject, including:
  - **Physical:** changes caused by the elements that can occur gradually or over a brief period of time
  - **Political:** regulations that affect property use
  - **Economic:** employment level; business start-ups, expansions, and failures; and other factors that influence the level of prosperity of a region

- **Social:** demographic and other trends in population that affect the demand for property
- **Environmental:** factors such as high pollution from fires following a drought, waste depositories, wetlands, or areas set aside for protected species

■ **Conformity:** individual properties in a residential neighborhood tend to have a higher value when they are of similar architecture, design, age, and size; the same principle applies generally to commercial property. Conformity of like kind use such as residential, retail, industrial, or other types may enhance value.

■ **Competition:** a result of increased demand as well as a cause of increased demand. For example, even though a regional mall may offer many stores selling similar products, it will benefit all storeowners by bringing more shoppers to the area.

■ **Highest and best use:** the legally allowed property use that makes maximum physical use of a site and generates the highest value or income.

■ **Law of decreasing returns:** in effect, this occurs when property improvements no longer bring a corresponding increase in property value.

■ **Law of increasing returns:** in effect, this occurs as long as property improvements bring a corresponding increase in property value.

■ **Progression:** the benefit to a property of being located in an area of more desirable properties; a small plain house on a street of mansions will benefit in value from proximity to them.

■ **Regression:** the detriment to property value of being located in a neighborhood of less desirable properties; a large, over-improved house on a street of small, plain houses will have a lower value than it would in a neighborhood of comparable houses.

■ **Substitution:** the principle that the typical buyer will pay no more for a property than would be required to buy another equivalent property. This principle, when applied to income-producing property, is called **opportunity cost**. In addition, an investor will pay no more for real estate than for another investment offering the same likely risk and potential reward.

■ **Supply and demand:** As the number of properties available for sale or rent goes up relative to the number of potential buyers or tenants, prices will fall. As the number of properties decline while the number of potential buyers or tenants remains the same or increase, prices will rise.

■ **Theory of distribution:** consideration of the contribution to value of each of the four factors of production—land (rent), labor (salaries), capital (interest), and management (profit). When these factors are in balance, property value will be at its highest.

Methods of Estimating Value: Appraisal Process

Typically, an appraiser uses three different approaches in developing a final estimate of value of a property: **sales comparison** or **market data approach**, **cost approach**, and **income approach**. In the final reconciliation, the appraiser will give the most weight to the value that would be most appropriate for the subject property.

Sales Comparison Approach (Market Data Approach)

If the property being appraised is a single-family residence, the most important determinant of value is the price that other similar properties have commanded in the open market. In using the sales comparison approach, the appraiser will select comparables (comps) to compare to the subject property (the property being appraised). For example, if several comparable properties sold for $200,000, the subject would most likely sell for about $200,000 as well. An appraiser would prefer to have at least three comps for a sales comparison approach.

Features that should be considered in choosing comps include:

- size (usually expressed as square footage)
- number of stories
- proximity to the subject
- quality of construction
- general condition of the property
- age
- number of bedrooms, bathrooms, and total rooms
- date of sale, preferably within the last six months
- similarity of features such as fireplaces, pools, spas, patios, and so on

The ideal comparable would be a house that sold very recently and is the same size; number of stories; in the same condition; the same age; on the same block in the same subdivision; with the same number of bedrooms, bathrooms, and total rooms; and with all of the same features as the subject. Typically, an appraiser will use sales within the last six months only.

Obviously, the chances of finding such a comparable are not very likely. The appraiser must secure the best comparables available and make adjustments to bring the comparables as close to the subject as possible. For example, Comparable A has three bedrooms and sold for $200,000. The subject has four bedrooms. In this subdivision, historically, one more bedroom has added $12,000 to the purchase price of a home. So the appraiser would assume that Comparable A, if it had had four instead of three, would have sold for $12,000 more, or $212,000. When a comparable is inferior as in this case, the adjustment is upward. If a comparable is superior to the subject, the adjustment is downward. If the only comparable available sold more than six months previously, the appraiser will use a time adjustment based on the market price trend in the area.

In analyzing the adjusted comparable sales, the appraiser would give the most weight to the comparable with the fewest adjustments.

Cost Approach

When the property is not an income-producing property and it is difficult to find market comparables, the cost approach to value is often used. This approach is most often used with unique properties. For instance, if you had to appraise a mosque located in Nagodoches, Texas, you would have a hard time finding three comparable properties in the same area. The cost approach would also be useful in appraising properties such as a college campus, an abandoned fire station, or a state capitol building.

The formula for determining value using the cost approach is as follows:

Value = Replacement or Reproduction Cost –
Accrued Depreciation + Land Value

The appraiser begins by estimation the **replacement cost** of the improvements. Replacement cost is the cost at today's prices and using today's methods of construction, for an improvement having the same or equivalent usefulness as the subject property. Or, the appraiser may estimate the **reproduction cost**, the cost of creating an exact replica of the improvements.

This would show the value of a new building. Because the subject property is not new, adjustments must be made for depreciation. The amount of adjustment depends on the amount and type of depreciation. There are **three types of depreciation**.

1. **Physical deterioration** results from wear and tear through use, such as carpet that is worn thin or a heating and cooling system that must be replaced. Nature, neglect, vandalism, and other factors contribute to physical deterioration.
2. **Functional obsolescence** results from outmoded equipment, faulty or outmoded design, inadequate structural facilities, or over-adequate structural facilities.
3. **External obsolescence** may be economic or environmental depreciation that results from factors outside the property over which the owner has no control.

Physical and functional obsolescence can be either **curable** or **incurable. Curable obsolescence** can be fixed at a reasonable cost. Examples include worn carpeting or outdated kitchen appliances. **Incurable obsolescence** cannot be fixed at a reasonable cost. For example, an illogical room layout or a building that will not accommodate a central heating and air conditioning system would be considered incurable obsolescence.

The value of the land must also be considered in determining value by the cost approach. The value of the land is established as though it were vacant using the sales comparison approach. While land value can decrease, land does not depreciate in the sense that it is subject to physical or functional obsolescence.

Income Approach

If a property produces income in the form of rent or other revenues, its value is estimated by analyzing the amount of stability of the income it can produce. The **income approach**, used to value properties such as apartment projects, shopping centers, and office buildings, considers the monetary returns a property can be expected to produce and then converts that amount into a value the property should sell for if placed on the market. This is called **capitalization** of the income stream.

The formula for determining value by the income approach is as follows:

Value = Net Operating Income ÷ Capitalization Rate

The income is the net income that the property produces after allowing for vacancy and loss of revenue and deducting all maintenance and operating expenses of the subject property. The **capitalization rate (cap rate)** is determined by the appraiser as a function of the market and the type and location of the property.

Purpose and Use of Appraisal

An appraisal is defined under federal law as "a written statement used in connection with a federally related transaction that is independent and impartially prepared by a licensed, certified appraiser that states an opinion of the defined value of an adequately described property as of a specific date that is supported by the presentation and analysis of relevant market information." The real estate practitioner defines appraisal more simply as "the act or process of estimating value."

Market value, or **fair market value**, is the highest price that a property will bring if all of the following apply:

1. The payment is made in cash or its equivalent.
2. The property is exposed on the open market for a reasonable length of time.
3. The buyer and seller are fully informed as to market conditions and the uses to which the property may be put.
4. Neither buyer nor seller is under abnormal pressure to conclude a transaction.
5. The seller is capable of conveying marketable title.

Role of the Appraiser

There are seven major steps in the appraisal process.

1. **State the problem.** The nature of the appraisal assignment must be clearly understood. The assignment may be to find a market value of the subject property. If so, that should be stated.

2. **Determine the kinds and sources of data necessary.**
   - What are the characteristics of the subject property?
   - What economic or other factors will play a role in determining property value?
   - What approach(es) will be most appropriate in this appraisal, and what kind of data will be necessary?

3. **Determine the highest and best use of the site.**

4. **Estimate the value of the site.**

5. **Estimate the property's value by the appropriate approaches (sales comparison, cost, and/or income).**

6. **Reconcile the different values reached** by the different approaches to estimate the property's most probable market value. This process is called **reconciliation** or **correlation**.

7. **Report the estimate of value to the client in writing.** There are several types of documents that may be prepared.
   - The **narrative appraisal report** provides a lengthy discussion of the factors considered in the appraisal and the reasons for the conclusion of value.
   - The **form report** is used most often for one- to four-family residential appraisals. A **Uniform Residential Appraisal Report (URAR)** is required by various agencies and organizations. Computerized appraisal generation is possible and is increasingly expected by lenders.
   - Reports may be written in other formats, which are defined by the **Uniform Standards of Professional Appraisal Practice (USPAP)**. The **self-contained report** is as complete as the narrative appraiser's conclusion. The **summary report** is less detailed than the self-contained report, and the **restricted report**, which reveals only minimal information, is less detailed than the summary report. Using either of the two latter types of reports will require the consent of the client.

Competitive or Comparative Market Analysis (CMA)

Real estate licensee do not generally prepare appraisals, although in some states, licensed brokers are permitted to do so provided they follow the uniform standards. Licensees must be careful to state that a **CMA is not an appraisal** and should not be regarded as such. All CMAs must include a notice to this effect.

The CMA is a tool used by the licensee to enable prospective sellers or buyers to identify a range of value in a given area in a given time frame. A **comparative** market analysis uses sold properties. A **competitive** market analysis also identifies the properties currently listed, those that have been on the market without success and have expired, as well as those that have sold.

The client can then choose an asking or offering price that is realistic and within the appropriate value range. Sellers who establish an asking price above the upper end of the range will make their properties invisible to many of the best potential buyers for their properties. Buyers who offer too little, or "low ball," will often insult the sellers and make it impossible to negotiate with them.

► Financing

The Loan Documents

Promissory Note
A lender will require a borrower to sign a note that is the promise to pay a certain sum of money according to certain terms. The note is the evidence of the borrower's debt, which is secured by a mortgage or deed of trust.

Mortgage
The mortgage is a legal document used to secure the property as collateral for the debt evidenced in the promissory note. It is a two-party instrument in which a mortgagor (the borrower) pledges property as security to the mortgagee (lender). The property may be sold at auction (foreclosure) when the borrower defaults and fails to fulfill the promises made in the mortgage instrument. The mortgage is given for the benefit of the mortgagee.

Caution! Remember that in legal terminology, words ending in *-or* refer to the person giving something, such as the borrower giving the pledge to repay. The words ending in *-ee* refer to the person receiving something, such as the lender receiving the promise from the borrower to repay the loan. Forget about the fact that the lender gives the money. It is the pledge of collateral that is important in this discussion.

The borrower remains in possession of the pledged property through a legal function known as **hypothecation**. There are two legal theories regarding the mortgaged property. Some states recognize the **title theory,** and some recognize the **lien theory**.

In a **title theory state**, the mortgagor conveys title to the lender but retains the use of the property. This conveyance of title in the mortgage agreement is conditional. The mortgage states that if the debt is repaid on time, title returns to the borrower. This is known as the **defeasance clause**, and title is returned by a **deed of reconveyance**.

In a **lien theory state**, the mortgagor retains legal title to the property and the mortgagee, the lender, has an equitable interest in and a lien on the property. When the mortgage is fully repaid, the lender gives a **release of lien** to the borrower.

A defaulting borrower faces penalties of varying severity. **Late charges** will be incurred if the borrower is late in making a payment. If the borrower remains in default, an **acceleration clause** may be invoked by the lender. An acceleration clause gives the lender the right to collect the balance of the loan immediately. Finally, if the debt remains unpaid, the formal process of **foreclosure** will begin. This will be through a court process or **judicial foreclosure**.

Deed of Trust (Trust Deed)
In some states, lenders use the **deed of trust (trust deed)** form of mortgage document whereby the borrower pledges the collateral as security for the loan. The deed of trust is a three-party instrument. The lender is the **beneficiary**, the borrower is the **trustor**, and a third party selected by the lender is the **trustee**. The borrower conveys the "power of sale" to the trustee, and upon any default by the borrower, the trustee will proceed with the foreclosure process.

This three-party system does not require a court action to proceed with foreclosure and is **nonjudicial foreclosure**. In this case, state law applies and there will be specific notice and procedural requirements. When the property is sold, a **trustee's deed** is used to convey title to the new owner.

If the proceeds of the foreclosure sale of either the mortgage or the deed of trust do not cover the amount owed on the loan, some states allow the lender to obtain a **deficiency judgment** against the borrower. This means that other assets can be claimed by the lender to satisfy the remaining indebtedness. Other states provide homeowners with anti-deficiency protection in the event that the proceeds of the sale on loan default do not cover the amount owed.

Real estate can be pledged as collateral for a loan using any of the following four methods.

1. The **standard**, or **regular mortgage**, is the most common. The borrower conveys title to the lender as security for the debt. The mortgage contains a statement that the mortgage will become void if the debt is secures is paid in full and on time.

2. An **equitable mortgage** is a written agreement that does not follow the form of a regular mortgage, but is still considered by the courts to be one. An **equitable mortgage**, or **equitable**, **lien** can arise in a number of ways. For example, a prospective buyer may give the seller a money deposit along with an offer to purchase property. If the seller refuses the offer and also refuses to return the deposit, the court will hold that the purchaser has an equitable mortgage in the amount of the deposit against the seller's property.

3. In some cases, the borrower may convey the deed to the pledged property to the lender as a **deed as security** for a loan. If the loan is repaid in full and on time, the borrower can force the lender to convey the real property back to him or her. Like the equitable mortgage, a deed used a security is treated according to its intent, not its label.

4. A **deed of trust** is a three-party agreement including a beneficiary (lender), a trustor (borrower), and a trustee (neutral third party). The key aspect of this method is that the borrower executes a deed to the trustee rather than to the lender. If the borrower pays the debt in full and on time, the trustee delivers a **release of liability** or **deed of reconveyance** to the borrower.

Primary and Secondary Mortgage Markets

The **primary mortgage market** is where lenders originate loans and directly fund them. The participants in the primary market are commercial banks, savings and loan associations, mutual banks, credit unions, insurance companies, and mortgage bankers. Mortgage brokers originate loans and match borrowers with appropriate lenders, but mortgage brokers do not fund loans.

The **secondary mortgage market** is where closed loans are bought and sold. Some participants in the secondary market are Fannie Mae (Federal National Mortgage Association, or FNMA), Freddie Mac (Federal Home Loan Mortgage Corporation, or FHLMC), Ginnie Mae (Government National Mortgage Association, or GNMA), and others. Some are closely regulated by the federal government, and some are strictly private purchasers of mortgage loans. The secondary market provides liquidity for primary lenders by purchasing pools of closed loans. The primary lender is then able to fund more loans and repeat the process.

Government and Conventional

Loans can be divided into two overall categories, **government programs** and nongovernment programs, or **conventional loans**.

Government loan programs consist of two major types, the **FHA loan** and the **VA loan**. The **Federal Housing Administration (FHA)** was created in 1934 to provide a way to get as many people into homes as possible. It is designed to reduce the lender's risk when low down payment loans are made. FHA is administered by the Housing and Urban Development Department (HUD) and is an insurance program requiring the borrower to pay an insurance premium protecting the lender in the event of default by the borrower.

FHA mortgage insurance requires the payment of a **premium**, a sum of money paid in addition to the amount of the loan. In 2006, the up-front premium was 1.5% of the loan amount paid in cash at closing or financed with the loan. The annual premium of 0.5% of the loan balance is payable over the life of the loan. FHA insurance covers the entire loan balance for the life of the loan.

The **VA program** is designed to encourage lenders to make loans to qualified veterans. Basically, the **VA guarantees** a portion of the loan in sufficient amount to entice lenders to make loans. Depending on eligibility, a veteran may be able to borrow 100% of the purchase price up to approximately $417,000 (in 2007). Rather than a premium, the VA charges a funding fee. The amount of the funding fee ranges from 1.25% to 3.30% depending on the amount of down payment, veteran's service status, and whether it is the first or subsequent use of the veteran's entitlement.

Conventional loans consist of two major types: conforming and non-conforming.

Conforming loans meet the Fannie Mae and Freddie Mac guidelines regarding loan maximums, borrower qualification, use of application and verification forms, and the appraisal process. These entities control how the loan origination or primary market operates in the conforming loan market. Fannie Mae and Freddie Mac purchase only conforming loans.

Non-conforming loans are anything that does not meet Fannie Mae and Freddie Mac guidelines, including loan amounts over the conforming limit. These are referred to as **jumbo loans**. Borrowers who do not meet the income or credit requirements for a conforming loan may qualify for non-conforming loans known as **subprime loans**. Private investors determine the guidelines for subprime loans and pur-

chase them on the secondary market from loan originators in the primary market.

Types of Loan Payment Plans

There are several ways to structure the repayment of borrowed funds.

1. **Term or straight loan**—This is an **interest-only** loan with the entire loan amount payable at the maturity date of the loan.
2. **Fully amortized loan**—The loan payments include both principal and interest and will be **paid in full** at the maturity date.
3. **Partially amortized loan**—The loan payments include both principal and interest, but the term is not long enough to retire the debt fully, resulting in a **balloon payment** at the maturity date.
4. **Fixed rate loan**—This loan has a permanent fixed interest rate over the life of the loan and can be used with a term, fully amortized or partially amortized loan.
5. **Adjustable or variable rate loan**—The interest rate on this loan adjusts periodically according to the terms of the note. Adjustable-rate mortgages (ARMs) have three primary factors to consider: (a) the **adjustment period** or how often the rate is changed; (b) the **index**, an economic indicator to which the loan regularly adjusts; and (c) the **margin**, a percentage added to the index and results in the fully indexed rate charged to the borrower.

Types of Mortgages

There is a variety of mortgage plans available to borrowers.

1. **Blanket mortgage**—More than one parcel of real estate is pledged as collateral. The mortgage document typically contains a **partial release**

clause, allowing the borrower to sell a parcel of the property and maintain the mortgage on the remaining parcels.

2. **Buydown mortgage**—By paying the lender up-front points on the loan, the interest rate is temporarily reduced.

3. **Graduated payment mortgage**—Payment in the first one to three years is paid at a reduced rate and may result in negative amortization, that is, unpaid interest being added back to the principal.

4. **Growing equity mortgage**—The borrower agrees to increase the principal payment a certain percentage each year, thereby growing equity at a faster rate.

5. **Package mortgage**—This mortgage includes personal property, such as furnishings and appliances, and is common in financing condominiums.

6. **Participation mortgage**—More than one lender funds the loan and each holds an equal lien position.

7. **Reverse mortgage**—This loan is for seniors over age 62. The homeowner receives regular payments drawn from the equity in the home and repayment becomes due when the senior no longer lives in the home.

8. **Shared equity mortgage**—A lender may offer a very favorable interest rate to the borrower in exchange for an equity interest in the property.

Financing/Credit Laws

Truth-in-Lending Act (TILA)

The Federal Consumer Credit Protection Act includes the Truth-in-Lending Act and went into effect in 1969. It is implemented by the **Federal Reserve Board's Regulation Z**. The law requires that borrowers be clearly shown how much they are paying for credit in both dollar terms and percentage terms before committing to the loan.

The borrower is also given the **right to rescind** certain transactions under provisions of the law. The lender must notify the borrower of the right to rescind regarding a transaction in which the borrower is pledging his or her principal dwelling as security for the loan. The borrower may rescind in writing until midnight of the third business day following the loan settlement.

Exempt transactions under the rule of rescission are:

- a residential mortgage at the time of purchase
- a refinancing or consolidation by the same creditor or an extension of credit already secured by the consumer's principal dwelling
- a transaction in which a state agency is the lender

The act requires certain disclosures in advertising anything that involves financing. If an advertisement contains any one of the TILA list of financing terms (called **trigger terms**), the ad must also include five disclosures. Here are some of the trigger terms:

- amount of down payment in dollars or percentage
- amount of any additional payments
- number of payments
- period of payments
- dollar amount of any finance charge
- statement that there is no interest charged

If the ad contains any one of these trigger terms, the ad must also include all of these disclosures:

- cash price or the amount of the loan
- amount of down payment or a statement that none is required

- number, amount, and frequency of repayments
- annual percentage rate (APR)
- deferred payment price or total of all payments

Equal Credit Opportunity Act (ECOA)

The Equal Credit Opportunity Act was passed in 1974 and is Title VII of the Federal Consumer Credit Protection Act. It first protected the categories of **sex** (gender) and **marital status** against discrimination. In 1976, the act was amended to include **color, race, religion, national origin, age,** and those applicants who receive all or part of their **income from public assistance.** It is administered under the **Federal Reserve Board's Regulation B.**

Factors that can legitimately be considered are the applicant's income, stability of the source of the income, total assets and liabilities, and credit score.

Home Mortgage Disclosure Act (HMDA)

The Home Mortgage Disclosure Act was enacted in 1975 and is implemented by the **Federal Reserve Board's Regulation C.** The purpose of the act is to ensure that banks provide regular reports to the federal government that they are serving the housing needs of the communities in which they do business. The reports also may identify possible discriminatory lending patterns.

Community Reinvestment Act (CRA)

The CRA was enacted in 1977 to regulate banks and require them to demonstrate that their deposit facilities serve the needs of the communities in which they are chartered to do business. Along with HMDA, the CRA also is intended to prevent the practice of **redlining.** Redlining is defined as refusing to make loans in particular geographic areas and may be used as a means of discrimination.

Fair Credit Reporting Act (FCRA)

Congress enacted the Fair Credit Reporting Act in 1970 to protect consumers from the reporting of inaccurate credit information to credit reporting agencies. This legislation is administered by the Federal Trade Commission. It requires that if a buyer of real estate is denied credit because of an unfavorable credit report, the lender refusing to make the loan must reveal to the buyer the identity of the credit agency reporting the information that was the basis of the rejection. Most negative items are to be dropped from the report after a period of seven years; an exception is bankruptcy information, which may be held for ten years.

Fair and Accurate Credit Transactions Act (FACT Act)

This law was passed by Congress in 2003 as an amendment to the Fair Credit Reporting Act. Consumers can request and obtain a free credit report once every 12 months from each of the three nationwide consumer credit reporting companies (Equifax, Experian, and TransUnion).

This law also addresses the disposal of private information. Businesses must use "reasonable procedures" in the disposal of credit reports and other similar information.

Gramm-Leach-Bliley Act (GLBA)

Under the jurisdiction of the Federal Trade Commission, this law requires companies to give consumers privacy notices explaining the company's privacy policies regarding the sharing of information. The GLBA applies to banks and lending institutions.

► Contracts/Agency Relationships

General

A **contract** is a legally enforceable agreement between two parties to do something (**performance**) or to refrain from certain acts (**forbearance**). To create a real estate contract, there are seven requirements. A contract must:

1. involve legally competent parties
2. be in writing as required by the Statute of Frauds (One notable exception is a lease for one year or less.)
3. be signed by the parties to the agreement
4. have a lawful objective
5. include consideration (does not need to be money)
6. mention offer and acceptance and notification of the acceptance
7. contain a legal description of the property

Offers/Purchase Agreements

The **sales contract** (sometimes called an **earnest money contract**) is arguably the most important document used in a real estate transaction. Because a defective contract can allow either buyer or seller to end the transaction, real estate practitioners must be thoroughly familiar with contract law.

A **contract** is a legally enforceable agreement to do or not do a certain thing. Most contracts are based on promises by the parties involved to act in some manner. Examples of such acts would be to pay money, to provide services, or to deliver title. However, a contract can also contain a promise to **forbear** (not to act) by one or more of its parties. For example, a lender may agree not to foreclose on a delinquent mortgage loan if the borrower agrees to a new payment schedule.

A contract may be either **express** or **implied**.

- An **express contract** occurs when the parties to the contract declare their intentions either orally or in writing. Leases and contracts to purchase real estate are examples of express contracts. The Statute of Frauds requires that all documents affecting title to or an interest in real estate be expressed in writing except for a lease of one year or less.
- An **implied contract** is created by the actions of the parties rather than by words. An example of an implied contract is the agreement between you and a restaurant when you walk in and sit down. The presence of tables, silverware, and menus implies that you will be served food. When you order, you imply that you are going to pay the bill.

A contract may be **bilateral** or **unilateral**.

- A **bilateral contract** results when a promise is exchanged for a promise. A bilateral contract is essentially an agreement that says, "I will do this, and you will do that." A real estate sales contract is a good example of a bilateral contract.
- A **unilateral contract** results when a promise is exchanged for performance. It is essentially an agreement that says, "I will do this *if* you do that." If the sales manager offers a bonus if you sell $3,000,000 worth of real estate, you are not obligated to sell $3,000,000 worth of real estate—but the sales manager is obligated to pay you the bonus if you do.

A contract can be construed by the courts to be **valid**, **void**, **voidable**, or **unenforceable**.

- A **valid contract** meets all the requirements of law. It is binding upon its parties and legally enforceable in a court of law.

- A **void contract** has no legal effect and, in fact, is not a contract at all. Even though the parties may have intended to enter into a contract, no legal rights are created and no party is bound. The word *void* means the absence of something.

- A **voidable contract** binds one party but not the other. For example, when one party is guilty of fraud, the other party may void the contract. But if the offended party wishes to fulfill the contract, then the party who committed fraud is still bound to the terms of the contract. A contract with a minor is voidable at the option of the minor party.

- An **unenforceable contract** is one that may once have been valid, but its enforcement is barred by a statute of limitations or a change of law.

Counteroffers/Multiple Counteroffers

Purpose of Offer and Counteroffer

The real estate sales contract begins as a written **offer** from buyer to seller and will typically include:

- identity of all parties to the transaction
- full legal description of the real estate, as well as a listing of any personal property to be included
- sales price, including the amount of down payment and an indication of how the remainder of the price will be paid at closing
- financing contingency giving details of the type of financing the buyer hopes to obtain and stipulating a deadline for release of the contingency
- statement that the transaction is contingent on a sale of other property of the buyer (the seller will want a deadline for release of the contin-

gency, particularly if a noncontingent offer is made while the transaction is pending)
- name of the escrow agent for the transaction and by whom the fee for this service will be paid
- list of property inspections to be made and by whom, including deadlines for the inspections as well as the appropriate notifications to buyer and/or seller (the seller will want a limit on expenditures for any pest control treatment or necessary repairs)
- list of applicable categories of disclosure required by state and federal law, which may include location in a flood, earthquake, or other zone, and the presence of hazardous materials, such as lead-based paint
- provision for arbitration or mediation of disputes that may arise between the parties
- remedies, including suit for specific performance, money damages, or acceptance of liquidated damages, in the event one of the parties breaches the agreement
- statement of compliance with the federal **Foreign Investment in Real Property Tax Act (FIRPTA)**
- statement of compliance with all applicable fair housing laws
- statement of compliance with any other state or federal law not already mentioned
- provision for a final walk-through by the buyer to ensure that the property has been adequately maintained before closing
- statement of who will bear the risk of loss in the event of property damage or destruction between the time the contract is signed and the transaction is closed
- statement of the agency representation and commission owed
- signature of the buyer(s) and space for signature of the seller(s)

An offer will **expire** (end) if it is not accepted by the deadline specified in its terms. If no deadline is specified, a reasonable time period will be implied. An offer can be withdrawn at any time prior to the offeror being notified of its **acceptance**.

Any change to the terms of an offer is a **counteroffer** and has the effect of rejecting the initial offer and making a new offer. The offer and acceptance must both be made voluntarily (without coercion) and without misrepresentation.

Valid Methods of Communicating Offers

Although verbal negotiations may appear to save time and to be efficient, a licensee needs to remember that agreements for the sale of real estate must be reduced to writing to be enforceable. The Statute of Frauds requires that there be a written offer and written acceptance. As soon as the written acceptance is obtained, the offeror must be notified of the acceptance. The notification is accomplished by delivering a copy of the accepted document to the offeror.

Remember that a party making an offer or a counteroffer may revoke that offer or counteroffer at any time prior to acceptance by the other party. Revocation of a written offer or counteroffer must be made in writing to be effective.

When one party fails to perform as required by the contract, a **breach of contract** or **default** has occurred. The wronged or innocent party has six possible remedies.

1. **Accept partial performance**. If the purchaser was expecting 25 acres to be conveyed, but the survey showed that there were only 23.57 acres in the tract, the purchaser may accept the property as is.
2. **Rescind the contract unilaterally**. The wronged party can simply rescind or cancel the contract and return to the status prior to executing the contract.
3. **Sue for specific performance**. *Specific performance* means doing exactly what the contract requires. The party seeking specific performance must have acted in good faith and not committed a material breach of the contract.
4. **Sue for money damages**. For example, if a seller cannot perform, but the buyer has already spent a large amount of money on inspections, appraisals, and so on, the buyer could sue to recover the money spent.
5. **Accept liquidated money damages**. This remedy, available only to the seller, means retaining the earnest money.
6. **Mutually rescind the contract**. Sometimes both parties are better off just walking away from the contract and canceling the agreement. A mutual rescission must be expressed in writing.

Before closing a real estate transaction, the parties involved must be assured that certain conditions are met. By signing a contract, the parties affirm their mutual agreement. Once they are bound to the terms of the agreement, they can then take the time to ensure that these conditions are met. If there was no contract, and the parties were not bound to honor their agreement, one or both of the parties might spend considerable time and money on a transaction that could fall through.

There are three basic contingencies.

1. **Buyer's ability to obtain suitable financing**. When buyers start looking at properties, they typically meet with a lender to determine what loan amount they would likely qualify for. Once they have selected a specific property, they must get lender approval for a loan on that property.

This takes time, so it is important to have the property tied to a specific contractual agreement.

2. **Buyer's approval of title matters**. Buyers generally will not take the time and effort to examine the title until they have a firm agreement from the seller.

3. **Buyer's acceptance of the property condition**. A property may appear to be in good condition when the buyer initially views it, but the buyer will likely require a thorough inspection of the property after negotiating with the seller. The inspection, too, will take time to complete.

Leases as Contracts

A lease is a contract wherein a property owner (**lessor**) transfers the rights of possession, quiet enjoyment, and use to the tenant (**lessee**) for a period of time, thus creating a **leasehold estate**. When property ownership transfers during the term of a lease, the lease remains binding upon the new owner.

This topic will be discussed in more detail under "Property Management" on page 93.

Options

An **option** is a unilateral contract. An option to purchase enables a purchaser to purchase a property at a set price within a given time frame. An option to terminate grants a purchaser the unrestricted right to terminate a contract without penalty within a given time frame.

To create a valid option, the property owner must be paid some cash (valuable consideration), and **time is of the essence**.

Rescission and Cancellation Agreements

Contracts usually come to an end by completion of the objective of the contract or by expiration of the term specified in the agreement. On occasion, the parties will decide to end the agreement and to restore each other to the position enjoyed prior to entering into the agreement. This is identified in legal terms as **mutual rescission**.

Agency appointments may be ended early by termination or withdrawal. If a property owner has entered into an exclusive right to sell listing agreement and decides to terminate, he or she may withdraw the listing and request that the agent stop marketing the property. If the owner then sells the property during the term of the listing, the broker is still entitled to receive the agreed upon compensation.

The seller may terminate with the agreement and consent of the agent. To effect a termination, the broker may require some compensation to cover expenses incurred through the date of the termination. If all parties can reach agreement, the termination becomes a mutual rescission. When an agreement cannot be reached, the property owner should seek legal counsel before attempting to fire the agent and the agent should seek legal counsel before quitting or renouncing the agency appointment.

With regard to leases and purchase agreements, the parties may cancel an agreement through mutual rescission or may create a substitute agreement to replace the original contract. The substitution of a new agreement for an existing contract is known as a **novation**. The new agreement should reference the agreement that it is replacing and clearly state that it replaces the original agreement.

Broker-Salesperson Agreements

Most salespersons function as **independent contractors** rather that as employees of the primary broker. A licensee holding a broker license may also be associated with the primary broker of a firm as an independent contractor. The federal tax code requires that the broker and salesperson or broker-associate enter into a written contract to create the working relationship.

The agreement should clearly stipulate that the salesperson or broker-associate is an independent contractor and that:

- he or she has paid his or her own licensing and trade association fees
- he or she is free to work on his or her own time schedule
- he or she may perform the tasks of the business where he or she wishes
- compensation is based solely on production and that no salary, hourly wages, or benefits are paid or provided
- the salesperson or broker-associate is responsible for paying quarterly federal income tax payments and the full 15.3% of gross wages for FICA taxes

This agreement also needs to define compensation amounts and issues such as payment of commissions generated prior to termination of the agreement but not yet paid.

Law, Definition, and Nature of Agency Relationships

Type of Agencies and Agents

When one person agrees to act on behalf of another, an agency relationship is established. Agency relationships are regulated by a body of laws collectively known as the **law of agency**. This is **common law**. States have also enacted **statutory laws** regulating agency in their respective states.

An agency is a **legal, fiduciary relationship** where the agent works for and under the direction and control of a principal or client. Two kinds of agency relationships are common in real estate practice.

1. **General agency**—Real estate brokers typically have licensees who act as their agents in working for the broker's principals/clients. It is broad in power, extends for transaction after transaction, and gives the agent authority to bind the principal to certain agreements within the scope of the business. The relationship between a primary broker and an associate or the relationship between a property manager and owner are examples of general agency.
2. **Special agency**—A principal to a transaction (seller/landlord and buyer/tenant) secures the advice and assistance of a real estate broker and the broker's associates. The authority is limited in scope and does not allow the agent to bind the principal to any agreement and generally is limited to one transaction per agreement.

Creation of Agency and Agency Agreements

An agency relationship is established when a buyer or seller delegates authority to a broker and the broker accepts the authority to act on behalf of the principal. Although the delegation may be given orally, the best method of establishing an agency relationship is by an express written agreement called a listing agreement to represent a seller and a buyer's representation agreement.

Listing Agreements

A real estate transaction that makes use of the services of one or more real estate licensees usually begins with an agreement between property owner and broker to list the property for sale, lease, or trade.

Under contract law, an agreement to represent a seller (listing agreement) should contain the following:

- identity of the parties
- legal description of the property
- object of the agreement (sale, exchange, lease)

- term (definite length of time) of the agreement
- definition of the agent's role and list of the agent's obligations
- statement of compensation to which the agent is entitled on fulfilling his or her obligations
- safety clause or protection period stipulating that the agent's compensation is to be paid if a sale is transacted with a buyer who was introduced to the owner by the agent within a stated period after termination of the listing agreement
- authorization for the agent to use multiple listing systems, Internet listing systems, or other marketing forums
- authorization for the use of subagents or for the broker to function as an intermediary
- authorization for the agent to retain a key to the property or to use a lock box or other means of property entry in the owner's absence
- authorization to receive a deposit or other funds on behalf of the buyer and stipulation as to how those funds are to be handled
- arbitration or mediation provision to be used in the event of a contract dispute
- statement of compliance with all applicable fair housing laws
- any other provision required by law
- signature of seller and signature of broker or the broker's associate (general agent)

There are four basic types of listing agreements in common use.

1. **Exclusive Right to Sell**—From the broker's point of view, this is the best type of listing. During the period set out in the agreement, **the listing broker has the exclusive right** to produce a ready, willing, and able buyer at the price and terms agreed upon in the listing agreement. If any other person—including the seller or another broker—procures a buyer, the listing broker is still entitled to the commission stipulated in the listing agreement. However, if another broker procures a buyer, most listing brokers are happy to share the commission with the procuring broker in a cooperative or **"co-op" sale**. With this type of listing, brokers will exert maximum effort in marketing property, because they have strong assurance that they will be compensated. Under the exclusive right to sell agreement, the listing broker is entitled to a commission when the broker procures a buyer who will meet the seller's price and terms even if the seller then refuses to sell the property.

2. **Exclusive Agency**—This listing is similar to an exclusive right to sell listing except that it gives the **seller the right to sell the property without paying** the broker a commission. This agreement is nevertheless an exclusive agency agreement because the seller cannot give the listing to another broker during the term of the listing.

3. **Open Listing**—This agreement is simply a **nonexclusive agreement** that a commission will be paid if the broker is the procuring cause in producing a ready, willing, and able buyer. A seller may enter into an open listing with an unlimited number of brokers. The only real benefit to the brokers is that they know they will be compensated if they are the procuring cause of the sale. In residential transactions, brokers rarely accept open listings because of the strong possibility that another broker or the seller will find a buyer. However, the seller of a multimillion dollar commercial property is not as likely to give an exclusive listing, so commercial brokers are more likely to accept open listings. Such brokers typically have clients with

whom he or she has worked in the past to whom the broker can present the property.

4. **Net Listing**—This can be an exclusive or non-exclusive listing and is actually a method of structuring the compensation. If offers the property owner a guaranteed net amount at closing, with the listing broker taking any part of the purchase price over that amount. Net listings often leave brokers open to charges of fraud or misconduct, and should therefore be avoided if possible. For example, an owner may tell a broker, "I want $400,000 for my property. You can keep anything over that amount that the property sells for." The broker knows the property will sell for $480,000 in the current market, so he thinks he has a great opportunity. But when the broker brings an offer for $480,000 and the transaction closes, the broker may be sued for violating his fiduciary duty of loyalty and disclosure to a client. The broker should have informed the seller of the true market value of the property. On the contrary, the only offer received might have been for only $400,000 and complying with the legal requirement to present all offer, the broker submits the offer and the seller accepts. The broker is then left without a commission.

Listing Procedures

Evaluating Property

An agent needs to be totally honest with the client who is getting ready to sell or purchase a property. A competitive market analysis (CMA) should be prepared to help the seller client or buyer client identify the "right" asking or offering price. The agent should advise the seller how to get the property ready to show to its best advantage and to be attractive to buyers. Although the agent must never take on the role of property inspec-

tor, an agent should also point out potential problem areas relating to the structural and mechanical systems of the property improvements.

Disclosure of Property Conditions

Both property owners and real estate licensees are required to reveal any material facts about the property that may be known to one or the other but may not easily be observed by an untrained person. These deficiencies are known as **latent structural defects** or **property defects**.

In a growing number of states, a real estate licensee is responsible for conducting a reasonable visual inspection of property to be listed, noting any defects or conditions that could affect the property's value or desirability (termed **red flags**) and revealing those facts to prospective buyers. Part of this process includes questioning the property owner about conditions that may not be apparent in a visual inspection.

In some states, the owner of a previously occupied single-family residential dwelling unit must complete a statement disclosing the condition of the property to the best of the owner's knowledge.

Fraud and Misrepresentation

A broker or salesperson commits fraud when the licensee deliberately deceives the consumer. For instance, a broker might encourage a consumer to part with something of value or to enter into a contract that the consumer would not have entered into had truthful information been provided. **Misrepresentation**, more correctly called **innocent misrepresentation**, is unintentional rather than deliberate.

Often, real estate professionals are found guilty of one of the above because of what they fail to reveal. Failure to disclose a property defect and/or giving wrong information constitutes fraud or **misrepresentation by omission**.

Brokers and salespersons must avoid making any representation when they do not have the correct answer. Instead, real estate professionals should guide buyers and sellers to a source from which they may obtain the information they need to make an intelligent and informed decision.

Authority

Ostensible authority or **apparent authority** may establish an agency relationship. This occurs when a principal gives a third party reason to believe that another person is the principal's agent even though that person is unaware of the appointment. If the third party accepts the principal's representation as true, the principal may have established **ostensible authority** and, therefore, may be bound by the acts of his or her agent.

Agency can also be established by **ratification**. For example, a broker might bring an offer to a property owner who had no knowledge of the broker's attempt to sell his property. If the owner accepts the offer (which generally entitles the broker to a commission), then it could be held that an agency was created when negotiations started.

An **agency by estoppel** can result when a principal fails to maintain due diligence over an agent and the agent exercises powers not granted to her. If this causes a third party to believe the agent has these powers, an agency of estoppel has been created.

Within any agency relationship, **implied authority** can sometimes be exercised. Implied authority can arise, for example, from custom in the industry. If a broker lists a house, there may not be an express agreement concerning advertising the property in the newspaper. However, because this is a customary practice, the broker may have the implied authority to advertise. In some states, express authority in writing is required to be able to erect a "For Sale" sign or to share one's agency with another licensee.

Buyer-Broker Agreements

In recent years, it has become common for buyers to appoint exclusive agents to represent them in real estate transactions. The contract that appoints an exclusive buyer agency should contain the basic elements found in a listing agreement with a few minor changes. The subjects to be addressed include but are not limited to the following:

- the name of the client and the agent
- a clearly defined market area
- how and by whom the agent will be compensated
- the term of the agreement
- the authority of the agent
- the duties of the agent
- the duties of the client
- provisions of dispute resolution
- notices relating to fair housing, antitrust, and other related law
- signatures of the parties

Cooperative Transactions

Often, two brokers of different firms cooperate in the sale or lease of a property. This may occur in one of two ways as follows.

Buyer Agency

When the broker of one firm represents a buyer under a buyer representation agreement and sells that buyer a property listed with another broker in a different firm, each client is exclusively represented by his or her respective broker/agent. The following diagram illustrates this.

Subagency

When the broker of one firm sells the listing of another broker's firm to a buyer that is not represented, the selling broker is the subagent of the listing broker. The following diagram illustrates this.

The Residential Real Estate Transaction
Listing Broker and Subagent

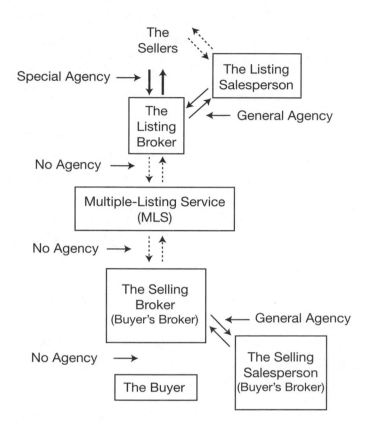

Responsibilities of the Agent to the Seller/Buyer as Principal

Accepting an appointment as a seller's or buyer's agent imposes obligations and creates liabilities. A licensee who fails to fulfill his or her fiduciary duties or oversteps the bounds of the agent's authority may face disciplinary action by the state's licensing authority or even a civil suit brought by an unhappy buyer or seller. The agent appointed by a listing agreement or a buyer representation agreement is a **special agent** and has not been granted the authority to speak or sign on behalf of the principal or client.

It is very important to know when and if an agency relationship has been created. When someone becomes an agent for another person, a dramatic change in duties and obligation occurs. The agency creates a **fiduciary relationship**, requiring that the agent exhibit trust, honesty, and good business judgment when working on behalf of the principal. This fiduciary relationship imposes the following duties:

- **Obedience** (also called **faithful performance**). The agent must obey all legal instructions given by the principal, applying best efforts and diligence in carrying out the objectives of the agency (for example, selling the property).
- **Loyalty.** The agent must put the interests of the principal above his or her own interests. This is perhaps the most difficult duty for the agent, which may be why failure of the agent to uphold this duty causes so many lawsuits.

- **Disclosure.** The agent must keep the principal informed on all pertinent facts. Because just about anything relating to the transaction could be pertinent to a principal, the agent basically is obligated to investigate and disclose everything related to the situation.
- **Confidentiality.** The agent must keep confidential information about the principal and the principal's motivations and financial interests.
- **Accounting.** The agent may not place the principal's funds in the agent's own account. This practice, called **commingling**, is grounds for suspension or revocation of the broker's real estate license.
- **Reasonable care.** The agent must exercise competence and expertise. The agent must not be party to any fraud or misrepresentation likely to affect the sound judgment of the principal.

Termination of Agency

Agencies are created when the principal or client delegates authority to the agent and the agent accepts the appointment. Most agencies come to a successful, happy conclusion through completion of the purpose of the agency—the property sells and the transaction closes. On occasion, the agent is not successful within the time established in the listing or buyer representation agreement, and the agency ends because the agreement expires. Other events that can terminate an agency are:

- destruction of the property
- condemnation of the property
- mutual agreement (**rescission**) by the parties
- bankruptcy of the owner
- death or incapacity of the principal or the agent (Note: The death of a subagent would not affect the status of the agency.)

Commission and Fees

Compensation paid by sellers and buyers is always negotiable between the parties and can be calculated and paid in a variety of ways.

1. **Success fees** (**contingent fees**) are usually paid at the closing of the transaction and are usually a percentage of the sales price or a flat fee. The agent gets paid only if the transaction closes.
2. **Noncontingent fees** may be calculated on an hourly basis or on a fee for specific or limited services basis. Some brokers require a nonrefundable retainer fee before beginning work for the principal.

Federal antitrust laws prohibit price fixing! Licensees should exercise caution to make certain that they do not say anything about fees that might give someone the idea that fees are standard or fixed in a particular market.

▶ Settlement/Transfer of Property

The real estate agent does not create the instruments that transfer title. The real estate agent does assist the buyer and the seller in defining and setting down what, when, and how the title of the property will be transferred in an agreement of purchase. Most real estate closings involve transferring title from the seller (**grantor**) to the buyer (**grantee**) by the delivery of a **general warranty deed**, executed by the seller and delivered to the buyer. A **general warranty deed** is an instrument by which the grantor guarantees the grantee that the title being conveyed is free from other claims or encumbrances.

Title Insurance

Title insurance has become the most common method of protecting the property buyer. A **title company** issues a **preliminary title report** or **title commitment**. It will indicate the present condition of the title based on examination of the documents contained in the public records as well as any exceptions to the coverage that the title company is willing to provide. The title company will defend the buyer's title in a title dispute covered by the policy.

Title insurance is necessary to indemnify the new owner against financial loss in the event an error was made when the title was searched and examined. There is no guarantee that the finished abstract, or its certification, is completely accurate. Many problems can arise in the recorded chain of ownership. For example:

- What if a recorded deed in the title chain is a forgery?
- What if a minor or an otherwise legally incompetent person executed a deed?
- What if a document was misfiled, or there were undisclosed heirs, or a missing will later came to light, or there was confusion because of similar names on documents?

These situations can result in substantial losses to property owners and lenders, yet the fault may not lie with the title closer, abstracter, or attorney, so there is no one to sue for damages. The solution has been the organization of private companies to sell insurance against losses arising from title defects such as those previously mentioned as well as from errors in title examination.

Essentials of Title Insurance

Numerous details must be handled between the time a buyer and seller sign a sales contract and the day the title is conveyed to the buyer. Ask yourself:

- What is the status of the title? It must be checked thoroughly.
- What is the property tax status? Are the taxes up to date? Are there any special assessments? What is the tax bill for the current year?
- Are there any judgments against the seller that may encumber the property? Are there any liens that must be paid off?

The most expeditious method of preparing for the closing is to place all of these matters in the hands of a neutral third party. Because the title insurance provider has a high level of interest in having these matters handled correctly, it makes sense that it should be chosen as the closing agent or escrow agent, as noted previously.

Deeds

A **deed** is a written document that conveys property from the grantor (owner) to the grantee (buyer). State law dictates the form that a deed must take. There are a number of requirements for a valid deed.

- It must be in writing.
- The grantor(s) must be of sound mind (legally capable).
- It must identify the parties, preferably by full name and marital status (single, married, widow, and so on).
- It must identify the property by legal description.
- It must contain a **granting clause**—also called **words of conveyance**—that contains the appropriate words ("I hereby grant and convey").
- It must be signed by the grantor(s).
- It must be delivered to *and* accepted by the grantee. A deed held by a third party until the grantor dies, for instance, will have no effect during the grantor's life and on the grantor's

death will be invalid. Even after a valid delivery, the fact that the deed is in the hands of the grantee does not mean that it is accepted. Many charitable donations of real estate have ultimately been rejected because of the high cost of their maintenance or remediation (as in the case of contaminated property).

There are many different **types of deeds**.

- A **bargain and sale deed** states the consideration paid by the grantee. There may or may not be a warranty that the grantor actually has an interest in the described property.
- A **gift deed** requires no consideration to be paid by the grantee.
- A **grant deed** (using the words "I hereby grant and convey" or similar) carries three implied promises of the grantor:
  1. The grantor has good title.
  2. There are no encumbrances other than those noted.
  3. The grantor will convey any after-acquired title (ownership interest received after the grant deed is delivered) to the grantee.
- A **quitclaim deed** transfers whatever interest the grantor may own but does not warrant that the grantor actually has any interest in the described property.
- A **sheriff's deed** conveys title to property sold at public auction following a judicial foreclosure sale or other court action.
- A **tax deed** conveys title to property sold at public auction to cover unpaid taxes.
- A **trust deed** (**deed of trust**) is used to make real estate security for the repayment of a debt. The **trust deed** conveys conditional title from the **trustor** (property owner) to the **trustee** to

be held for the benefit of the named **beneficiary** (the lender).

Recording Title

In most states, a deed must be **acknowledged** (signed before a notary public or other official) in order to be **recorded** (made a part of the public records of the county in which the property is located).

A recorded deed provides **constructive notice** or **legal notice** of the conveyance. Recording establishes the priority of interests in or claims against a property.

Settlement Procedures

Each person attending the **closing**, the point in a real estate transaction when the buyer receives a deed and the seller receives the purchase price, is responsible for bringing certain documents.

The seller is typically responsible for some or all of the following:

- the deed
- recent property tax certificates
- insurance policies
- termite inspections
- survey maps
- keys, garage door openers, and the like

If an income-producing property is being sold, then the seller may also need to bring:

- leases
- operating statements
- estoppel letters from the tenants
- maintenance contracts

The buyer needs to bring adequate monies in the form of a cashier's check or other form of good funds and may need to provide a(n):

- survey
- insurance policy
- flood insurance policy
- termite certificate

As the closing proceeds, many signatures are required. Both the buyer and the seller sign a closing statement. The seller signs the deed, and the buyer signs the note, the deed of trust, and numerous other documents required by the lender.

The closing **agent** or **closing officer** has several responsibilities at the closing or settlement meeting, including:

- monitoring all the signatures and making copies of the documents for the buyer, seller, and brokers
- distributing checks, if so authorized by the lender (in a process called **table funding**, as funds are distributed at the closing table); table funding is now authorized in the majority of real estate closings
- sending the deed and deed of trust for recording to the county courthouse of the county in which the property is located

Most lenders require that termite inspections be made prior to closing. Because the property is their collateral, they want to be assured that the property will not be destroyed by termites. Lenders also insist on an appraisal to ensure that their collateral is sufficient value to cover the loan. Finally, lenders typically require insurance policies to cover the property from fire, casualty, flood, or wind damage.

Also at the closing, documents may have to be presented on mandatory disclosures, such as the presence of lead-based paint in a house built before 1978.

Purpose of Closing/Settlement

Immediately before closing, buyers typically do a final **walk-through** of the property they are about to purchase. The buyer's broker (if any) will typically accompany the client. The purpose of the walk-through is to verify the condition of the property after the sellers have moved out and to determine if any items have been improperly removed.

In addition to the buyer and seller, the following people usually attend a closing:

- attorneys for the seller and buyer, to ascertain that everything promised in the sales contract has been carried out
- real estate brokers
- title company closer (serving as the escrow agent), who will conduct the closing

Legal Requirements (includes RESPA)

Congress passed the **Real Estate Settlement and Procedures Act** (**RESPA**) in response to consumer complaints regarding real estate closing costs and procedures. The purpose of RESPA is to regulate and standardize real estate settlement practices when federally related first-mortgage loans are made on one- to four-family residences, condominiums, and cooperatives.

Almost all residential transactions come under RESPA because most home loans are sold in the secondary mortgage market to federally related organizations. The most important of these are:

- Federal National Mortgage Association (FNMA, or Fannie Mae)
- Government National Mortgage Association (GNMA, or Ginnie Mae)
- Federal Home Loan Mortgage Corporation (FHLMC, or Freddie Mac)

One of the most important provisions of RESPA is a prohibition of kickbacks and fees for services not performed during the closing. Prior to the act, attorneys and closing agents in some areas routinely channeled title business to certain title companies in return for a fee. This increased closing costs to the buyer without adding services. RESPA requires that there must be a justifiable service rendered for each closing fee charged.

The act also prohibits the seller from requiring that the buyer purchase title insurance from a particular title company.

Finally, RESPA places restrictions on the amount of advance property tax and insurance payments a lender can collect and place in an impound or reserve account. The amount that may be collected in advance is limited to one-sixth, or two months' worth, of annual property taxes.

Tax Aspects

In many jurisdictions, a transfer tax is assessed when ownership of real estate occurs. The tax is based on the sales price and is calculated in mils or dollars per $100, $500, or $1,000.

Legal vs. Equitable Title

Equitable title is an interest held by a purchaser (vendee) under a purchase contract or a contract for deed. The vendee may demand that legal title be transferred upon full payment of the contract purchase price.

Legal title is title that is fully vested in the owner as evidenced by a deed, will, or court document. Legal title to land and its appurtenances encompasses the entire bundle of rights that an owner possesses. The best title or greatest bundle of rights that an individual can own and hold is **fee simple** ownership.

Special Processes

Probate

Probate is the legal process of finalizing the affairs of a deceased person and distributing the real and personal property left by the decedent. A person who dies with a will, **testate**, will have his or her property distributed as specified in the will. A person who dies without having written a will, **intestate**, will have his or her property administered and distributed by the probate court under the provisions of the state's Law of Decent and Intestate Succession.

Foreclosure

Foreclosure is covered in the Financing section.

▶ Business Practices

Fair Housing and Anti-Discrimination Laws

In addition to the U.S. Constitution, two major federal laws prohibit discrimination in housing.

The **Civil Rights Act of 1866** states that "all citizens of the United States shall have the same right in every State and every Territory, as is enjoyed by the white citizens thereof to inherit, purchase, lease, sell, hold, and convey real and personal property." In 1968, the Supreme Court affirmed that the 1866 act prohibits "all racial discrimination, private as well as public, in the sale of real property." The 1866 law prohibits discrimination based on skin color. Later laws and rulings prohibit discrimination based on race.

The **Federal Fair Housing Act** (**Title VIII of the Civil Rights Act of 1968**) makes it illegal to discriminate on the basis of race, color, religion, sex, or national origin in connection with the sale or rental of housing or vacant land offered for residential construction or use. The law specifically prohibits the following **discriminatory acts**:

- **refusing to sell** to, rent to, or negotiate with any person who is a member of a protected class, or otherwise making a dwelling unavailable to such a person
- **changing terms**, conditions, or services for different individuals as a means of discrimination against a member of a protected class
- practicing discrimination through any statement or **advertisement** that restricts the sale or rental of residential property
- representing to any person, as a means of discrimination, that a dwelling is **unavailable** for sale or rental
- making a profit by inducing owners of housing to sell or rent by representing that persons of a protected category are moving into the neighborhood
- altering the conditions of a home loan to any person, or otherwise denying such a loan as a means of discrimination
- denying persons membership or limiting their participation in any multiple-listing service, real estate broker's organization, or other facility related to the sale or rental of dwellings

A **protected class** is any group of people designated as such by the Department of Housing and Urban Development (HUD) in consideration of federal and state civil rights legislation. Protected classes currently include color, race, religion or creed, ancestry or national origin, gender, handicap, and familial status.

The Fair Housing Amendment defines a handicapped person as one who meets one of the following criteria:

- has a physical or mental impairment that substantially limits one or more major life activities
- has a record of having such an impairment
- is regarded as having such an impairment

The current use of illegal substances is not considered a handicap under the law. However, a person undergoing treatment for drug abuse is considered handicapped. AIDS and HIV-positive status are defined as handicaps.

Protected familial status applies to any household with one or more individuals under the age of 18 living with a parent or legal guardian. This status also applies to anyone who is pregnant or is in the process of obtaining legal custody of an individual under the age of 18. In other words, it is illegal to discriminate against families with children.

The most common violations of federal fair housing laws involve steering, blockbusting, advertising, and less favorable treatment.

Steering (also called **channeling**) is the practice of directing home seekers to or away from particular neighborhoods based on race, color, religion, sex, national origin, handicap, or familial status. Steering includes both efforts to exclude minorities from one area of a city and efforts to direct minorities to minority or changing areas. Steering accounts for many of the complaints filed against real estate agents under the Fair Housing Act.

Examples of steering include:

- showing only certain neighborhoods
- slanting property descriptions
- downgrading neighborhoods
- implying that certain properties are no longer available when, in reality, they are available

Blockbusting (also called **panic peddling**) is the illegal practice of inducing panic selling in a neighborhood for financial gain. Blockbusting typically starts when someone induces one homeowner to sell cheaply by implying that an impending change in the racial or religious composition of the neighborhood will cause property values to fall. The first home thus acquired is sold at a mark-up to a minority family. The process quickly snowballs as residents panic and sell at progressively lower prices.

Less favorable treatment occurs when members of a protected category are provided with fewer services and less information than other people. This violation involves the claim that a minority client received inferior service, was unable to negotiate, or was offered different terms and conditions than a comparable nonminority client. Less favorable treatment is often very subtle, but it has the same discriminatory effects as steering or blockbusting.

Two types of housing are covered by the 1968 Fair Housing Act: **single-family houses** and **multifamily dwellings**.

A **single-family house** is covered if one of the following is true:

- It is owned by a private individual who uses a real estate broker or other person in the business of selling or renting dwellings or who advertises the dwelling.
- It is not owned by private individuals.
- It is owned by a private individual who owns more than three such houses or who, in any two-year period, sells more than one dwelling in which the individual was not the most recent resident.

A **multifamily dwelling** is covered if one of the following is true:

- It consists of five units or more.
- It consists of four or fewer units, and the owner does not reside in one of the units.

The act does not cover:

- rentals of rooms or units in owner-occupied multifamily dwellings of two to four units, as long as discriminatory advertising and the services of a real estate agent are not used
- restricting the sale, rental, or occupancy of dwellings owned or operated by a religious organization for a noncommercial purpose to persons of the same religion, as long as membership in that religion is not restricted on account of race, color, or national origin
- restricting the rental or occupancy of lodgings operated by a private club for its members for other than commercial purposes
- housing for the elderly that meets certain Department of Housing and Urban Development (HUD) guidelines

A person who believes he or she has been discriminated against can pursue one of three avenues. He or she can:

1. file a written complaint with HUD
2. file a civil action directly in a U.S. District Court or state or local court
3. file a complaint with the U.S. Attorney General

The burden of proof is on the person filing the complaint. A person found guilty of a fair housing violation may face:

- an injunction to stop the sale or rental of the property to someone else, making it available to the complainant

- monetary fines for actual damages caused by the discrimination
- unlimited punitive damages
- court costs
- criminal penalties against those who coerce, intimidate, threaten, or interfere with a person's buying, renting, or selling of housing
- state penalties including the loss of the real estate license

Anti-Trust Compliance

The **Sherman Anti-Trust Act** prohibits certain business practices that could place unfair restrictions on free competition in the marketplace. Prohibitions against restraint of trade that directly affect the real estate industry include the following:

- There can be no price fixing. Agency fees or commission are always subject to negotiation between a principal and an agent. Agents for different companies are not allowed to agree to predetermined fees or to agree on a range of fees for specific services. Even discussion of such matters could subject licensees to civil and criminal penalties including fines and/or imprisonment.
- Realty firms cannot agree to provide service only in a designated geographic area.
- Realty firms cannot agree to **boycott** (direct business away from) certain companies or other realty firms.
- Agents are not to form exclusive organizations (such as **property listing services**) that arbitrarily prevent nonmembers from gaining access to sales and marketing information. Membership criteria must be designed so as not to unfairly exclude otherwise qualified brokers from participation.

Advertising

At all times, real estate licensees must make a diligent effort to make certain that all of their advertising creates an accurate and truthful picture. There is no place in the real estate business for falsehoods and inaccuracies.

When advertising credit terms, be sure to comply with the federal Truth-in-Lending Law and give complete information including the Annual Percentage Rate (APR) whenever any **trigger term** is used. For a list of trigger terms, please review the Financing/Credit Laws section.

▶ Property Management

Property Management and Landlord/Tenant and Commercial/Income Property

Tenancies and Leasehold Estates

A **lease** is a contract that transfers a possessory interest in real estate. The **leasehold estate** conveys to the tenant a right to occupy the property for the term of the lease.

Leases may be oral or written, but the Statute of Frauds requires that leases of real estate, except for residential leases of one year or less, be in writing to be enforceable.

Leases must be signed by the landlord and the tenant but need not be recorded to be enforceable. An individual who wishes to notify the public of a leasehold interest may record a **memorandum of lease**.

A lease must include a sufficient property description. A legal description as used in a deed is appropriate, although in certain residential leases, a street address and apartment number are sufficient.

There are several kinds of leases.

- A **gross lease** specifies that the landlord pay all expenses: property taxes, insurance, maintenance. This kind of lease is often used for apartments and other residential properties.

- A **net lease** specifies that the tenant pay certain expenses. The most common arrangement requires the tenant to pay property taxes, insurance, and maintenance. This is called a **net, net, net** or **triple net lease**.

- An **office-building lease** is a hybrid of a gross and a net lease. The landlord pays the first portion of the expenses, and each tenant pays a *pro rata* share of all expenses over that.

- A **percentage lease** requires the tenant to pay a percentage of gross sales as rent in addition to a base rental amount specified in the lease.

Several types of tenancies can be created by a lease.

- An **estate for years** is given for a specified term. This common type of lease agreement includes all leaseholds that continue for a specific period of time and have a definite termination date, such as a five-year office lease or a 20-year retail lease.

- A **periodic estate** is initially given for a specific term and then renews automatically until notice of termination is given. It does not have a definite termination date but runs from month to month or year to year. A periodic estate is generally created when the landlord and tenant contract to rent month to month, without specifying the number of months or years the lease will run.

- A **tenancy at will** extends indefinitely and may be terminated at any time by either the landlord or tenant by giving a notice equal to one rental period's notice.

- **Tenancy at sufferance** is created when a tenant takes possession of a property lawfully and continues to hold possession of the property after the right to remain has expired. However, if the holdover tenancy exists with the consent of the landlord, then a **periodic tenancy** is created. When a lease is **assigned** to a third party, the third party assumes all the obligations of the lessee (**tenant**). The right of the tenant to assign the lease must be granted in writing by the landlord.

- If a tenant **subleases** some or all of the leased space (commonly referred to as the **demised premises**) to a third party, the original tenant's relationship with the landlord does not change. All of the tenant's obligations remain binding even though the tenant no longer occupies the premises. The sublease is created between the tenant (who now acts as the landlord) and the third party (who now becomes the tenant). The original lease should specify whether a sublet is allowed.

Property Manager and Owner Relationships

The range of services that the **property manager** can perform for the landlord (property owner) includes marketing, leasing, maintenance, and rent collection.

A major activity of the property manager will be the cost-effective marketing of vacant units, primarily by ongoing advertising in selected publications. This usually will include classified ads in local newspapers, but may also include specialty publications as well as Internet rental listing services. Use of rental listing agencies, particularly for residential property, will require compliance with specific state laws intended to safeguard the consumer. On-site posting of unit availability will help attract the drive-by prospect.

The **law of supply and demand** applies in the leasing as well as the sale of real estate. Continuing surveys of the number of units and vacancies available on the market and rents charged will help the property remain competitive.

Advertising through newspapers, use of billboards, and posting on Internet and other listing services should attract a steady flow of prospective tenants, provided the units have been competitively priced and offer amenities expected in the area. The applicant review process should be conducted in a personal interview on-site, for the benefit of both property manager and prospective tenant.

Laws Affecting Property Management

All or part of the wording of the rental application, as well as the time frame in which the applicant must be notified of acceptance or nonacceptance, may be mandated by state law. Federal law regarding the use of a credit report may also apply.

A property manager must comply with all federal and state fair housing laws to avoid charges of unlawful discrimination.

State law governs many of the provisions in a residential lease (or **rental agreement**). The **typical lease** will include:

- the identity of the lessor (landlord) and lessee (tenant)
- a description of the premises to be leased
- the terms of the lease, including beginning and ending times
- the amount of rent to be paid and when payment is due—a grace period may be specified, as well as the penalty for late payment due after that time
- the obligations of the lessor, which will include compliance with an express or implied warranty of habitability

- the obligations of the lessee, which will include payment of the stated rent as well as maintenance of the premises
- a provision for arbitration or mediation clause to be enforced in the event of a dispute in the terms of the agreement
- the signature of the lessee and signature of the lessor (or agent)

In most states, the **Statute of Frauds** requires that a lease that will terminate one year or more from the date of its signing must be in writing.

Federal law now requires compliance with the **Lead-Based Paint Disclosure Law**. This law is applicable for a new or renewal lease on residential property constructed prior to 1978.

The state may require specific disclosures as part of the rental agreement, such as whether or not a smoke alarm has been installed in the rental unit. The state may require dead-bolt locks on exterior doors of rental units. A sprinkler system may be a requirement in a commercial building or a fire hazard area.

Common Interest Ownership Properties

Many properties are owned by multiple owners. Here are three types of these properties.

1. **Cooperatives** are apartments owned by a **corporation** that holds titles to the entire cooperative property and is liable for the mortgage obligations and the ad valorem taxes for the entire property.

    Each purchaser of an apartment unit is a stockholder in the corporation and obtains the right to occupy through a **proprietary lease**. Each block of stock is tied to a specific right to occupy and carries a lease payment financial obligation that represents a *pro rata* share of the total cost of the operations expense and mortgage payments on the building.

2. **Condominiums** are created under state laws that permit a multi-tenant building to be divided into air lots and that are declared as separate parcels of real estate by recording a vertical and horizontal plot. The **condominium declaration** identifies each condominium and the percentage ownership that the individual owns in the land and the common elements of the structures. Some of the common elements will be defined as **limited common** elements and will be designated as for the exclusive use of a specific unit.

An advantage of condominium ownership over cooperative ownership is that default in payment of taxes, mortgage payment, or monthly assessment affects only the specific unit. Each unit is defined as a separate parcel of real estate and is owned fee simple.

3. **Time shares** are agreements by which multiple owners own a proportional interest in a single condominium unit with the exclusive right to use and occupy the unit for a specified period of time each year. The individual owners pay common expense and maintenance costs based on the ratio between the ownership period and the total number of ownership periods available in the property. This type of ownership can be either a fee simple or leasehold interest.

Subdivisions

When larger tracts of land are divided into smaller parcels that will be owned by multiple owners, the tract will be converted into a subdivision. The **subdivider** divides the tract into smaller lots for sale. The **developer** will improve the land by installing utilities, building roads, and preparing the sites for the activities of the builders who will construct the buildings.

The subdivision of the tract may be regulated by local, state, and federal regulations. The subdivision will be evidenced by the recording of a plat that shows lots, blocks, streets, and common amenities. The plat will also identify easements on each lot, easements in gross, for the purpose of bringing necessary utilities to the lots.

When the lots are offered for sale across state lines, the Federal Interstate Land Sales Full Disclosure Act enforced by HUD will require the filing of various reports. This law applies only to subdivisions with more than 25 lots and lots in excess of 20 acres.

Frequently subdividers and developers will place restrictive covenants on the lots that will control use of the land and establish standards for the improvements to be constructed on the lots.

5 ▶ Real Estate Math Review

CHAPTER SUMMARY

In most states, math accounts for almost 10% of a real estate sales exam, so you should take this topic seriously. But even if math is not your favorite subject, this chapter will help you do your best. It not only covers arithmetic, algebra, geometry, and word problems, but also has practice problems for each of the real estate math topics.

 ERE ARE SOME types of math questions you may encounter on your exam.

- Percents
- Areas
- Property Tax
- Loan-to-Value Ratios
- Points
- Equity
- Qualifying Buyers
- Prorations
- Commissions
- Sale Proceeds

- Transfer Tax/Conveyance Tax/Revenue Stamps
- Competitive Market Analyses (CMA)
- Income Properties
- Depreciation

Keep in mind that although the math topics are varied, you will be using the same math skills to complete each question. But before you review your math skills, take a look at some helpful strategies for doing your best.

▶ Strategies for Math Questions

Answer Every Question

You should answer every single question, even if you don't know the answer. There is usually no penalty for a wrong answer, and, if there are four answer choices, you have a 25% chance of guessing correctly. If one or two answers are obviously wrong, the odds may be even higher for selecting the correct one.

Bring a Calculator

Your state *may* allow you to bring calculator to your exam. **You must check with your exam center to find out exactly what type of calculator is permitted.** In general, permissible calculators are battery operated, do not print, are not programmable, and do not have a keypad with letters. As a precaution, you should bring an extra battery with you to your exam. Try not to rely entirely on the calculator. Although using one can prevent simple adding and subtracting errors, it may take longer for you to use the calculator than to figure it out yourself.

Use Scratch Paper

Resist the temptation to "save time" by doing all your work on your calculator. The main pitfall with calculators is the temptation to work the problem all the way through to the end on the calculator. At this point, if none of the answers provided is correct, there is no way to know where the mistake lies. Use scratch paper to avoid this problem.

Check Your Work

Checking your work is always good practice, and it's usually quite simple. Even if you come up with an answer that is one of the answer choices, you should check your work. Test writers often include answer choices that are the results of common errors, which you may have made.

► Real Estate Math Review

Here's a quick review of some basic arithmetic, algebra, geometry, and word problem skills you will need for your exam.

Arithmetic Review

Symbols of Multiplication

When two or more numbers are being multiplied, they are called **factors**. The answer that results is called the **product**.

> *Example:*
> $5 \times 6 = 30$ 5 and 6 are **factors** and 30 is the **product**.

> There are several ways to represent multiplication in a mathematical statement.

- A dot between factors indicates multiplication:

  $5 \cdot 6 = 30$

- Parentheses around any part of the one or more factors indicates multiplication:

  $(5)6 = 30, 5(6) = 30,$ and $(5)(6) = 30$

- Multiplication is also indicated when a number is placed next to a variable:

  $5a = 30$ In this equation, 5 is being multiplied by a.

Divisibility

Like multiplication, division can be represented in a few different ways:

$8 \div 3$ $3\overline{)8}$ $\frac{8}{3}$

In each expression, 3 is the **divisor** and 8 is the **dividend**.

How to Round

If the number after the one you need to round to is 5 or more, make the preceding number one higher. If it is less than 5, drop it and leave the preceding number the same. (Information about rounding is usually provided in the exam instructions or in the exam bulletin.)

Example:

0.0135 = .014, or .01

Decimals

The most important thing to remember about decimals is that the first place value to the right begins with tenths. The place values are as follows:

1	2	6	8	.	3	4	5	7
THOUSANDS	HUNDREDS	TENS	ONES	DECIMAL POINT	TENTHS	HUNDREDTHS	THOUSANDTHS	TEN THOUSANDTHS

In expanded form, this number can also be expressed as . . .

$1{,}268.3457 = (1 \times 1{,}000) + (2 \times 100) + (6 \times 10) + (8 \times 1) + (3 \times .1) + (4 \times .01) + (5 \times .001) + (7 \times .0001)$

Fractions

To do well when working with fractions, you must understand some basic concepts. Here are some math rules for fractions using variables:

$$\frac{a}{b} \times \frac{c}{d} = \frac{a \times c}{b \times d}$$

$$\frac{a}{b} + \frac{c}{b} = \frac{a + c}{b}$$

$$\frac{a}{b} \div \frac{c}{d} = \frac{a}{b} \times \frac{d}{c} = \frac{a \times d}{b \times c}$$

$$\frac{a}{b} + \frac{c}{d} = \frac{ad + bc}{bd}$$

Multiplying Fractions

Multiplying fractions is one of the easiest operations to perform. To multiply fractions, simply multiply the numerators and the denominators, writing each in the respective place over or under the fraction bar.

Example:

$$\frac{4}{5} \times \frac{6}{7} = \frac{24}{35}$$

Dividing Fractions

Dividing fractions is the same thing as multiplying fractions by their **reciprocals**. To find the reciprocal of any number, switch its numerator and denominator. For example, the reciprocals of the following numbers are:

$$\frac{1}{3} \rightarrow \frac{3}{1} = 3$$

$$x \rightarrow \frac{1}{x}$$

$$\frac{4}{5} \rightarrow \frac{5}{4}$$

$$5 \rightarrow \frac{1}{5}$$

When dividing fractions, simply multiply the dividend (what is being divided) by the divisor's (what is doing the dividing) reciprocal to get the answer.

Example:

$$\frac{12}{21} \div \frac{3}{4} = \frac{12}{21} \times \frac{4}{3} = \frac{48}{63} = \frac{16}{21}$$

Adding and Subtracting Fractions

To add or subtract fractions with like denominators, just add or subtract the numerators and leave the denominator as it is. For example,

$$\frac{1}{7} + \frac{5}{7} = \frac{6}{7} \quad \text{and} \quad \frac{5}{8} - \frac{2}{8} = \frac{3}{8}$$

To add or subtract fractions with unlike denominators, you must find the **least common denominator**, or **LCD**.

For example, if given the denominators 8 and 12, 24 would be the LCD because $8 \times 3 = 24$ and $12 \times 2 = 24$. In other words, the LCD is the smallest number divisible by each of the denominators.

Once you know the LCD, convert each fraction to its new form by multiplying both the numerator and denominator by the necessary number to get the LCD, and then add or subtract the new numerators.

Example:

$$\frac{1}{3} + \frac{2}{5} = \frac{5(1)}{5(3)} + \frac{3(2)}{3(5)} = \frac{5}{15} + \frac{6}{15} = \frac{11}{15}$$

Percent

A **percent** is a measure of a part to a whole, with the whole being equal to 100.

- To change a decimal to a percentage, move the decimal point two units to the right and add a percentage symbol.

    Example:
    .45 = 45%   .07 = 7%   .9 = 90%

- To change a fraction to a percentage, first change the fraction to a decimal. To do this, divide the numerator by the denominator. Then change the decimal to a percentage.

    Example:

    $\frac{4}{5} = .80 = 80\%$

    $\frac{2}{5} = .4 = 40\%$

    $\frac{1}{8} = .125 = 12.5\%$

- To change a percentage to a decimal, simply move the decimal point two places to the left and eliminate the percentage symbol.

    Example:
    64% = .64   87% = .87   7% = .07

- To change a percentage to a fraction, divide by 100 and reduce.

    Example:

    $64\% = \frac{64}{100} = \frac{16}{25}$

    $75\% = \frac{75}{100} = \frac{3}{4}$

    $82\% = \frac{82}{100} = \frac{41}{50}$

- Keep in mind that any percentage that is 100 or greater will need to reflect a whole number or mixed number when converted.

    Example:

    $125\% = 1.25$, or $1\frac{1}{4}$

    $350\% = 3.5$, or $3\frac{1}{2}$

Here are some conversions you should be familiar with:

Fraction	Decimal	Percentage
$\frac{1}{2}$	.5	50%
$\frac{1}{4}$	.25	25%
$\frac{1}{3}$	.333 . . .	$33.\overline{3}$%
$\frac{2}{3}$	.666 . . .	$66.\overline{6}$%
$\frac{1}{10}$	.1	10%
$\frac{1}{8}$	.125	12.5%
$\frac{1}{6}$	.1666 . . .	$16.\overline{6}$%
$\frac{1}{5}$	.2	20%

Algebra Review

Equations

An **equation** is solved by finding a number that is equal to an unknown variable.

Simple Rules for Working with Equations

1. The equal sign separates an equation into two sides.
2. Whenever an operation is performed on one side, the same operation must be performed on the other side.
3. Your first goal is to get all of the variables on one side and all of the numbers on the other.
4. The final step often will be to divide each side by the coefficient, leaving the variable equal to a number.

Checking Equations

To check an equation, substitute the number equal to the variable in the original equation.

Example:

To check the following equation, substitute the number 10 for the variable x.

$$\frac{x}{6} = \frac{x + 10}{12}$$

$$\frac{10}{6} = \frac{10 + 10}{12}$$

$$\frac{10}{6} = \frac{20}{12}$$

$$1\frac{2}{3} = 1\frac{2}{3}$$

$$\frac{10}{6} = \frac{10}{6}$$

Because this statement is true, you know the answer $x = 10$ must be correct.

Special Tips for Checking Equations

1. If time permits, be sure to check all equations.
2. Be careful to answer the question that is being asked. Sometimes, this involves solving for a variable and then performing an operation.

Example:
If the question asks the value of $x - 2$, and you find $x = 2$, the answer is not 2, but $2 - 2$. Thus, the answer is 0.

Algebraic Fractions

Algebraic fractions are very similar to fractions in arithmetic.

Example:
Write $\frac{x}{5} - \frac{x}{10}$ as a single fraction.

Solution:
Just like in arithmetic, you need to find the LCD of 5 and 10, which is 10. Then change each fraction into an equivalent fraction that has 10 as a denominator.

$$\frac{x}{5} - \frac{x}{10} = \frac{x(2)}{5(2)} - \frac{x}{10}$$
$$= \frac{2x}{10} - \frac{x}{10}$$
$$= \frac{x}{10}$$

Geometry Review

Area	the space inside a two-dimensional figure
Circumference	the distance around a circle
Perimeter	the distance around a figure
Radius	the distance from the center point of a circle to any point on the circle

Area

Area is the space inside of the lines defining the shape.

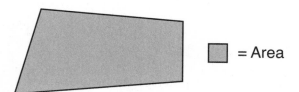

This geometry review will focus on the area formula for three main shapes: circles, rectangles/squares, and triangles.

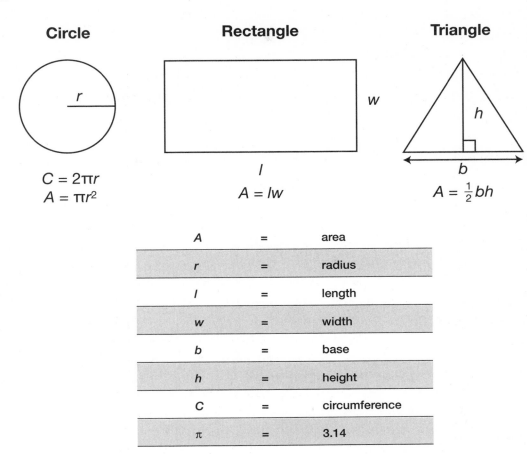

Circle

$C = 2\pi r$
$A = \pi r^2$

Rectangle

$A = lw$

Triangle

$A = \frac{1}{2} bh$

A	=	area
r	=	radius
l	=	length
w	=	width
b	=	base
h	=	height
C	=	circumference
π	=	3.14

Perimeter

The **perimeter** of an object is simply the sum of all of its sides.

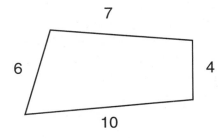

Perimeter = 6 + 7 + 4 + 10 = 27

The **circumference** is the perimeter of a circle.

$C = 2\pi r$

Word Problem Review

Because many of the math problems on any real estate sales exam will be word problems, pay extra attention to the following review.

Translating Words into Numbers

The most important skill needed for word problems is being able to translate words into mathematical operations. The following will assist you by giving you some common examples of English phrases and their mathematical equivalents.

- "Increase" means add.

  Example:
  A number increased by five $= x + 5$.

- "Less than" means subtract.

  Example:
  10 less than a number $= x - 10$.

- "Times" or "product" means multiply.

  Example:
  Three times a number $= 3x$.

- "Times the sum" means to multiply a number by a quantity.

  Example:
  Five times the sum of a number and three $= 5(x + 3)$.

- Two variables are sometimes used together.

  Example:
  A number y exceeds 5 times a number x by 10.
  $y = 5x + 10$

- "Of" means multiply.

  Example:
  10% of 100 is 10 $= 10\% \times 100 = 10$.

- "Is" means equals.

Example:

15 is 14 plus 1 becomes 15 = 14 + 1.

Assigning Variables in Word Problems

It may be necessary to create and assign variables in a word problem. To do this, first identify an unknown and a known. You may not actually know the exact value of the "known," but you will know at least something about its value.

Examples:

Max is three years older than Ricky.

Unknown = Ricky's age = x

Known = Max's age is three years older.

Therefore,

Ricky's age = x and Max's age = $x + 3$.

Heidi made twice as many cookies as Rebecca.

Unknown = number of cookies Rebecca made = x

Known = number of cookies Heidi made = $2x$

Jessica has five more than three times the number of books that Becky has.

Unknown = the number of books Becky has = x

Known = the number of books Jessica has = $3x + 5$

Percentage Problems

There is one formula that is useful for solving the three types of percentage problems:

$$\frac{\#\ \text{part}}{\text{whole}} = \frac{\%}{100}$$

When reading a percentage problem, substitute the necessary information into this formula based on the following:

- 100 is always written in the denominator of the percentage sign column.
- If given a percentage, write it in the numerator position of the number column. If you are not given a percentage, then the variable should be placed there.
- The denominator of the number column represents the number that is equal to the whole, or 100%. This number always follows the word *of* in a word problem.

- The numerator of the number column represents the number that is the percent.
- In the formula, the equal sign can be interchanged with the word *is*.

Examples:
- Finding a percentage of a given number.

What number is equal to 40% of 50?

$$\frac{\overset{\#}{x}}{50} = \frac{\overset{\%}{40}}{100}$$

Cross multiply:

$100(x) = (40)(50)$

$100x = 2,000$

$\frac{100x}{100} = \frac{2,000}{100}$

$x = 20$ Therefore, 20 is 40% of 50.

- Finding a number when a percentage is given:
  40% of what number is 24?

$$\frac{\overset{\#}{24}}{x} = \frac{\overset{\%}{40}}{100}$$

Cross multiply:

$(24)(100) = (40)(x)$

$2,400 = 40x$

$\frac{2,400}{40} = \frac{40x}{40}$

$60 = x$ Therefore, 40% of 60 is 24.

- Finding what percentage one number is of another:
  What percentage of 75 is 15?

$$\frac{\overset{\#}{15}}{75} = \frac{\overset{\%}{x}}{100}$$

$$\textbf{Rate} = \frac{x \text{ units}}{y \text{ units}}$$

A percentage problem simply means that *y* units is equal to 100. This is important to remember that a percentage problem may be worded using the word *rate*.

Cross multiply:

$15(100) = (75)(x)$

$1{,}500 = 75x$

$\frac{1{,}500}{75} = \frac{75x}{75}$

$20 = x$ Therefore, 20% of 75 is 15.

Rate Problems

You may encounter a couple of different types of rate problems on your state's real estate sales exam: cost per unit, interest rate, and tax rate. Rate is defined as a comparison of two quantities with different units of measure.

$$\textbf{Rate} = \frac{x \text{ units}}{y \text{ units}}$$

Examples: $\frac{\text{dollars}}{\text{square foot}}, \frac{\text{interest}}{\text{year}}$

Cost Per Unit

Some problems on your exam may require that you calculate the cost per unit.

Example:

If 100 square feet cost $1,000, how much does 1 square foot cost?

Solution:

$= \frac{1{,}000}{100} = \$10/\text{square foot}$

Interest Rate

The formula for simple interest is Interest = principal × rate × time or $I = PRT$. If you know certain values, but not others, you can still find the answer using algebra. In simple interest problems, the value of T is usually 1, as in one year. There are three basic kinds of interest problems, depending on which number is missing.

Equivalencies

Here are some equivalencies you may need to use to complete some questions. Generally, any equivalencies you will need to know for your exam are provided for you.

Equivalencies

12 inches (in. or ") = 1 foot (ft. or ')

3 feet = 36 inches = 1 yard (yd.)

1,760 yards = 1 mile (mi.)

5,280 feet = 1 mile

144 square inches (sq. in. or in^2) = 1 square foot (sq. ft. or $ft.^2$)

9 square feet = 1 square yard (sq. yd. or $yd.^2$)

43,560 feet = 1 acre

640 acres = 1 square mile (sq. mi. or $mi.^2$)

Percents

You may be asked a basic percentage problem.

Example:

What is 86% of 1,750?

Solution:

Start by translating words into math terms.

$x = (86\%)(1,750)$

Change the percent into a decimal by moving the decimal point two spaces to the left.

$86\% = .86$

Now you can solve.

$x = (.86)(1,750)$

$x = 1,505$

Other percentage problems you may find on your state's real estate sales exam will come in the form of rate problems. Keep reading for more examples of these problems.

Interest Problems

Let's take a look at a problem in which you have calculate the interest rate (R). Remember, the rate is the same as the percentage.

Example:

Mary Valencia borrowed $5,000, for which she is paying $600 interest per year. What is the rate of interest being charged?

Solution:

Start with the values you know.

Principal = $5,000

Interest = $600

Rate = x

Time = 1 year

Using the formula $I = PRT$, insert the values you know, and solve for x.

$600 = 5,000(x)(1)$

$600 = 5,000x$

$\frac{600}{5,000} = \frac{x}{5,000}$

$.12 = x$

To convert .12 to a percent, move the decimal point two places to the right.

$.12 = 12\%$

Area

Some of the problems on your exam may ask you to figure the area of a piece of land, a building, or some other figure. Here are some formulas and how to use them.

Rectangles

Remember the formula Area = (length)(width).

Example:

A man purchased a lot that is 50 feet by 10 feet for a garden. How many square feet of land does he have?

Solution:

Using the formula Area = (length)(width), you have:

$A = (50)(10) = 500$ square feet

Example:

The Meyers family bought a piece of land for a summer home that was 2.75 acres. The lake frontage was 150 feet. What was the length of the lot?

Solution:

When you take your salesperson exam, you may be provided with certain equivalencies. You will need to refer to the equivalencies list on the previous page to answer this question. First, find the area of the land in square feet.

$(2.75)(43,560) = 119,790$ square feet

In the previous example, you were given the length and the width. In this example, you are given the area and the width, so you are solving for the length. Because you know the area and the width of the lot, use the formula to solve.

Area = (length)(width)

119,790 = (x)(150)

Divide both sides by 150.

$\frac{119,790}{150} = \frac{(x)(150)}{150}$

$x = \frac{119,790}{150}$

$x = 798.6$ feet

Triangles

Although it may not be as common, you may be asked to find the area of a triangle. If you don't remember the formula, see page 105.

Example:

The Baron family is buying a triangular piece of land for a gas station. It is 200 feet at the base, and the side perpendicular to the base is 200 feet. They are paying $2 per square foot for the property. What will it cost?

Solution:

Start with the formula Area = $\frac{1}{2}$(base)(height).

Now, write down the values you know.

Area = x

Base = 200

Height = 200

If it's easier, you can change $\frac{1}{2}$ to a decimal.

$\frac{1}{2} = .5$

Now you can plug these values into the formula.

x = (.5)(200)(200)

x = (.5)(40,000)

x = 20,000 square feet

Don't forget that the question is not asking for the number of square feet, but of the *cost* of the property per square foot. This is a rate problem, so you need to complete one more step: (20,000 square feet)($2 per square foot) = $40,000.

Example:

Victor and Evelyn Robinson have an outlot that a neighbor wants to buy. The side of the outlot next to their property is 86 feet. The rear line is perpendicular to their side lot, and the road frontage is 111 feet. Their plat shows they own 3,000 square feet in the outlot. What is the length of the rear line of the outlot? Round your answer to the nearest whole number.

Solution:

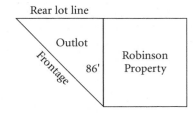

It helps to draw the figure to conceive shapes. The rear lot line is perpendicular to the side lot line. This makes the side lot line the base and the rear lot line the height (altitude).

Area = $\frac{1}{2}$(base)(height)

Area = 3,000 square feet

Base = 86 feet

Height = x

If it's easier, you can change $\frac{1}{2}$ to a decimal.

$\frac{1}{2} = .5$

Now you can plug these values into the formula.

$3,000 = (.5)(86)(x)$

$3,000 = (43)(x)$

Divide both sides by 43.

$\frac{3,000}{43} = \frac{(43)(x)}{43}$

$x = 69.767$ feet

Don't forget the question says to round your answer to the nearest whole number. The answer is 70 feet.

Circles

Remember the formula Area $= \pi r^2$.

Example:

Murray Brodman, a contractor, has been awarded the job to put up a circular bandstand in the town square. The radius of the circular area for the bandstand is 15 feet. What is the area of the bandstand? Use 3.14 for π.

Solution:

Area = πr^2

Start with the values you know.

Area = x

$\pi = 3.14$

radius = 15

Now plug these values into the formula.

Area = $(3.14)(15)(15) = 706.5$ sq. ft.

Property Tax

To solve property tax questions, you will be using percents and rates.

Example:

The tax rate in your county is $4.17 per hundred of assessed valuation, and Mr. Brown, a possible client, has told you his taxes are $1,100. What is his property assessment? (Round your answer to the nearest 10 cents.)

Solution:

Start off with the values you know.

Taxes = $1,100

Assessment = x

Tax rate = $4.17 per hundred (%)

If you remember the definition of percent as being an amount per hundred, then $4.17 per hundred is actually 4.17%. To make this equation more manageable, convert this percent to a decimal by moving the decimal point two spaces to the left. Now the tax rate is .0417.

.0417 of the assessed value of the house is $1,100. Translate the words into math terms. This means:

$(.0417)(x) = 1,100$

To solve the equation, divide both sides by .0417.

$$\frac{.0417x}{.0417} = \frac{1,100}{.0417}$$

$x = \$26,378.896$

Remember, the question asks you round to the nearest 10 cents. That means that .896 needs to be rounded up to 90. So the answer is $26,378.90.

Example:

Mr. Smith knew his own taxes were $975 and his property assessment was $17,000 for the house and $6,000 for the land. He wanted to know the tax rate (%).

Note that you may be asked for monthly amounts certain problems. Most calculations are on an annual basis—unless you divide by 12.

Solution:

Start with the values you know.

Taxes = $975

Assessment for house = $17,000 plus assessment for land = $6,000. Therefore, the total = $23,000.

Rate (%) = x

According to the question, $23,000 at a rate of x is $975. Convert this statement into an equation.

($23,000)($x$) = 975

Solve the equation by dividing both sides by 23,000.

$$\frac{23,000x}{23,000} = \frac{975}{23,000}$$

x = .0423913

To make this equation more simple, round the answer to .0424.

Remember that you are looking for the rate. Therefore, you need to convert this decimal to a percent by moving the decimal point two places to the right. The rate is 4.24%. (This can also be expressed as $4.24 per hundred.)

Loan-to-Value Ratios

These problems often deal with percentages.

Example:

A mortgage loan for 10% is at a 75% loan-to-value ratio. The interest on the original balance for the first year is $6,590. What is the value of the property securing the loan? Round to the nearest cent.

Solution:

First, find out the loan amount.

$6,590 is 10% of the loan amount. Let x equal the loan amount. Now, translate these words into math terms.

$6,590 = (10%)($x$)

Change 10% into a decimal by moving the decimal point two places to the left.

10% = .1

Now your equation looks like this.

$6,590 = (.1)($x$)

Divide both sides by (.1).

x = $65,900

Now that you know the loan amount ($65,900), use this information to find the value of the property.

Write down the values you know.

Loan amount = $65,900

Loan-to-value ratio = 75%

Value = x

We know that 75% of the value is $65,900.

Translate this into math terms.

$(75\%)(x) = \$65,900$

Change the percent into a decimal (75% = .75) and solve.

$(.75)(x) = 65,900$

Divide both sides by .75.

$$\frac{(.75)(x)}{(.75)} = \frac{65,900}{(.75)}$$

$x = 87,866.66666$

When rounded to the nearest cent, the answer is $87,866.67.

Points

Loan discounts are often called *points*, or loan placement fees, *one point* meaning 1% of the face amount of the loan. The service fee of 1% paid by buyers of government-backed loans is called a *loan origination fee*.

Example:

A homebuyer may obtain a $50,000 FHA mortgage loan, provided the seller pays a discount of five points. What is the amount of the discount?

Solution:

The definition of one point is 1% of the face amount of the loan.

Therefore, 5 points = 5% of face of loan. First, change the percent to a decimal.

5% = .05

Now you can use these values to solve.

Amount of discount = x

Points = .05

Amount of loan = $50,000

So, $x = (.05)(50,000)$

$x = \$2,500$

Example:

A property is listed at $74,000. An offer is made for $72,000, provided the seller pays three points on a loan for 80% of the purchase price. The brokerage commission rate is 7%. How much less will the seller receive if he accepts the offer than he would have received if he sold at all cash at the original terms?

Solution:

Here are the values you know:

Sold for original terms—price	$74,000	
Less 7% commission	− 5,180	(.07)(74,000) = 5,180
Seller's net	$68,820	

This question becomes more difficult, because in order to find the seller's net on the offered price, you must calculate the discount. The provision is that the seller pays three points (or .03) on a loan for 80% (or .8) of the price.

Start by finding 80% of the price.

$(.8)(72,000) = \$57,600$

Now, the points are applied to this amount. This means .03 of $57,600 is the discount.

So, $(.03)(57,600) = $ discount $= 1,728$.

You know these values:

Sold at offered terms—price	$72,000	
Less 7% commission	− 5,040	(.07)(72,000) = 5,040
Less discount	− 1,728	
Seller's net	$65,232	

$72,000	Sales price		Net at original	$68,820
× .80	Loan-to-value ratio		Net at offered	− 65,232
$57,600	Loan amount		Difference	$3,588
× .03	Points			
$1,728	Discount			

Equity

Example:

If a homeowner has a first mortgage loan balance of $48,350, a second mortgage loan balance of $18,200, and $26,300 equity, what is the value of her home?

Solution:

In this case, the value of the home is determined by the total loan balance plus the equity. Add the three numbers to find the value of the home.

$48,350 loan balance + $18,200 loan balance + $26,300 = value of the home

$92,850 = value of the home

Qualifying Buyers

Example:

A buyer is obtaining a conventional loan that requires 29/33 ratios. He earns $66,000 a year and has a $1,350 car payment. What is his maximum principal, interest, taxes, and insurance (PITI) payment?

  a. $1,612.50

  b. $1,812.50

  c. $465

  d. $2,475

Solution:

$66,000 divided by 12 = $5,500 monthly income

($5,500)(.29) = $1,595 front-end qualifier

($5,500)(.33) = $1,815 − $1,350 debt = $465 back-end qualifier

Maximum PITI is the lower of these two qualifiers, $465.

Prorations

At the time of settlement, there must be a reconciliation or adjustment of any monies owed by either party as of that date. The important fact to bear in mind is that *the party who used the service pays for it*. If you will keep this firmly in mind, you will not have any difficulty deciding whom to credit and whom to debit.

Example:

Mr. Seller's taxes are $1,200 a year paid in advance on a calendar year. He is settling on the sale of his house to Mr. Buyer on August 1. Which of them owes how much to the other?

Solution:

Ask yourself some questions:

How many months has the seller paid for?	12	($1,200)
How many months has the seller used?	7	($700)
How many months should the seller be reimbursed for?	5	($500)
How many months will the buyer use?	5	($500)
How many months has he paid for?	0	($0)
How many months should he reimburse the seller for?	5	($500)

Credit Mr. Seller $500.

Debit Mr. Buyer $500.

What would the answer be if the taxes were paid in arrears? In other words, the seller has used the service for seven months but hasn't paid anything. The buyer will have to pay it all at the end of the year. In that case, the seller owes the buyer for seven months, or $700.

Commissions

Let's look at a commission problem. They are typically rate (percentage) problems.

Example:

Broker Jones sold the Smith house for $65,000. The total commission came to $4,000. What was Jones's commission rate? Round to the nearest whole percent.

Solution:

You see the word *rate* and decide to solve this problem using percentages.

Start with the values you know.

Price of house = 65,000

Commission rate = x

Commission = 4,000

Now, translate the word problem into an equation.

$65,000x = 4,000$

Divide both sides by 65,000

$x = \frac{4,000}{65,000}$

$x = 0.061$

Convert the decimal to a percent by moving the decimal two places to the right.

$0.061 = 6.1\%$

Example:

An agent received a 3% commission on $\frac{1}{4}$ of her total sales. On the remainder, she received a 6% commission. What was her average commission for all of her sales?

Solution:

Start off by asking yourself, how many fourths (parts) were there? Four, naturally.

3%   6%   6%   6%

To find the average, you add up all the numbers, and divide by the number of items you added together. In this case, there are four numbers.

So, $3 + 6 + 6 + 6 = 21$.

And $21\% \div 4 = 5.25\%$.

Sale Proceeds

Example:

Salesman Garcia was trying to list a house. The owner said he wanted to clear (net) $12,000 from the sale of the house. The balance of the mortgage was $37,000. It would cost about $1,200 to fix the house up to sell. How much would the owner have to sell the house for if the 7% commission was included? (Round your answer to the nearest cent.)

Solution:

Use a chart to clarify the problem.

Expenses	In Dollars	In Percentages
Seller's net	$12,000	
Loan balance	$37,000	
Repairs	$ 1,200	
Commission		7%
	$50,200	7%

If the sales price is 100% and the commission is 7% of the sales price, all the remaining items added together must make 93% of the sales price. The place where most people go wrong is in not including the seller's net when they add the expenses. The seller's net has to come out of the sales price. (Where else would it come from?) Therefore, it is part of the remaining 93%. You now have a percentage problem. As always, convert your percents to decimals.

Start with the values you know:

Expenses = $50,200

Sales price = x

Seller's net, loan balance, repairs = .93 of sales price

.93 of the sales price is $50,200.

Convert this statement into an equation.

$(.93)(x) = \$50,200$

Divide both sides by .93.

$\frac{(.93)(x)}{.93} = \frac{\$50,200}{.93}$

$x = \frac{\$50,200}{.93}$

$x = \$53,978.4945$

Don't forget to round to the nearest cent!

$x = \$53,978.49$

Transfer Tax/Conveyance Tax/Revenue Stamps

Here is a transfer tax question.

Example:

A property is sold for $135,800 in cash. The transfer tax is $441.35. If transfer taxes are calculated per $200 of value, what was the rate (per $200) of the transfer tax?

Solution:

Start with the values you know.

Selling price = $135,800

Transfer tax rate = x per $200

Transfer tax = $441.35

It's probably easiest to begin by dividing $200 because the rate is calculated per $200 of value.

So, $\frac{\$135,800}{\$200} = \$679$.

You know that $441.35 is some rate of $679. Translate this into math terms.

$\$441.35 = (x)(\$679)$

Divide both sides by $679 to get

$\frac{\$441.35}{(\$679)} = \frac{(x)(\$679)}{(\$679)}$

$.65 = x$

Therefore, the transfer tax rate is $.65 per $200.

Competitive Market Analyses (CMA)

To solve these problems, you will use measurements and other hypothetical features of the comparable property to arrive at a value. Remember, a CMA is not an appraisal.

Example:

If Building A measures 52' by 106' and Building B measures 75' by 85', how much will B cost if A costs $140,000 and both cost the same per square foot to build?

Solution:

Area = (length)(width)

Area of Building A = (52)(106) = 5,512 square feet

Area of Building B = (75)(85) = 6,375 square feet

Cost of Building A per square foot = $\frac{140,000}{5,512}$ = $25.40

Cost of Building B = (6,375)($25.40) = $161,925

Example:

Carson's house (B), which is being appraised, is an exact twin of the houses on either side of it, built by the same builder at the same time. House A was appraised for $45,000, but it has a 14 × 20 foot garage, which was added at a cost of about $18 per square foot. House C was recently sold for $43,000, with central air valued at $3,000. What would be a fair estimate of the value of Carson's house?

Solution:

Comparable C	$43,000	
– Air Conditioning	– 3,000	
	$40,000	

Comparable A	$45,000	Garage: 14' × 20' = 280 sq. ft.
– Cost of Garage	– 5,040	280 sq. ft. × $18 = $5,040
	$39,960	

Answer: $40,000

Income Properties

Example:

An investor is considering the purchase of an income property generating a gross income of $350,000. Operating expenses constitute 70% of gross income. If the investor wants a return of 14%, what is the maximum he can pay?

Solution:

Gross income = $350,000

Expenses = 70% of gross income

Net income = Gross income – Expenses

Desired return = 14%

Maximum buyer can pay = x

This is a multistep problem. Start by calculating the expenses, but remember, you will need to stop to calculate the net income. First, change the percent to a decimal.

70% = .70

Now, you know that expenses are 70% of the gross income of $350,000. Change the words to mathematical terms.

Expenses = (.7)(350,000) = $245,000

Gross income − Expenses = Net income

$350,000 − $245,000 = $105,000

The buyer wants the net income ($105,000) to be 14% of what he pays for the property.

Change the percent to a decimal (14% = .14) and then convert this statement to an equation.

$105,000 = (.14)(x)$

Divide both sides by .14.

$$\frac{\$105,000}{.14} = \frac{(.14)(x)}{.14}$$

$\$105,000 \div .14 = x$

$\$750,000 = x$

Depreciation

There are several methods of depreciation, but the only one you are likely to meet on your exam is the straight-line method. This method spreads the total depreciation over the useful life of the building in equal annual amounts. It is calculated by dividing the replacement cost by the years of useful life left.

$$\frac{\text{replacement cost}}{\text{years of useful life}} = \text{annual depreciation}$$

The depreciation rate may be given or may have to be calculated by the straight-line method. This means dividing the total depreciation (100%) by the estimated useful life given for the building.

$$\frac{100\%}{\text{years of useful life}} = \text{depreciated rate}$$

If a building has 50 years of useful life left, the depreciation rate would be computed as follows:

$$\frac{100\%}{50} = 2\%$$

In other words, it has a 2% depreciation rate annually.

Example:

The replacement cost of a building has been estimated at $80,000. The building is 12 years old and has an estimated 40 years of useful life left. What can be charged to annual depreciation? What is the total depreciation for 12 years? What is the present value of this building?

Solution:

Calculate the annual depreciation.

$\frac{\text{replacement cost}}{\text{years of useful life}} = $ annual depreciation

$\frac{\$80,000}{40} = \$2,000$

Find the total depreciation over the 12 years.

Annual depreciation of $\$2,000 \times 12$ years $= \$24,000$

Find the current value: replacement $-$ depreciation $=$ current value.

$\$80,000 - \$24,000 = \$56,000$

► Summary

Hopefully, with this review you have realized that real estate math is not as bad as it seems. If you feel you need more practice, check out LearningExpress's *Practical Math Success in 20 Minutes a Day* or *1,001 Math Problems*. Use the exams in the books to practice even more real estate math.

CHAPTER

6 ▶ Real Estate Glossary

CHAPTER SUMMARY

One of the most basic components in preparing for your real estate exam is making sure you know all the terminology. This glossary provides a list of the most commonly used real estate terms and their definitions.

THESE TERMS WILL help you not only as you study for your real estate exam, but also after you pass your exam and are practicing in the field. The terms are listed in alphabetical order for easy reference.

▶ A

abandonment the voluntary surrender of a right, claim, or interest in a piece of property without naming a successor as owner or tenant.

abstract of title a certified summary of the history of a title to a particular parcel of real estate that includes the original grant and all subsequent transfers, encumbrances, and releases.

abutting sharing a common boundary; adjoining.

acceleration clause a clause in a note, mortgage, or deed of trust that permits the lender to declare the entire amount of principal and accrued interest due and payable immediately in the event of default.

acceptance the indication by a party receiving an offer that they agree to the terms of the offer. In most states, the offer and acceptance must be reduced to writing when real property is involved.

accretion the increase or addition of land resulting from the natural deposit of sand or soil by streams, lakes, or rivers.

accrued depreciation (1) the amount of depreciation, or loss in value, that has accumulated since initial construction; (2) the difference between the current appraised value and the cost to replace the building new.

accrued items a list of expenses that have been incurred but have not yet been paid, such as interest on a mortgage loan, that are included on a closing statement.

acknowledgment a formal declaration before a public official, usually a notary public, by a person who has signed a deed, contract, or other document that the execution was a voluntary act.

acre a measure of land equal to 43,560 square feet or 4,840 square yards.

actual eviction the result of legal action brought by a landlord against a defaulted tenant, whereby the tenant is physically removed from rented or leased property by a court order.

actual notice the actual knowledge that a person has of a particular fact.

addendum any provision added to a contract, or an addition to a contract that expands, modifies, or enhances the clarity of the agreement. To be a part of the contract and legally enforceable, an addendum must be referenced within the contract.

adjacent lying near to but not necessarily in actual contact with.

adjoining contiguous or attached; in actual contact with.

adjustable-rate mortgage (ARM) a mortgage in which the interest changes periodically, according to corresponding fluctuations in an index. All ARMs are tied to indexes. For example, a seven-year, adjustable-rate mortgage is a loan in which the rate remains fixed for the first seven years, then fluctuates according to the index to which it is tied.

adjusted basis the original cost of a property, plus acquisition costs, plus the value of added improvements to the property, minus accrued depreciation.

adjustment date the date the interest rate changes on an adjustable-rate mortgage.

administrator a person appointed by a court to settle the estate of a person who has died without leaving a will.

ad valorem tax tax in proportion to the value of a property.

adverse possession a method of acquiring title to another person's property through court action after taking actual, open, hostile, and continuous possession for a statutory period of time; may require payment of property taxes during the period of possession.

affidavit a written statement made under oath and signed before a licensed public official, usually a notary public.

agency the legal relationship between principal and agent that arises out of a contract wherein an agent is employed to do certain acts on behalf of the principal who has retained the agent to deal with a third party.

agent one who has been granted the authority to act on behalf of another.

agreement of sale a written agreement between a seller and a purchaser whereby the purchaser agrees to buy a certain piece of property from the seller for a specified price.

air rights the right to use the open space above a particular property.

alienation the transfer of ownership of a property to another, either voluntarily or involuntarily.

alienation clause the clause in a mortgage or deed of trust that permits the lender to declare all unpaid principal and accrued interest due and payable if the borrower transfers title to the property.

allodial system in the United States, a system of land ownership in which land is held free and clear of any rent or services due to the government; commonly contrasted with the feudal system, in which ownership is held by a monarch.

amenities features or benefits of a particular property that enhance the property's desirability and value, such as a scenic view or a pool.

amortization the method of repaying a loan or debt by making periodic installment payments composed of both principal and interest. When all principal has been repaid, it is considered fully amortized.

amortization schedule a table that shows how much of each loan payment will be applied toward principal and how much toward interest over the lifespan of the loan. It also shows the gradual decrease of the outstanding loan balance until it reaches zero.

amortize to repay a loan through regular payments that consist of principal and interest.

annual percentage rate (APR) the total or effective amount of interest charged on a loan, expressed as a percentage, on a yearly basis. This value is created according to a government formula intended to reflect the true annual cost of borrowing.

anti-deficiency law laws used in some states to limit the claim of a lender on default on payment of a purchase money mortgage on owner-occupied residential property to the value of the collateral.

anti-trust laws laws designed to protect free enterprise and the open marketplace by prohibiting certain business practices that restrict competition. In reference to real estate, these laws would prevent such practices as price fixing or agreements by brokers to limit their areas of trade.

apportionments adjustment of income, expenses, or carrying charges related to real estate, usually computed to the date of closing so that the seller pays all expenses to date, then the buyer pays all expenses beginning on the closing date.

appraisal an estimate or opinion of the value of an adequately described property, as of a specific date.

appraised value an opinion of a property's fair market value, based on an appraiser's knowledge, experience, and analysis of the property, and based on comparable sales.

appraiser an individual qualified by education, training, and experience to estimate the value of real property. Appraisers may work directly for mortgage lenders, or they may be independent contractors.

appreciation an increase in the market value of a property.

appurtenance something that transfers with the title to land even if not an actual part of the property, such as an easement.

arbitration the process of settling a dispute in which the parties submit their differences to an impartial third party, on whose decision on the matter is binding.

ARELLO the Association of Real Estate License Law Officials.

assessed value the value of a property used to calculate real estate taxes.

assessment the process of assigning value on property for taxation purposes.

assessor a public official who establishes the value of a property for taxation purposes.

asset items of value owned by an individual. Assets that can be quickly converted into cash are considered "liquid assets," such as bank accounts and stock portfolios. Other assets include real estate, personal property, and debts owed.

assignment the transfer of rights or interest from one person to another.

assumption of mortgage the act of acquiring the title to a property that has an existing mortgage and agreeing to be liable for the payment of any debt still existing on that mortgage. However, the lender must accept the transfer of liability for the original borrower to be relieved of the debt.

attachment the process whereby a court takes custody of a debtor's property until the creditor's debt is satisfied.

attest to bear witness by providing a signature.

attorney-in-fact a person who is authorized under a power of attorney to act on behalf of another.

avulsion the removal of land from one owner to another when a stream or other body of water suddenly changes its channel.

▶ B

balloon mortgage a loan in which the periodic payments do not fully amortize the loan, so that a final payment (a balloon payment) is substantially larger than the amount of the periodic payments that must be made to satisfy the debt.

balloon payment the final, lump-sum payment that is due at the termination of a balloon mortgage.

bankruptcy an individual or individuals can restructure or relieve themselves of debts and liabilities by filing in federal bankruptcy court. Of the many types of bankruptcies, the most common for an individual is "Chapter 7 No Asset," which relieves the borrower of most types of debts.

bargain and sale deed a deed that conveys title but does not necessarily carry warranties against liens or encumbrances.

baseline one of the imaginary east-west lines used as a reference point when describing property with the rectangular or government survey method of property description.

benchmark a permanently marked point with a known elevation, used as a reference by surveyors to measure elevations.

beneficiary (1) one who benefits from the acts of another; (2) the lender in a deed of trust.

bequest personal property given by provision of a will.

betterment an improvement to property that increases its value.

bilateral contract a contract in which each party promises to perform an act in exchange for the other party's promise also to perform an act.

bill of sale a written instrument that transfers ownership of personal property. A bill of sale cannot be used to transfer ownership of real property, which is passed by deed.

binder an agreement, accompanied by an earnest money deposit, for the purchase of a piece of real estate to show the purchaser's good faith intent to complete a transaction.

biweekly mortgage a mortgage in which payments are made every two weeks instead of once a month. Therefore, instead of making 12 monthly payments during the year, the borrower makes the equivalent of 13 monthly payments. The extra payment reduces the principal, thereby reducing the time it takes to pay off a 30-year mortgage.

blanket mortgage a mortgage in which more than one parcel of real estate is pledged to cover a single debt.

blockbusting the illegal and discriminatory practice of inducing homeowners to sell their properties by suggesting or implying the introduction of members of a protected class into the neighborhood.

bona fide in good faith, honest.

bond evidence of personal debt secured by a mortgage or other lien on real estate.

boot money or property provided to make up a difference in value or equity between two properties in an exchange.

branch office a place of business secondary to a principal office. The branch office is a satellite office generally run by a licensed broker, for the benefit of the broker running the principal office, as well as the associate broker's convenience.

breach of contract violation of any conditions or terms in a contract without legal excuse.

broker in real estate terms, it is the owner-manager of a business who brings together the parties to a real estate transaction for a fee. The roles of brokers and brokers' associates are defined by state law. In the mortgage industry, *broker* usually refers to a company or individual who does not lend the money for the loans directly, but who brokers loans to larger lenders or investors.

brokerage the business of bringing together buyers and sellers or other participants in a real estate transaction.

broker's price opinion (BPO) a broker's opinion of value based on a comparative market analysis rather than a certified appraisal.

building code local regulations that control construction, design, and materials used in construction that are based on health and safety regulations.

building line the distance from the front, rear, or sides of a building lot beyond which no structures may extend.

building restrictions limitations listed in zoning ordinances or deed restrictions on the size and type of improvements allowed on a property.

bundle of rights the concept that ownership of a property includes certain rights regarding the property, such as possession, enjoyment, control of use, and disposition.

buydown usually refers to a fixed-rate mortgage where the interest rate is "bought down" for a temporary period, usually one to three years. After that time and for the remainder of the term, the borrower's payment is calculated at the note rate. In order to buy down the initial rate for the temporary payment, a lump sum is paid and held in an account used to supplement the borrower's monthly payment. These funds usually come from the seller as a financial incentive to induce someone to buy his or her property.

buyer's broker real estate broker retained by a prospective buyer; this buyer becomes the broker's client to whom fiduciary duties are owed.

bylaws rules and regulations adopted by an association—for example, a condominium.

▶ C

cancellation clause a provision in a lease that confers on one or all parties to the lease the right to terminate the parties' obligations, should the occurrence of the condition or contingency set forth in the clause happen.

canvassing the practice of searching for prospective clients by making unsolicited phone calls and/or visiting homes door to door.

cap the limit on fluctuation rates regarding adjustable rate mortgages. Caps, or limitations, may apply to how much the loan may adjust over a six-month period, an annual period, and over the life of the loan. There is also a limit on how much that payment can change each year.

capital money used to create income, or the net worth of a business as represented by the amount by which its assets exceed its liabilities.

capital expenditure the cost of a betterment to a property.

capital gains tax a tax charged on the profit gained from the sale of a capital asset.

capitalization the process of estimating the present value of an income-producing piece of property by dividing anticipated future income by a capitalization rate.

capitalization rate the rate of return a property will generate on an owner's investment.

cash flow the net income produced by an investment property, calculated by deducting operating and fixed expenses from gross income.

caveat emptor a phrase meaning "let the buyer beware."

CC&R covenants, conditions, and restrictions of a cooperative or condominium development.

certificate of discharge a document used when the security instrument is a mortgage.

certificate of eligibility a document issued by the Veterans Administration that certifies a veteran's eligibility for a VA loan.

certificate of reasonable value (CRV) once the appraisal has been performed on a property being bought with a VA loan, the Veterans Administration issues a CRV.

certificate of sale the document given to a purchaser of real estate that is sold at a tax foreclosure sale.

certificate of title a report stating an opinion on the status of a title, based on the examination of public records.

chain of title the recorded history of conveyances and encumbrances that affect the title to a parcel of land.

chattel personal property, as opposed to real property.

chattel mortgage a loan in which personal property is pledged to secure the debt.

city a large municipality governed under a charter and granted by the state.

clear title a title that is free of liens and legal questions as to ownership of a property that is a requirement for the sale of real estate; sometimes referred to as *just title*, *good title*, or *free and clear*.

closing the point in a real estate transaction when the purchase price is paid to the seller and the deed to the property is transferred from the seller to the buyer.

closing costs there are two kinds: (1) nonrecurring closing costs and (2) prepaid items. Nonrecurring closing costs are any items paid once as a result of buying the property or obtaining a loan. Prepaid items are items that recur over time, such as property taxes and homeowners insurance. A lender makes an attempt to estimate the amount of nonrecurring closing costs and prepaid items on the good faith estimate, which is issued to the borrower within three days of receiving a home loan application.

closing date the date on which the buyer takes over the property.

closing statement a written accounting of funds received and disbursed during a real estate transaction. The buyer and seller receive separate closing statements.

cloud on the title an outstanding claim or encumbrance that can affect or impair the owner's title.

clustering the grouping of home sites within a subdivision on smaller lots than normal, with the remaining land slated for use as common areas.

codicil a supplement or addition to a will that modifies the original instrument.

coinsurance clause a clause in an insurance policy that requires the insured to pay a portion of any loss experienced.

collateral something of value hypothecated (real property) or pledged (personal property) by a borrower as security for a debt.

collection when a borrower falls behind, the lender contacts the borrower in an effort to bring the loan current. The loan goes to "collection."

color of title an instrument that gives evidence of title, but may not be legally adequate to actually convey title.

commercial property property used to produce income, such as an office building or a restaurant.

commingling the illegal act of an agent mixing a client's monies, which should be held in a separate escrow account, with the agent's personal monies; in some states, it means placing funds that are separate property in an account containing funds that are community property.

commission the fee paid to a broker for services rendered in a real estate transaction.

commitment letter a pledge in writing affirming an agreement.

common areas portions of a building, land, and amenities owned (or managed) by a planned unit development or condominium project's homeowners association or a cooperative project's cooperative corporation. These areas are used by all of the unit owners, who share in the common expenses of their operation and maintenance. Common areas may include swimming pools, tennis courts, and other recreational facilities, as well as common corridors of buildings, parking areas, and lobbies.

common law the body of laws derived from local custom and judicial precedent.

community property a system of property ownership in which each spouse has equal interest in property acquired during the marriage; recognized in nine states.

comparable sales recent sales of similar properties in nearby areas that are used to help estimate the current market value of a property.

comparative market analysis (CMA) an analysis of market value used to determine a probable selling price using recently sold properties most like the subject property.

competent parties people who are legally qualified to enter a contract, usually meaning that they are of legal age, of sound mind, and not under the influence of drugs or other mind-altering substances.

competitive market analysis (CMA) an analysis of market value used to assist a seller in determining an asking price, using currently active listings, expired listings, and sold properties comparable to the subject property.

condemnation the judicial process by which the government exercises its power of eminent domain.

condominium a form of ownership in which an individual owns a specific unit in a multiunit building and shares ownership of common areas with other unit owners.

condominium conversion changing the ownership of an existing building (usually a multi-dwelling rental unit) from single ownership to condominium ownership.

conformity an appraisal principle that asserts that property achieves its maximum value when a neighborhood is homogeneous in its use of land; the basis for zoning ordinances.

consideration something of value that induces parties to enter into a contract, such as money or services.

construction mortgage a short-term loan used to finance the building of improvements to real estate.

constructive eviction action or inaction by a landlord that renders a property uninhabitable, forcing a tenant to move out with no further liability for rent.

constructive notice notice of a fact given by making the fact part of the public record. All persons are responsible for knowing the information, whether or not they have actually seen the record.

contingency a condition that must be met before a contract is legally binding. A satisfactory home inspection report from a qualified home inspector is an example of a common type of contingency.

contract an agreement between two or more legally competent parties to do or to refrain from doing some legal act in exchange for a consideration.

contract for deed a contract for the sale of a parcel of real estate in which the buyer makes periodic payments to the seller and receives title to the property only after all, or a substantial part, of the purchase price has been paid, or regular payments have been made for one year or longer.

conventional loan a loan that is neither insured nor guaranteed by an agency of government.

conversion option an option in an adjustable-rate mortgage to convert it to a fixed-rate mortgage.

convertible ARM an adjustable-rate mortgage that allows the borrower to change the ARM to a fixed-rate mortgage at a specific time.

conveyance the transfer of title from the grantor to the grantee.

cooperative a form of property ownership in which a corporation owns a multiunit building and stockholders of the corporation may lease and occupy individual units of the building through a proprietary lease.

corporation a legal entity with potentially perpetual existence that is created and owned by shareholders who appoint a board of directors to direct the business affairs of the corporation.

cost approach an appraisal method whereby the value of a property is calculated by estimating the cost of constructing a comparable building, subtracting depreciation, and adding land value.

counteroffer an offer submitted in response to an offer. It has the effect of overriding the original offer.

covenant an agreement or promise between parties to do or not do specifies acts.

covenant of seisin the seller of real estate promises he or she has rightful title and is delivering that title to the buyer.

credit an agreement in which a borrower receives something of value in exchange for a promise to repay the lender.

credit history a record of an individual's repayment of debt.

cul-de-sac a dead-end street that widens at the end, creating a circular turnaround area.

curtesy the statutory or common law right of a husband to all or part of real estate owned by his deceased wife, regardless of will provisions, recognized in some states.

curtilage area of land occupied by a building, its outbuildings, and yard, either actually enclosed or considered enclosed.

▶ D

damages the amount of money recoverable by a person who has been injured by the actions of another.

datum a specific point used in surveying.

DBA the abbreviation for "doing business as."

debt an amount owed to another.

debt service the amount of money needed to make payments of principal and interest on a loan.

decedent a person who dies.

dedication the donation of private property by its owner to a governmental body for public use.

deed a written document that, when properly signed and delivered, conveys title to real property from the grantor to the grantee.

deed-in-lieu a foreclosure instrument used to convey title to the lender when the borrower is in default and wants to avoid foreclosure.

deed of trust (**trust deed**) a deed in which the title to property is transferred to a third-party trustee to secure repayment of a loan; three-party mortgage arrangement.

deed restriction an imposed restriction for the purpose of limiting the use of land, such as the size or type of improvements to be allowed. Also called a *restrictive covenant*.

default the failure to perform a contractual duty.

defeasance clause a clause in a mortgage that renders the mortgage void where all obligations have been fulfilled.

deficiency judgment a personal claim against a borrower when mortgaged property is foreclosed and sale of the property does not produce sufficient funds to pay off the mortgage. Deficiency judgments may be prohibited in some circumstances by anti-deficiency protection.

delinquency failure to make mortgage or loan payments when payments are due.

density zoning a zoning ordinance that restricts the number of houses or dwelling units that can be built per acre in a particular area, such as a subdivision.

depreciation a loss in value because of physical deterioration or functional or external obsolescence.

descent the transfer of property to an owner's heirs when the owner dies intestate.

devise the transfer of title to real estate by will.

devisee one who receives a bequest of real estate by will.

devisor one who grants real estate by will.

directional growth the direction toward which certain residential sections of a city are expected to grow.

discount point one percent of the loan amount charged by a lender at closing to increase a loan's effective yield and lower the fare rate to the borrower.

discount rate the rate that lenders pay for mortgage funds—a higher rate is passed on to the borrower.

dispossess to remove a tenant from property by legal process.

dominant estate (tenement) property that includes the right to use an easement on adjoining property.

dower the right of a widow in the property of her husband upon his death in noncommunity property states.

down payment the part of the purchase price that the buyer pays in cash and is not financed with a mortgage or loan.

dual agency an agent who represents both parties in a transaction.

due-on-sale clause a provision in a mortgage that allows the lender to demand repayment in full if the borrower sells the property that serves as security for the mortgage.

duress the use of unlawful means to force a person to act or to refrain from an action against his or her will.

▶ **E**

earnest money down payment made by a buyer of real estate as evidence of good faith.

easement the right of one party to use the land of another for a particular purpose, such as to lay utility lines.

easement by necessity an easement, granted by law and requiring court action that is deemed necessary for the full enjoyment of a parcel of land. An example would be an easement allowing access from landlocked property to a road.

easement by prescription a means of acquiring an easement by continued, open, and hostile use of someone else's property for a statutorily defined period of time.

easement in gross a personal right granted by an owner with no requirement that the easement holder own adjoining land.

economic life the period of time over which an improved property will generate sufficient income to justify its continued existence.

effective age an appraiser's estimate of the physical condition of a building. The actual age of a building may be different than its effective age.

emblements cultivated crops; generally considered to be personal property.

eminent domain the right of a government to take private property for public use upon payment of its fair market value. Eminent domain is the basis for condemnation proceedings.

encroachment a trespass caused when a structure, such as a wall or fence, invades another person's land or airspace.

encumbrance anything that affects or limits the title to a property, such as easements, leases, mortgages, or restrictions.

equitable title the interest in a piece of real estate held by a buyer who has agreed to purchase the property, but has not yet completed the transaction; the interest of a buyer under a contract for deed.

equity the difference between the current market value of a property and the outstanding indebtedness due on it.

equity of redemption the right of a borrower to stop the foreclosure process.

erosion the gradual wearing away of land by wind, water, and other natural processes.

escalation clause a clause in a lease allowing the lessor to charge more rent based on an increase in costs; sometimes called a pass-through clause.

escheat the claim to property by the state when the owner dies intestate and no heirs can be found.

escrow the deposit of funds and/or documents with a disinterested third party for safekeeping until the terms of the escrow agreement have been met.

escrow account a trust account established to hold escrow funds for safekeeping until disbursement.

escrow analysis annual report to disclose escrow receipts, payments, and current balances.

escrow disbursements money paid from an escrow account.

estate an interest in real property. The sum total of all the real property and personal property owned by an individual.

estate for years a leasehold estate granting possession for a definite period of time.

estate tax federal tax levied on property transferred upon death.

estoppel certificate a document that certifies the outstanding amount owed on a mortgage loan, as well as the rate of interest.

et al. abbreviation for the Latin phrase *et alius*, meaning "and another."

et ux. abbreviation for Latin term *et uxor*, meaning "and wife."

et vir Latin term meaning "and husband."

eviction the lawful expulsion of an occupant from real property.

evidence of title a document that identifies ownership of property.

examination of title a review of an abstract to determine current condition of title.

exchange a transaction in which property is traded for another property, rather than sold for money or other consideration.

exclusive agency listing a contract between a property owner and one broker that only gives the broker the right to sell the property for a fee within a specified period of time but does not obligate the owner to pay the broker a fee if the owner produces his or her own buyer without the broker's assistance. The owner is barred only from appointing another broker within this time period.

exclusive right to sell a contract between a property owner and a broker that gives the broker the right to collect a commission regardless of who sells the property during the specified period of time of the agreement.

exculpatory clause a statement that absolves or waives a right or obligation.

execution the signing of a contract.

executor/executrix a person named in a will to administer an estate. The court will appoint an administrator if no executor is named. *Executrix* is the feminine form.

executory contract a contract in which one or more of the obligations have yet to be performed.

executed contract a contract in which all obligations have been fully performed.

express contract an oral or written contract in which the terms are expressed in words.

extension agreement an agreement between mortgagor and mortgagee to extend the maturity date of the mortgage after it is due.

external obsolescence a loss in value of a property because of factors outside the property, such as a change in surrounding land use.

▶ **F**

fair housing law a term used to refer to federal and state laws prohibiting discrimination in the sale or rental of residential property.

fair market value the highest price that a buyer, willing but not compelled to buy, would pay, and the lowest a seller, willing but not compelled to sell, would accept.

Federal Housing Administration (FHA) an agency within the U.S. Department of Housing and Urban Development (HUD) that insures mortgage loans by FHA-approved lenders to make loans available to buyers with limited cash.

Federal National Mortgage Association (Fannie Mae) a privately owned corporation that buys existing government-backed and conventional mortgages.

Federal Reserve System the central banking system of the United States, which controls the monetary policy and, therefore, the money supply, interest rates, and availability of credit.

fee simple the most complete form of ownership of real estate.

FHA-insured loan a loan insured by the Federal Housing Administration.

fiduciary relationship a legal relationship with an obligation of trust, as that of agent and principal.

finder's fee a fee or commission paid to a mortgage broker for finding a mortgage loan for a prospective borrower.

first mortgage a mortgage that has priority to be satisfied over all other mortgages.

fixed-rate loan a loan with an interest rate that does not change during the entire term of the loan.

fixture an article of personal property that has been permanently attached to the real estate so as to become an integral part of the real estate.

foreclosure the legal process by which a borrower in default of a mortgage is deprived of interest in the mortgaged property. Usually, this involves a forced sale of the property at public auction, where the proceeds of the sale are applied to the mortgage debt.

forfeiture the loss of money, property, rights, or privileges because of a breach of legal obligation.

franchise in real estate, an organization that lends a standardized trade name, operating procedures, referral services, and supplies to member brokerages.

fraud a deliberate misstatement of material fact or an act or omission made with deliberate intent to deceive (active fraud) or gross disregard for the truth (constructive fraud).

freehold estate an estate of ownership in real property.

front foot a measurement of property taken by measuring the frontage of the property along the street line.

functional obsolescence a loss in value of a property due to causes within the property, such as faulty design, outdated structural style, or inadequacy to function properly.

future interest ownership interest in property that cannot be enjoyed until the occurrence of some event; sometimes referred to as a household or equitable interest.

▶ **G**

general agent an agent who is authorized to act for and obligate a principal in a specific range of matters, as specified by their mutual agreement.

general lien a claim on all property, real and personal, owned by a debtor.

general warranty deed an instrument in which the grantor guarantees the grantee that the title being conveyed is good and free of other claims or encumbrances.

government-backed mortgage a mortgage that is insured by the Federal Housing Administration (FHA) or guaranteed by the Department of Veterans Affairs (VA) or the Rural Housing Service (RHS). Mortgages that are not government loans are identified as conventional loans.

Government National Mortgage Association (Ginnie Mae) a government-owned corporation within the U.S. Department of Housing and Urban Development (HUD). Ginnie Mae manages and liquidates government-backed loans and assists HUD in special lending projects.

government survey system a method of land description in which meridians (lines of longitude) and baselines (lines of latitude) are used to divide land into townships and sections.

graduated lease a lease that calls for periodic, stated changes in rent during the term of the lease.

grant the transfer of title to real property by deed.

grant deed a deed that includes three warranties: (1) that the owner has the right to convey title to the property, (2) that there are no encumbrances other than those noted specifically in the deed, and (3) that the owner will convey any future interest that he or she may acquire in the property.

grantee one who receives title to real property.

grantor one who conveys title to real property; the present owner.

gross income the total income received from a property before deducting expenses.

gross income multiplier a rough method of estimating the market value of an income property by multiplying its gross annual rent by a multiplier discovered by dividing the sales price of comparable properties by their annual gross rent.

gross lease a lease in which a tenant pays only a fixed amount for rental and the landlord pays all operating expenses and taxes.

gross rent multiplier similar to *gross income multiplier,* except that it looks at the relationship between sales price and monthly gross rent.

ground lease a lease of land only, on which a tenant already owns a building or will construct improvements.

guaranteed sale plan an agreement between a broker and a seller that the broker will buy the seller's property if it does not sell within a specified period of time.

guardian one who is legally responsible for the care of another person's rights and/or property.

▶ **H**

habendum clause the clause in a deed, beginning with the words "to have and to hold," that defines or limits the exact interest in the estate granted by the deed.

hamlet a small village.

heir one who is legally entitled to receive property when the owner dies intestate.

hereditament any type of inheritable property both real and personal.

highest and best use the legally permitted use of a parcel of land that will yield the greatest return to the owner in terms of money or amenities.

holdover tenancy a tenancy where a lessee retains possession of the property after the lease has expired, and the landlord, by continuing to accept rent, agrees to the tenant's continued occupancy.

holographic will a will that is entirely handwritten, dated, and signed by the testator.

home equity conversion mortgage (HECM) often called a reverse-annuity mortgage; instead of making payments to a lender, the lender makes payments to you. It enables older homeowners to convert the equity they have in their homes into cash, usually in the form of monthly payments. Unlike traditional home equity loans, a borrower does not qualify on the basis of income but on the value of his or her home. In addition, the loan does not have to be repaid until the borrower no longer occupies the property.

home equity line of credit a mortgage loan that allows the borrower to obtain cash drawn against the equity of his or her home, up to a predetermined amount.

home inspection a thorough inspection by a professional that evaluates the structural and mechanical condition of a property. A satisfactory home inspection is often included as a contingency by the purchaser.

homeowner's insurance an insurance policy specifically designed to protect residential property owners against financial loss from common risks such as fire, theft, and liability.

homeowner's warranty an insurance policy that protects purchasers of newly constructed or pre-owned homes against certain structural and mechanical defects.

homestead the parcel of land and improvements legally qualifying as the owner's principal residence.

HUD an acronym for the Department of Housing and Urban Development, a federal agency that enforces federal fair housing laws and oversees agencies such as FHA and GNMA.

hypothecate the act of pledging property as collateral for a loan without giving up possession of the pledged property.

► I

implied contract a contract whereby the agreement of the parties is created by their conduct.

improvement human-made addition to real estate.

income capitalization approach a method of estimating the value of income-producing property by dividing its expected annual net operating income of the property by a capitalization rate.

income property real estate developed or improved to produce income.

incorporeal right intangible, non-possessory rights in real estate, such as an easement or right of way.

indemnify to hold harmless and to reimburse or compensate someone for a loss.

independent contractor one who is retained by another to perform a certain task and is not subject to the control and direction of the hiring person with regard to the end result of the task. Individual contractors receive a fee for their services but pay their own expenses and taxes and receive no employee benefits.

index a number used to compute the interest rate for an adjustable-rate mortgage (ARM). The index is a published number or percentage, such as the average yield on Treasury bills. A margin is added to the index to determine the interest rate to be charged on the ARM. This interest rate is subject to any caps that are associated with the mortgage.

industrial property buildings and land used for the manufacture and distribution of goods, such as a factory.

inflation an increase in the amount of money or credit available in relation to the amount of goods or services available, which causes an increase in the general price level of goods and services.

initial interest rate the beginning interest rate of the mortgage at the time of closing. This rate changes for an adjustable-rate mortgage (ARM).

installment the regular, periodic payment that a borrower agrees to make to a lender, usually related to a loan.

installment contract see *contract for deed*.

installment loan borrowed money that is repaid in periodic payments, known as installments.

installment sale a transaction in which the sales price is paid to the seller in two or more installments over more than one calendar year.

insurance a contract that provides indemnification from specific losses in exchange for a periodic payment. The individual contract is known as an insurance policy, and the periodic payment is known as an insurance premium.

insurance binder a document that states that temporary insurance is in effect until a permanent insurance policy is issued.

insured mortgage a mortgage that is protected by the Federal Housing Administration (FHA) or by private mortgage insurance (PMI). If the borrower defaults on the loan, the insurer must pay the lender the insured amount.

interest a fee charged by a lender for the use of the money loaned; or a share of ownership in real estate.

interest accrual rate the percentage rate at which interest accrues on the mortgage.

interest rate the rent or rate charged to use funds belonging to another.

interest rate buydown plan an arrangement in which the property seller (or any other party) deposits money into an account so that it can be released each month to reduce the mortgagor's monthly payments during the early years of a mortgage. During the specified period, the mortgagor's effective interest rate is "bought down" below the actual interest rate.

interest rate ceiling the maximum interest rate that may be charged for an adjustable-rate mortgage (ARM), as specified in the mortgage note.

interest rate floor the minimum interest rate for an adjustable-rate mortgage (ARM), as specified in the mortgage note.

interim financing a short-term loan made during the building phase of a project; also known as a construction loan.

intestate to die without having authored a valid will.

invalid not legally binding or enforceable.

investment property a property not occupied by the owner.

▶ J

joint tenancy co-ownership that gives each tenant equal interest and equal rights in the property, including the right of survivorship.

joint venture an agreement between two or more parties to engage in a specific business enterprise.

judgment a decision rendered by court determining the rights and obligations of parties to an action or lawsuit.

judgment lien a lien on the property of a debtor resulting from a court judgment.

judicial foreclosure a proceeding that is handled as a civil lawsuit and conducted through court; used in some states.

jumbo loan a loan that exceeds Fannie Mae's mortgage amount limits. Also called a *non-conforming loan.*

junior mortgage any mortgage that is inferior to a first lien and that will be satisfied only after the first mortgage; also called a *secondary mortgage.*

▶ L

laches a doctrine used by a court to bar the assertion of a legal claim or right, based on the failure to assert the claim in a timely manner.

land the earth from its surface to its center, and the airspace above it.

landlocked property surrounded on all sides by property belonging to another.

lease a contract between a landlord and a tenant wherein the landlord grants the tenant possession and use of the property for a specified period of time and for a consideration.

leased fee the landlord's interest in a parcel of leased property.

lease option a financing option that allows homebuyers to lease a home with an option to buy. Each month's rent payment may consist of rent, plus an additional amount that can be applied toward the down payment on an already specified price.

leasehold a tenant's right to occupy a parcel of real estate for the term of a lease.

legal description a description of a parcel of real estate specific and complete enough for an independent surveyor to locate and identify it.

lessee the one who receives that right to use and occupy the property during the term of the leasehold estate.

lessor the owner of the property who grants the right of possession to the lessee.

leverage the use of borrowed funds to purchase an asset.

levy to assess or collect a tax.

license (1) a revocable authorization to perform a particular act on another's property; (2) authorization granted by a state to act as a real estate broker or salesperson.

lien a legal claim against a property to secure payment of a financial obligation.

life estate a freehold estate in real property limited in duration to the lifetime of the holder of the life estate or another specified person.

life tenant one who holds a life estate.

liquidity the ability to convert an asset into cash.

lis pendens a Latin phrase meaning "suit pending"; a public notice that a lawsuit has been filed that may affect the title to a particular piece of property.

listing agreement a contract between the owner and a licensed real estate broker wherein the broker is employed to sell real estate on the owner's terms within a given time, for which service the owner agrees to pay the broker an agreed-upon fee.

listing broker a broker who contracts with a property owner to sell or lease the described property; the listing agreement typically may provide for the broker to make property available through a multiple-listing system.

littoral rights landowner's claim to use water in large, navigable lakes and oceans adjacent to property; ownership rights to land-bordering bodies of water up to the high-water mark.

loan a sum of borrowed money, or principal, that is generally repaid with interest.

loan officer also known as a lender; serves several functions and has various responsibilities, such as soliciting loans; a loan officer both represents the lending institution and represents the borrower to the lending institution.

lock-in an agreement in which the lender guarantees a specified interest rate for a certain amount of time.

lock-in period the time period during which the lender has guaranteed an interest rate to a borrower.

lot and block description a method of describing a particular property by referring to a lot and block number within a subdivision recorded in the public record.

▶ **M**

management agreement a contract between the owner of an income property and a firm or individual who agrees to manage the property.

margin the difference between the interest rate and the index on an adjustable-rate mortgage. The margin remains stable over the life of the loan, while the index fluctuates.

market data approach a method of estimating the value of a property by comparing it to similar properties recently sold and making monetary adjustments for the differences between the subject property and the comparable property.

market value the amount that a seller may expect to obtain for merchandise, services, or securities in the open market.

marketable title title to property that is free from encumbrances and reasonable doubts and that a court would compel a buyer to accept.

mechanic's lien a statutory lien created to secure payment for those who supply labor or materials for the construction of an improvement to land.

metes and bounds a method of describing a parcel of land using direction and distance.

mill one-tenth of one cent; used by some states to express or calculate property tax rates.

minor a person who has not attained the legal age of majority.

misrepresentation a misstatement of fact, either deliberate or unintentional.

modification the act of changing any of the terms of the mortgage.

money judgment a court order to settle a claim with a monetary payment, rather than specific performance.

month-to-month tenancy tenancy in which the tenant rents for only one month at a time.

monument a fixed, visible marker used to establish boundaries for a survey.

mortgage a written instrument that pledges property to secure payment of a debt obligation as evidenced by a promissory note. When duly recorded in the public record, a mortgage creates a lien against the title to a property.

mortgage banker an entity that originates, funds, and services loans to be sold into the secondary money market.

mortgage broker an entity that, for a fee, brings borrowers together with lenders.

mortgage lien an encumbrance created by recording a mortgage.

mortgagee the lender who benefits from the mortgage.

mortgagor the borrower who pledges the property as collateral.

multi-dwelling units properties that provide separate housing units for more than one family that secure only a single mortgage. Apartment buildings are also considered multi-dwelling units.

multiple-listing system (MLS—also multiple-listing service) the method of marketing a property listing to all participants in the MLS.

mutual rescission an agreement by all parties to a contract to release one another from the obligations of the contract.

▶ **N**

negative amortization occurs when an adjustable rate mortgage is allowed to fluctuate independently of a required minimum payment. A gradual increase in mortgage debt happens when the monthly payment is not large enough to cover the entire principal and interest due. The amount of the shortfall is added to the remaining balance to create negative amortization.

net income the income produced by a property, calculated by deducting operating expenses from gross income.

net lease a lease that requires the tenant to pay maintenance and operating expenses, as well as rent.

net listing a listing in which the broker's fee is established as anything above a specified amount to be received by the seller from the sale of the property.

net worth the value of all of a person's assets.

no cash-out refinance a refinance transaction in which the new mortgage amount is limited to the sum of the remaining balance of the existing first mortgage.

non-conforming use a use of land that is permitted to continue, or grandfathered, even after a zoning ordinance is passed that prohibits the use.

nonliquid asset an asset that cannot easily be converted into cash.

notarize to attest or certify by a notary public.

notary public a person who is authorized to administer oaths and take acknowledgments.

note a written instrument acknowledging a debt, with a promise to repay, including an outline of the terms of repayment.

note rate the interest rate on a promissory note.

notice of default a formal written notice to a borrower that a default has occurred on a loan and that legal action may be taken.

novation the substitution of a new contract for an existing one; the new contract must reference the first and indicate that the first is being replaced and no longer has any force and effect.

▶ O

obligee a person on whose favor an obligation is entered.

obligor a person who is bound to another by an obligation.

obsolescence a loss in the value of a property because of functional or external factors.

offer to propose as payment; to bid on property.

offer and acceptance two necessary elements for the creation of a contract.

open-end mortgage a loan containing a clause that allows the mortgagor to borrow additional funds from the lender, up to a specified amount, without rewriting the mortgage.

open listing a listing contract given to one or more brokers in which a commission is paid only to the broker who procures a sale. If the owner sells the house without the assistance of one of the brokers, no commission is due.

opinion of title an opinion, usually given by an attorney, regarding the status of a title to property.

option an agreement that gives a prospective buyer the right to purchase a seller's property within a specified period of time for a specified price.

optionee one who receives or holds an option.

optionor one who grants an option; the property owner.

ordinance a municipal regulation.

original principal balance the total amount of principal owed on a loan before any payments are made; the amount borrowed.

origination fee the amount charged by a lender to cover the cost of assembling the loan package and originating the loan.

owner financing a real estate transaction in which the property seller provides all or part of the financing.

ownership the exclusive right to use, possess, control, and dispose of property.

▶ P

package mortgage a mortgage that pledges both real and personal property as collateral to secure repayment of a loan.

parcel a lot or specific portion of a large tract of real estate.

participation mortgage a type of mortgage in which the lender receives a certain percentage of the income or resale proceeds from a property, as well as interest on the loan.

partition the division of property held by co-owners into individual shares.

partnership an agreement between two parties to conduct business for profit. In a partnership, property is owned by the partnership, not the individual partners, so partners cannot sell their interest in the property without the consent of the other partners.

party wall a common wall used to separate two adjoining properties.

payee one who receives payment from another.

payor one who makes payment to another.

percentage lease a lease in which the rental rate is based on a percentage of the tenant's gross sales. This type of lease is most often used for retail space.

periodic estate tenancy that automatically renews itself until either the landlord or tenant gives notice to terminate it.

personal property (hereditaments) all items that are not permanently attached to real estate; also known as chattels.

physical deterioration a loss in the value of a property because of impairment of its physical condition.

PITI principal, interest, taxes, and insurance—the components of a regular mortgage payment.

planned unit development (PUD) a type of zoning that provides for residential and commercial uses within a specified area.

plat a map of subdivided land showing the boundaries of individual parcels or lots.

plat book a group of maps located in the public record showing the division of land into subdivisions, blocks, and individual parcels or lots.

plat number a number that identifies a parcel of real estate for which a plat has been recorded in the public record.

plottage combining two or more parcels of real estate resulting in increased usage and value.

PMI private mortgage insurance.

point a point is one percent of the loan.

point of beginning the starting point for a survey using the metes and bounds method of description.

police power the right of the government to enact laws, ordinances, and regulations to protect the public health, safety, welfare, and morals.

power of attorney a legal document that authorizes someone to act on another's behalf. A power of attorney can grant complete authority or can be limited to certain acts and/or certain periods of time.

preapproval condition where a borrower has completed a loan application and provided debt, income, and savings documentation that an underwriter has reviewed and approved. A preapproval is usually done at a certain loan amount, making assumptions about what the interest rate will actually be at the time the loan is actually made, as well as estimates for the amount that will be paid for property taxes, insurance, and so on.

prepayment amount paid to reduce the outstanding principal balance of a loan before the due date.

prepayment penalty a fee charged to a borrower by a lender for paying off a debt before the term of the loan expires.

prequalification a lender's opinion on the ability of a borrower to qualify for a loan, based on furnished information regarding debt, income, and available capital for down payment, closing costs, and prepaids. Prequalification is less formal than preapproval.

prescription a method of acquiring an easement to property by prolonged, unauthorized use.

primary mortgage market the financial market in which loans are originated, funded, and serviced.

prime rate the short-term interest rate that banks charge to their preferred customers. Changes in prime rate are used as the indexes in some adjustable-rate mortgages, such as home equity lines of credit.

principal (1) one who authorizes another to act on his or her behalf; (2) one of the contracting parties to a transaction; (3) the amount of money borrowed in a loan, separate from the interest charged on it.

principal meridian one of the 36 longitudinal lines used in the rectangular survey system method of land description.

probate the judicial procedure of proving the validity of a will.

procuring cause the action that brings about the desired result. For example, if a broker takes actions that result in a sale, the broker is the procuring cause of the sale.

promissory note a document that details the terms of the loan and is the debt instrument.

property management the operating of an income property for another.

property tax a tax levied by the government on property, real or personal.

prorate to divide ongoing property costs such as taxes or maintenance fees proportionately between buyer and seller at closing.

pur autre vie a phrase meaning "for the life of another." In a life estate *pur autre vie*, the term of the estate is measured by the life of a person other than the person who holds the life estate.

purchase agreement a written contract signed by the buyer and seller stating the terms and conditions under which a property will be sold.

purchase money mortgage a mortgage given by a buyer to a seller to secure repayment of any loan used to pay part or all of the purchase price.

▶ Q

qualifying ratios calculations to determine whether a borrower can qualify for a mortgage. There are two ratios. The "top" ratio is a calculation of the borrower's monthly housing costs (principle, taxes, insurance, mortgage insurance, homeowner's association fees) as a percentage of monthly income. The "bottom" ratio includes housing costs as well as all other monthly debt.

quitclaim deed a conveyance whereby the grantor transfers without warranty or obligations whatever interest or title he or she may have.

▶ R

range an area of land six miles wide, numbered east or west from a principal meridian in the rectangular survey system.

ready, willing, and able description of someone who is able to pay the asking price for a property and is prepared to complete the transaction.

real estate land, the earth below it, the air above it, and anything permanently attached to it.

real estate agent a real estate broker who has been appointed to market a property for and represent the property owner (listing agent); or a broker who has been appointed to represent the interest of the buyer (buyer's agent).

real estate board an organization whose members consist primarily of real estate sales agents, brokers, and administrators.

real estate broker a licensed person, association, partnership, or corporation who negotiates real estate transactions for others for a fee.

Real Estate Settlement Procedures Act (RESPA) a consumer protection law that requires lenders to give borrowers advance notice of closing costs and prohibits certain abusive practices against buyers using federally related loans to purchase their homes.

real property the rights of ownership to land and its improvements.

REALTOR® a registered trademark for use by members of the National Association of REALTORS® and affiliated state and local associations.

recording entering documents, such as deeds and mortgages, into the public record to give constructive notice.

rectangular survey system a method of land description based on principal meridians (lines of longitude) and baselines (lines of latitude). Also called the *government survey system*.

redemption period the statutory period of time during which an owner can reclaim foreclosed property by paying the debt owed plus court costs and other charges established by statute.

redlining the illegal practice of lending institutions refusing to provide certain financial services, such as mortgage loans, to property owners in certain areas.

refinance transaction the process of paying off one loan with the proceeds from a new loan using the same property as security or collateral.

Regulation Z a Federal Reserve regulation that implements the federal Truth-in-Lending Act.

release clause a clause in a mortgage that releases a portion of the property upon payment of a portion of the loan.

remainder estate a future interest in an estate that takes effect upon the termination of a life estate.

remainderman a person entitled to take an estate in remainder. For example, Louis grants a life estate to Marla that will pass to Shana upon Marla's death. Shana is the remainderman.

remaining balance in a mortgage, the amount of principal that has not yet been repaid.

remaining term the original amortization term minus the number of payments that have been applied to it.

rent a periodic payment paid by a lessee to a landlord for the use and possession of leased property.

replacement cost the estimated current cost to replace an asset similar or equivalent to the one being appraised.

reproduction cost the cost of building an exact duplicate of a building at current prices.

rescission canceling or terminating a contract by mutual consent or by the action of one party on default by the other party.

restriction (restrict covenant) a limitation on the way a property can be used.

reversion the return of interest or title to the grantor of a life estate.

reversionary interest a person has a reversionary interest in land when he or she has a right to take back property that he or she granted to another. For example, a landlord has a reversionary interest in leased property to take back possession at the termination of the lease. Here's another example: Gerry grants a life estate to Jessika that will revert back to Gerry upon Jessika's death. The person, Gerry in this case, is holding the reversionary right.

reverse annuity mortgage an agreement in which a homeowner receives monthly checks or a lump sum with no repayment until property is sold; usually between a mortgagor and elderly homeowners.

revision a revised or new version, as in a contract.

right of egress (or ingress) the right to enter or leave designated premises.

right of first refusal the right of a person to have the first opportunity to purchase property before it is offered to anyone else.

right of redemption the statutory right to reclaim ownership of property after a foreclosure sale.

right of survivorship in joint tenancy, the right of survivors to acquire the interest of a deceased joint tenant.

riparian rights the rights of a landowner whose property is adjacent to a flowing waterway, such as a river, to access and use the water.

▶ S

safety clause a contract provision that provides a time period following expiration of a listing agreement, during which the agent will be compensated if there is a transaction with a buyer who was initially introduced to the property by the agent.

sale-leaseback a transaction in which the owner sells improved property and, as part of the same transaction, signs a long-term lease to remain in possession of its premises, thus becoming the tenant of the new owner.

sales contract a contract between a buyer and a seller outlining the terms of the sale.

salesperson one who is licensed to sell real estate in a given territory.

salvage value the value of a property at the end of its economic life.

satisfaction an instrument acknowledging that a debt has been paid in full.

second mortgage a mortgage that is in less than first lien position; see *junior mortgage*.

section as used in the rectangular survey system, an area of land measuring one square mile, or 640 acres.

secured loan a loan that is backed by property or collateral.

security property that is offered as collateral for a loan.

seisin the possession of a freehold estate in land by a person having the title.

selling broker the broker who secures a buyer for a listed property; the selling broker may be the listing agent, a subagent, or a buyer's agent.

separate property property owned individually by a spouse, as opposed to community property.

servient tenement a property on which an easement or right-of-way for an adjacent (dominant) property passes.

setback the amount of space between the lot line and the building line, usually established by a local zoning ordinance or restrictive covenants; see *deed restrictions*.

settlement statement (HUD-1) the form used to itemize all costs related to closing of a residential transaction covered by RESPA regulations.

severalty the ownership of a property by only one legal entity.

special assessment a tax levied against only the specific properties that will benefit from a public improvement, such as a street or sewer; an assessment by a homeowners' association for a capital improvement to the common areas for which no budgeted funds are available.

special warranty deed a deed in which the grantor guarantees the title only against the defects that may have occurred during the grantor's ownership and not against any defects that occurred prior to that time.

specific lien a lien, such as a mortgage, that attaches to one defined parcel of real estate.

specific performance a legal action in which a court compels a defaulted party to a contract to perform according to the terms of the contract, rather than awarding damages.

standard payment calculation the method used to calculate the monthly payment required to repay the remaining balance of a mortgage in equal installments over the remaining term of the mortgage at the current interest rate.

statute of frauds the state law that requires that certain contracts to be in writing in order to be enforceable.

statute of limitations the state law that requires that certain actions be brought to court within a specified period of time.

statutory lien a lien imposed on property by statute, such as a tax lien.

steering the illegal practice of directing prospective homebuyers to or away from particular areas.

straight-line depreciation a method of computing depreciation by decreasing value by an equal amount each year during the useful life of the property.

subdivision a tract of land divided into lots as defined in a publicly recorded plat that complies with state and local regulations.

sublet the act of a lessee transferring part or all of his or her lease to a third party while maintaining responsibility for all duties and obligations of the lease contract.

subordinate to voluntarily accept a lien position of lower priority than one to which one would normally be entitled.

substitution the principle in appraising that a buyer will be willing to pay no more for the property being appraised than the cost of purchasing an equally desirable property.

subrogation the substitution of one party into another's legal role as the creditor for a particular debt.

suit for possession a lawsuit filed by a landlord to evict a tenant who has violated the terms of the lease or retained possession of the property after the lease expired.

suit for specific performance a lawsuit filed for the purpose of compelling a party to perform particular acts to settle a dispute, rather than pay monetary damages.

survey a map that shows the exact legal boundaries of a property, the location of easements, encroachments, improvements, rights of way, and other physical features.

syndicate a group formed by a syndicator to combine funds for real estate investment.

▶ T

tax deed in some states, an instrument given to the purchaser at the time of sale.

tax lien a charge against a property created by law or statue. Tax liens take priority over all other types of liens.

tax rate the rate applied to the assessed value of a property to determine the property taxes.

tax sale the court-ordered sale of a property after the owner fails to pay *ad valorem* taxes owed on the property.

tenancy at sufferance the tenancy of a party who unlawfully retains possession of a landlord's property after the term of the lease has expired.

tenancy at will an indefinite tenancy that can be terminated by either the landlord or the tenant at any time by giving notice to the other party one rental period in advance of the desired termination date.

tenancy by the entirety ownership by a married couple of property acquired during the marriage with right of survivorship; not recognized by community property states.

tenancy in common a form of co-ownership in which two or more persons hold an undivided interest in property without the right of survivorship.

tenant one who holds or possesses the right of occupancy title.

tenement the space that may be occupied by a tenant under the terms of a lease.

testate to die having created a valid will directing the testator's desires with regard to the disposition of the estate.

"time is of the essence" phrase in a contract that requires strict adherence to the dates listed in the contract as deadlines for the performance of specific acts.

time sharing undivided ownership of real estate for only an allotted portion of a year.

title a legal document that demonstrates a person's right to, or ownership of, a property. **Note:** Title is *not* an instrument. The instrument, such as a deed, gives evidence of title or ownership.

title insurance an insurance policy that protects the holder from defects in a title, subject to the exceptions noted in the policy.

title search a check of public records to ensure that the seller is the legal owner of the property and that there are no liens or other outstanding claims.

Torrens system a system of registering titles to land with a public authority, who is usually called a registrar.

township a division of land, measuring 36 square miles, in the government survey system.

trade fixtures an item of personal property installed by a commercial tenant and removable upon expiration of the lease.

transfer tax a state or municipal tax payable when the conveyancing instrument is recorded.

trust an arrangement in which title to property is transferred from a grantor to a trustee, who holds title but not the right of possession for a third party, the beneficiary.

trustee a person who holds title to property for another person designated as the beneficiary.

Truth-in-Lending Law also known as Regulation Z; requires lenders to make full disclosure regarding the terms of a loan.

▶ **U**

underwriting the process of evaluating a loan application to determine the risk involved for the lender.

undivided interest the interest of co-owners to use of an entire property despite the fractional interest owned.

unilateral contract a one-sided contract in which one party is obligated to perform a particular act completely, before the other party has any obligation to perform.

unsecured loan a loan that is not backed by collateral or security.

useful life the period of time a property is expected to have economic utility.

usury the practice of charging interest at a rate higher than that allowed by law.

► **V**

VA-guaranteed loan a mortgage loan made to a qualified veteran that is guaranteed by the Department of Veterans Affairs.

valid contract an agreement that is legally enforceable and binding on all parties.

valuation estimated worth.

variance permission obtained from zoning authorities to build a structure that is not in complete compliance with current zoning laws. A variance does not permit a non-conforming use of a property.

vendee a buyer.

vendor a seller; the property owner.

village an incorporated minor municipality usually larger than a hamlet and smaller than a town.

void contract a contract that is not legally enforceable; the absence of a valid contract.

voidable contract a contract that appears to be valid but is subject to cancellation by one or both of the parties.

► **W**

waiver the surrender of a known right or claim.

warranty deed a deed in which the grantor fully warrants a good clear title to the property.

waste the improper use of a property by a party with the right to possession, such as the holder of a life estate.

will a written document that directs the distribution of a deceased person's property, real and personal.

wraparound mortgage a mortgage that includes the remaining balance on an existing first mortgage plus an additional amount. Full payments on both mortgages are made to the wraparound mortgagee who then forwards the payments on the first mortgage to the first mortgagee.

writ of execution a court order to the sheriff or other officer to sell the property of a debtor to satisfy a previously rendered judgment.

► **Z**

zone an area reserved by authorities for specific use that is subject to certain restrictions.

zoning ordinance the exercise of regulating and controlling the use of a property in a municipality.

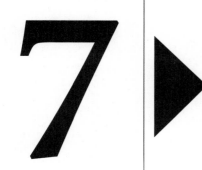

CHAPTER

7 ▶ Real Estate Sales Exam 2

CHAPTER SUMMARY

This is the second of four practice tests in this book. Because you have taken one practice test already, you should feel more confident with your test-taking skills. Use this test to see how knowing what to expect can make you feel better prepared.

F YOU ARE following the advice in this book, you've done some studying between the first exam and this one. This exam will give you a chance to see how much you have improved.

The answer sheet follows this page, and the test is followed by the answer key and explanations.

▶ Real Estate Sales Exam 2 Answer Sheet

1. ⓐ ⓑ ⓒ ⓓ	36. ⓐ ⓑ ⓒ ⓓ	71. ⓐ ⓑ ⓒ ⓓ
2. ⓐ ⓑ ⓒ ⓓ	37. ⓐ ⓑ ⓒ ⓓ	72. ⓐ ⓑ ⓒ ⓓ
3. ⓐ ⓑ ⓒ ⓓ	38. ⓐ ⓑ ⓒ ⓓ	73. ⓐ ⓑ ⓒ ⓓ
4. ⓐ ⓑ ⓒ ⓓ	39. ⓐ ⓑ ⓒ ⓓ	74. ⓐ ⓑ ⓒ ⓓ
5. ⓐ ⓑ ⓒ ⓓ	40. ⓐ ⓑ ⓒ ⓓ	75. ⓐ ⓑ ⓒ ⓓ
6. ⓐ ⓑ ⓒ ⓓ	41. ⓐ ⓑ ⓒ ⓓ	76. ⓐ ⓑ ⓒ ⓓ
7. ⓐ ⓑ ⓒ ⓓ	42. ⓐ ⓑ ⓒ ⓓ	77. ⓐ ⓑ ⓒ ⓓ
8. ⓐ ⓑ ⓒ ⓓ	43. ⓐ ⓑ ⓒ ⓓ	78. ⓐ ⓑ ⓒ ⓓ
9. ⓐ ⓑ ⓒ ⓓ	44. ⓐ ⓑ ⓒ ⓓ	79. ⓐ ⓑ ⓒ ⓓ
10. ⓐ ⓑ ⓒ ⓓ	45. ⓐ ⓑ ⓒ ⓓ	80. ⓐ ⓑ ⓒ ⓓ
11. ⓐ ⓑ ⓒ ⓓ	46. ⓐ ⓑ ⓒ ⓓ	81. ⓐ ⓑ ⓒ ⓓ
12. ⓐ ⓑ ⓒ ⓓ	47. ⓐ ⓑ ⓒ ⓓ	82. ⓐ ⓑ ⓒ ⓓ
13. ⓐ ⓑ ⓒ ⓓ	48. ⓐ ⓑ ⓒ ⓓ	83. ⓐ ⓑ ⓒ ⓓ
14. ⓐ ⓑ ⓒ ⓓ	49. ⓐ ⓑ ⓒ ⓓ	84. ⓐ ⓑ ⓒ ⓓ
15. ⓐ ⓑ ⓒ ⓓ	50. ⓐ ⓑ ⓒ ⓓ	85. ⓐ ⓑ ⓒ ⓓ
16. ⓐ ⓑ ⓒ ⓓ	51. ⓐ ⓑ ⓒ ⓓ	86. ⓐ ⓑ ⓒ ⓓ
17. ⓐ ⓑ ⓒ ⓓ	52. ⓐ ⓑ ⓒ ⓓ	87. ⓐ ⓑ ⓒ ⓓ
18. ⓐ ⓑ ⓒ ⓓ	53. ⓐ ⓑ ⓒ ⓓ	88. ⓐ ⓑ ⓒ ⓓ
19. ⓐ ⓑ ⓒ ⓓ	54. ⓐ ⓑ ⓒ ⓓ	89. ⓐ ⓑ ⓒ ⓓ
20. ⓐ ⓑ ⓒ ⓓ	55. ⓐ ⓑ ⓒ ⓓ	90. ⓐ ⓑ ⓒ ⓓ
21. ⓐ ⓑ ⓒ ⓓ	56. ⓐ ⓑ ⓒ ⓓ	91. ⓐ ⓑ ⓒ ⓓ
22. ⓐ ⓑ ⓒ ⓓ	57. ⓐ ⓑ ⓒ ⓓ	92. ⓐ ⓑ ⓒ ⓓ
23. ⓐ ⓑ ⓒ ⓓ	58. ⓐ ⓑ ⓒ ⓓ	93. ⓐ ⓑ ⓒ ⓓ
24. ⓐ ⓑ ⓒ ⓓ	59. ⓐ ⓑ ⓒ ⓓ	94. ⓐ ⓑ ⓒ ⓓ
25. ⓐ ⓑ ⓒ ⓓ	60. ⓐ ⓑ ⓒ ⓓ	95. ⓐ ⓑ ⓒ ⓓ
26. ⓐ ⓑ ⓒ ⓓ	61. ⓐ ⓑ ⓒ ⓓ	96. ⓐ ⓑ ⓒ ⓓ
27. ⓐ ⓑ ⓒ ⓓ	62. ⓐ ⓑ ⓒ ⓓ	97. ⓐ ⓑ ⓒ ⓓ
28. ⓐ ⓑ ⓒ ⓓ	63. ⓐ ⓑ ⓒ ⓓ	98. ⓐ ⓑ ⓒ ⓓ
29. ⓐ ⓑ ⓒ ⓓ	64. ⓐ ⓑ ⓒ ⓓ	99. ⓐ ⓑ ⓒ ⓓ
30. ⓐ ⓑ ⓒ ⓓ	65. ⓐ ⓑ ⓒ ⓓ	100. ⓐ ⓑ ⓒ ⓓ
31. ⓐ ⓑ ⓒ ⓓ	66. ⓐ ⓑ ⓒ ⓓ	
32. ⓐ ⓑ ⓒ ⓓ	67. ⓐ ⓑ ⓒ ⓓ	
33. ⓐ ⓑ ⓒ ⓓ	68. ⓐ ⓑ ⓒ ⓓ	
34. ⓐ ⓑ ⓒ ⓓ	69. ⓐ ⓑ ⓒ ⓓ	
35. ⓐ ⓑ ⓒ ⓓ	70. ⓐ ⓑ ⓒ ⓓ	

▶ Real Estate Sales Exam 2

1. Which of the following actions is legally permitted?
   a. advertising property for sale only to a special group
   b. altering the terms of a loan for a member of a minority group
   c. refusing to make a mortgage loan to a minority individual because of a poor credit history
   d. telling a minority individual that an apartment has been rented when, in fact, it has not been rented

2. The seller delivers the deed and the buyer pays the purchase price in the step referred to as
   a. commitment.
   b. underwriting.
   c. warehousing.
   d. closing.

3. The approach to value that considers depreciation is the
   a. cost approach.
   b. sales comparison approach.
   c. income approach.
   d. gross rent multiplier approach.

4. A building permit may be issued without question even if the proposed structure violates existing
   a. zoning laws.
   b. deed restrictions.
   c. building codes.
   d. setback requirements.

5. For a real estate agency relationship to be enforceable, which of the following is NOT required?
   a. The principal has the power to do what is being assigned.
   b. The principal has the funds to pay the agent.
   c. The agent must be authorized by a written agreement.
   d. The agent must be a real estate licensee.

6. Elderly homeowners can sometimes tap the equity in their home without having to make monthly payments by using a
   a. wraparound mortgage.
   b. reverse mortgage.
   c. conversion option.
   d. blanket mortgage.

7. Which of the following statements is true?
   a. FHA guarantees the lender against borrower default.
   b. FHA is a government credit life insurance program protecting the lender.
   c. A Section 203(b) FHA loan is for one- to four-family investment properties.
   d. FHA insures the lender against borrower default.

8. George Brown owns 150 acres of farmland and has posted "No Trespassing" signs on the fence surrounding the property. He can enforce this notice by virtue of his
   a. constitutional privilege.
   b. right to exclude.
   c. obligation of disposition.
   d. surface rights.

9. An oral agreement between a lessor and lessee is legally
   a. a valid tenancy for years.
   b. unenforceable because of the statute of frauds.
   c. a valid tenancy at will.
   d. unenforceable because of the statute of limitations.

10. Although the term *purchase money mortgage* applies to any loan that finances the purchase of real estate, it is commonly used to refer specifically to a
   a. loan taken back as part of the sales price by the seller.
   b. refinance loan.
   c. loan on property already owned that is used to finance the purchase of a second property.
   d. loan that is packaged for sale on the secondary market.

11. Any federally related loan may require the borrower to carry special insurance if the property is located in
   a. an earthquake area.
   b. a flood zone.
   c. an ocean hazard district.
   d. a desert.

12. Buyers who sign a document indicating the price and terms on which they are ready to purchase described property have created
   a. a purchase offer.
   b. an option.
   c. a contract of sale.
   d. a listing contract.

13. A tenant has a lease that begins on May 1 and terminates on the following April 30. What kind of lease is this?
   a. estate for years
   b. periodic estate
   c. estate at will
   d. estate of definition

14. A seller, anxious to sell, tells a cooperating agent during a showing that the agent will be given a riding lawnmower if he brings an acceptable offer by the end of the week. All of the following are true in this situation EXCEPT that the
   a. agent may accept the lawnmower because it is not cash.
   b. agent should report the incident to the listing broker.
   c. agent would be in violation of the law if he took the lawnmower.
   d. cooperating agent could legally receive the lawnmower from his broker.

15. The right to occupy a property without interference for a specified period of time is known as a
   a. trespass.
   b. prescriptive easement.
   c. leasehold.
   d. suit for possession.

16. Which of the following applies to a tenant's legal right to possession of a leased property against the claims of ownership by a third party?
   a. statute of frauds
   b. covenant of seisin
   c. covenant of quiet enjoyment
   d. tenancy at will

17. An appraiser is hired to estimate the value of a retail shopping center and will use the income approach to value. Which of the following items will NOT be used in her determination of value?
a. debt service
b. property taxes
c. insurance payments
d. maintenance expenses

18. A tenant is delinquent on his lease payments. The owner can
a. have her bill collector evict the tenant from the premises.
b. turn off the electricity and water.
c. personally evict the tenant after giving 24-hour constructive notice.
d. bring court action.

19. Which of the following is NOT associated with a mortgage/note?
a. a defeasible fee/indefeasible fee
b. an alienation/acceleration clause
c. a hypothecation/APR
d. a pledge of property/evidence of debt

20. The alienation clause found in most security instruments states that the full amount will be immediately due and payable if the
a. borrower is late with three monthly payments.
b. property is sold to a new owner.
c. hazard insurance policy is allowed to lapse.
d. homeowner borrows more money on the property.

21. A seller has $5,000 closing costs, a $93,000 loan balance, and pays 7% commission on a $125,000 sale. What are his net proceeds from the sale?
a. $81,490
b. $43,510
c. $23,250
d. $18,250

22. A broker may execute a contract on behalf of his or her principal when he or she is a(n)
a. special agent.
b. trustee.
c. attorney-at-law.
d. attorney-in-fact.

23. Even though the broker hires a salesperson as an independent contractor, the broker is still responsible for
a. payment of licensing and professional fees.
b. providing a desk and telephone for the salesperson.
c. the legal and ethical behavior of the salesperson.
d. seeing that the salesperson attends office meetings and training seminars.

24. Agent Evan is licensed in a state that requires residential sellers to provide a buyer with a statutory property disclosure statement, and Agent Robbins is licensed in a state that does not require such disclosures. In either case, the best way they can avoid misrepresentation of property condition to prospective buyers is to
 a. require buyers to sign a statement of understanding regarding *caveat emptor*.
 b. recommend that all buyers purchase a home warranty.
 c. recommend that all buyers discuss the property condition with the seller before closing.
 d. strongly recommend that all buyers have the property inspected by a qualified inspector.

25. When describing the particulars about a property, the agent does not disclose that a capital improvement project has been approved that will result in a special assessment to the owner in the near future. The broker has
 a. acted in accordance with the duties of a fiduciary.
 b. refrained from disclosing anything that would weaken the principal's bargaining position.
 c. committed a fraud.
 d. prevented future legal problems for the seller client.

26. The task of the appraiser is to
 a. establish market price.
 b. guess at the final contract price.
 c. estimate market value.
 d. evaluate the property for tax purposes.

27. Chris Salvano is the broker hired to sell Erin Miller's house. Chris shows the house to the Martins, who want to make an offer on it. At this point, what duty does Chris legally owe to the Martins?
 a. confidentiality and fairness
 b. fairness and honesty
 c. exclusivity
 d. those of a fiduciary

28. Within the agency agreement is a statement that binds the buyer to paying the broker's fee if, within a stated number of days, the buyer purchases a property that was shown to the buyer during the agency period. This clause is the called the
 a. limited coverage clause.
 b. broker protection clause.
 c. buyer liability clause.
 d. automatic extension clause.

29. In a real estate transaction, a broker does not affirmatively represent either the buyer or the seller as agent. She is acting as
 a. a transaction broker.
 b. an undisclosed dual agent.
 c. a nonrepresenting dual agent.
 d. an illegal real estate licensee.

30. Alex Rivera has an easement across Alice Dean's land to access his property because he has no other access to the property. Which of the following statements describes this arrangement?
- **a.** This is an easement in gross, and Alex has a servient easement.
- **b.** Alex has a dominant easement with license to use Alice's land.
- **c.** Alex has a servient easement, and Alice has a dominant easement.
- **d.** Alex has a dominant easement, and Alice has the servient easement.

31. Tenancy by the entirety differs from other forms of co-ownership in that
- **a.** neither owner can force a sale.
- **b.** each owner is free to devise his or her share to chosen heirs.
- **c.** shares may be acquired at different times.
- **d.** the property must be a principal residence.

32. To determine an encroachment, the purchaser should obtain
- **a.** a title search.
- **b.** title insurance.
- **c.** a survey.
- **d.** a current opinion from an attorney.

33. ABC Investments, Inc., the owner of an apartment building built in 1967, is required by federal law to furnish to all prospective tenants which of the following?
- **a.** disclosure of property condition
- **b.** environmental assessment report not more than one year old
- **c.** lead-based paint and lead-based paint hazards disclosure
- **d.** good faith estimate of rental and use charges

34. A corporation holds title in the name of its
- **a.** charter.
- **b.** board of directors.
- **c.** shareholders.
- **d.** creditors.

35. As the buyer's agent, your client is a person from China, who is moving to the United States to run a Chinese import business. You show properties only where it is obvious that the majority of residents are of Chinese ancestry. Have you violated any fair housing laws?
- **a.** No, as the buyer's agent, you're responsible to see that the buyer will be happy where he or she buys.
- **b.** Yes, this is an example of steering.
- **c.** No, even though the buyer never stated it, you felt he would be more comfortable in a Chinese community.
- **d.** Yes, this is an example of blockbusting.

36. The duties of the property manager include all of the following EXCEPT
- **a.** maintaining the property while preserving finances.
- **b.** marketing for a constant tenant base.
- **c.** seeking interested buyers.
- **d.** preparing budgets.

37. A mortgage broker
- **a.** originates, funds, and services home mortgage loans.
- **b.** is the same as a mortgage banker.
- **c.** brings borrowers together with mortgage lenders.
- **d.** originates and services home mortgage loans.

38. If a person dies leaving no will and no natural heirs, his or her property passes to
   a. local charities.
   b. the state.
   c. the Internal Revenue Service.
   d. the Department of Housing and Urban Development.

39. Sue Addison owns an apartment building that was constructed in 1965. According to federal law, which of the following must be attached to the leases Sue prepares for prospective tenants?
   a. a report of the building's radon level
   b. a lead-based paint disclosure statement
   c. an illustration of the building's location relative to electromagnetic fields (EMFs)
   d. any known instances of groundwater contamination in the building's water supply

40. A property is sold for $75,600 in cash. If transfer taxes are $0.55 per $300 of value, how much transfer tax is due?
   a. $138.60
   b. $1,384.20
   c. $1,525
   d. $152.50

41. If the buyer's agent splits his commission 50/50 with his broker, and the seller's agent receives 60% of his broker's 50% share, how much does the buyer's broker receive if the listing broker's fee is 6% of the $125,000 sales price of the house?
   a. $3,450
   b. $3,750
   c. $1,875
   d. $7,500

42. Jerry Wright, the owner of a commercial building, estimates the depreciation of the physical plant at $15,000, the furniture and fixtures at $8,000, and the machinery at $7,500. If he is in the 40% bracket, his tax savings would be
   a. $12,200
   b. $30,500
   c. $18,300
   d. $1,220

43. A residential property was built 75 years ago. Two of the five bedrooms have no closets, the basement floor is unpaved, and the original slate roof needs repairs. To the appraiser, the most important consideration is
   a. the sale price of a nearby similar property.
   b. how much it would cost to finish the basement floor.
   c. how the bedrooms could be reconfigured to provide some storage.
   d. the life expectancy of the roof.

44. Which of the following statements is true of a tenancy in common?
   a. When one of the tenants dies, his or her interest is spread among the survivors.
   b. Unless another form of ownership is described in the deed, co-owners who are not spouses of each other are presumed to be tenants in common.
   c. Sale of one of the interests will end the tenancy in common.
   d. Destruction of the property terminates the co-ownership.

45. Which of the following instruments would contain the loan amount, interest rate, term of the loan, and monthly payments?
a. note
b. mortgage
c. deed
d. lease

46. A seller is closing on August 21 and will pay off the balance of a 6.75% mortgage loan of $187,523. Having made the August 1 payment, what will be the prorated amount of accrued interest due at closing? (Use a banker's year.)
a. $1,265.78
b. $728.26
c. $795.36
d. $738.37

47. Using real property as collateral to secure a loan while retaining the property is called
a. mortgage.
b. encumbrance.
c. hypothecation.
d. promissory intent.

48. Dave Gates, a widower, died without leaving a will or other instruction. His surviving children received ownership of his real estate holdings by
a. adverse possession.
b. eminent domain.
c. escheat.
d. law of intestate succession.

49. In the event of default and foreclosure, which clause would require the lender to look only to the property for satisfaction of the debt?
a. defeasance clause
b. exculpatory clause
c. cognivit clause
d. subordination clause

50. Gratuities for referring prospects to a broker are legal if paid to a
a. salesperson affiliated with another firm.
b. relative of the buyer.
c. licensed broker.
d. federal employee.

51. Which of the following is NOT a participant in the secondary mortgage market?
a. Fannie Mae
b. RESPA
c. Ginnie Mae
d. FHLMC

52. Significant provisions of the Real Estate Settlement Procedures Act include all of the following EXCEPT
a. the lender's estimate of settlement costs.
b. a uniform settlement statement.
c. a settlement location.
d. the disclosure of controlled business.

53. Express covenants that protect the grantee are found in a
a. quitclaim deed.
b. bargain and sale deed.
c. sheriff's deed.
d. general warranty deed.

54. An elderly property owner dies testate. In the will, care of the family pet is assured by conveying ownership in the property to a grandson who may occupy and enjoy the property so long as the pet lives. Upon the death of the pet, ownership passes to a designated charity. Which of the following is true in this situation?
   a. The charity acquired legal title on the elderly property owner's death.
   b. The son may replace the pet with another of the same breed.
   c. The estate is one of a life tenancy *pur autre vie.*
   d. The son has a fee interest.

55. Rupert Labinsky borrowed $18,000 at 8% interest and paid it back in full at the end of two months. How much did Rupert pay?
   a. $1,440
   b. $18,240
   c. $19,440
   d. $240

56. What type of agency relationship exists between the primary broker of a firm and a sponsored salesperson licensee?
   a. general agency
   b. special agency
   c. universal agency
   d. No agency exists because the salesperson is an independent contractor.

57. A cap rate is used in what type of appraisal?
   a. reproduction
   b. income approach
   c. tax assessment
   d. competitive market analysis

58. Property managers often make management decisions about tenant selection and budgets for their clients. In these relationships, the property manager is acting as a(n)
   a. special agent.
   b. power of attorney.
   c. independent contractor.
   d. general agent.

59. What is the balance on an amortized loan of $340,000 after the first payment if the interest rate is 6% with principal and interest payments of $2,028?
   a. $319,600
   b. $338,300
   c. $337,972
   d. $339,672

60. Broker Peter Eklund listed Byron Hindley's house for $395,000. Byron is very anxious to sell the property and must close within 60 days. Peter showed the property to a prospective buyer and told the buyer he could most likely get the property for $15,000 below the asking price. Which of the following statements best describes this situation?
   a. Peter has represented his client Byron well by encouraging an offer.
   b. Peter has followed his agency obligation to bring a ready, willing, and able buyer to the seller.
   c. Peter has violated his fiduciary duties.
   d. Peter has not violated any duty to his client, Byron.

61. A type of lease that is common in retail proper-ties requires the tenant to pay a portion of gross sales to the landlord. This is commonly referred to as a
   a. net lease.
   b. sales lease.
   c. percentage lease.
   d. gross lease.

62. Which of the following listings is risky and open to fraudulent dealings?
   a. an open listing
   b. an exclusive right to sell
   c. an exclusive agency
   d. a net listing

63. In which appraisal approach is it necessary for the appraiser to estimate the value of the land separately?
   a. sales comparison approach
   b. cost depreciation approach
   c. income capitalization approach
   d. gross income multiplier

64. Mortgage insurance protects the
   a. borrower's family by paying off the loan in case of death.
   b. lending institution against loss if the loan goes into default.
   c. borrower in case of job loss or accident.
   d. veteran by allowing no-down-payment mortgage loans.

65. An appraiser is appraising a house that had an estimated economic life of 15 years when the property was purchased 10 years ago. If the appraiser currently estimates that the house is $\frac{1}{3}$ depreciated, what is the remaining economic life?
   a. 5 years
   b. 10 years
   c. 15 years
   d. none of the above

66. Jesse Ruiz is selling a tract of land that is 175 feet by 338 feet. The county recently paved the road in front of the property, and Mr. Ruiz will be charged special assessment tax at closing. How will this tax be computed?
   a. per square foot
   b. per acre
   c. per front foot
   d. per foot of perimeter

67. The appraisal principle that determines a value most likely to produce the highest price in the sale of a property is known as the principle of
   a. supply and demand.
   b. highest and best use.
   c. growth and decline.
   d. competition.

68. An acre contains approximately
   a. 5,270 square yards.
   b. 40,000 square feet.
   c. one-quarter square mile.
   d. 43,560 square feet.

69. Harold is an independent contractor and agent at Big Town Realty. He sold the listing of Country Time Realty to his client buyer. How will Harold be paid the 3.5% buyer's broker commission noted in the multiple-listing service (MLS) compensation field?

    a. Country Time Realty will pay Harold his portion of the fee and pay his broker the remainder of the fee.

    b. Country Time Realty will pay Big Town Realty the 3.5% commission, and the Big Town Realty broker will pay Harold.

    c. The escrow agent will pay Harold his fee at the closing.

    d. The fee will be paid to Harold through the MLS.

70. If a lender agrees to make a loan based on an 80% loan-to-value, what is the amount of a loan for a property appraised for $135,000 and a sale price of $137,800?

    a. $110,240

    b. $105,920

    c. $108,000

    d. $112,000

71. The buyer has been held to be in default on a contract of sale. If buyer and seller had not agreed on liquidated damage, the seller could

    a. obtain a court order preventing the buyer from purchasing another property.

    b. sue the buyer for compensatory damages.

    c. have the buyer incarcerated.

    d. require the buyer to find a substitute purchaser.

72. The house being appraised has no fireplace, but it does have a garage, and the appraiser estimates that a fireplace contributes $3,000 to the value of a home in that neighborhood. A nearby house that recently sold for $198,000 is similar except that it has a fireplace but no garage. The appraiser estimates that a garage contributes $12,000 to value. The adjusted sale price of the subject house is

    a. $213,000

    b. $183,000

    c. $207,000

    d. $189,000

73. Ownership of a property by only one person is known as

    a. entirety.

    b. remainder interest.

    c. reversionary interest.

    d. severalty.

74. A property sold for $57,300 and is subject to revenue stamp fees of $0.50 for each $500 (or portion thereof) of the sales price. What is the cost of the stamps?

    a. $571.50

    b. $57.50

    c. $95.50

    d. $955

75. The investor criterion for a home mortgage is an uninsured loan-to-value ratio of 90% of the appraisal. The sales agreement and appraisal is in the amount of $180,000. Following underwriting guidelines, the buyer qualifies for a loan of $145,000. How much of the purchase will be financed by this investor?
   a. $180,000
   b. $145,000
   c. $108,750
   d. $135,000

76. Ownership of chattels is most likely transferred by which of the following?
   a. special warranty deed
   b. bill of sale
   c. quitclaim deed
   d. chattel mortgage

77. Adjacent properties are combined into one large tract in order to enhance the utilization and the value of the larger tract. The term used to describe this is
   a. severalty.
   b. appurtenance.
   c. assemblage.
   d. plottage.

78. A seller entered into an agreement to sell his property, but six days before closing, he notified the buyer he was no longer willing to go through with the contract. The buyer sued the seller to compel him to do what he agreed to do in the contract. What type of suit is this?
   a. suit for compliance
   b. suit for deed
   c. suit for specific performance
   d. subrogation

79. A buyer makes an offer to purchase a property and specifies that the owner accept or reject the offer within 48 hours. Before hearing back from the owner, the buyer locates a more attractive property and withdraws the offer. Is the buyer legally entitled to withdraw the offer?
   a. Yes; either party may withdraw an offer or counteroffer at any time prior to its acceptance.
   b. No; the offer is binding until the 48-hour time period expires.
   c. Yes; an offer with a condition to respond in 48 hours is not valid.
   d. No; the owner must be allowed an opportunity to respond to the offer.

80. House A sold for $132,000. It had three bedrooms, two bathrooms, and a two-car garage. In the same neighborhood one month later, House B sold for $140,000. It had a three-car garage, but was otherwise very similar to House A. House C (the subject property) has a two-car garage. What would the appraiser adjust for the extra garage space on House B?
   a. $8,000 addition to the value of House A
   b. $8,000 deduction from the value of House A
   c. $8,000 addition to the value of House B
   d. $8,000 deduction from the value of House B

81. Which of the following conditions is NOT required for a real estate agent to be considered an independent contractor by the IRS?
   a. The agent must have a valid real estate license.
   b. All compensation is based on commission fees, not on hours worked.
   c. The agent must have a workspace or office in the broker's place of business.
   d. The agent's services are performed under a written contract between the broker and the agent.

82. The IRS requires that an independent contractor be
   a. paid on the basis of successful transactions rather than hours worked.
   b. covered by unemployment insurance.
   c. strictly regulated in the matter of attendance at sales meetings.
   d. allowed at least two weeks of paid vacation annually.

83. Jonathan paid an upfront mortgage insurance premium (MIP) of $2,566.50, which was financed with the loan and will also pay a monthly MIP premium to be included in his payment. What type of loan did Jonathan get?
   a. FHA
   b. VA
   c. conventional conforming
   d. interest-only term loan

84. Which statement is true with respect to the assignment of a lease?
   a. The original lessee is not responsible for the payment of the rent.
   b. It is the same as a sublease.
   c. The original lessee would still retain a right to use the property for a limited time.
   d. The entire leasehold is transferred.

85. Which of the following characteristics must a property have to be of value to a person for some purpose?
   a. improvements, accessibility, and demand
   b. scarcity, utility, and proper zoning
   c. transferability, utility, scarcity, and demand
   d. transferability, accessibility, and improvements

86. The Fair Housing Act of 1988, which addresses accessibility in new multifamily buildings for people with physical disabilities, mandates all of the following EXCEPT
   a. elevators or power lifts.
   b. doors, kitchens, and bathrooms that are wheelchair friendly.
   c. thermostats and lighting switches within easy reach.
   d. bathroom walls strong enough to support grab bars.

87. How will the accrued, prorated property taxes be shown on a closing statement?
   a. debit to seller and credit to buyer
   b. only as a debit to seller
   c. credit to seller and debit to buyer
   d. debit to seller and credit to tax district

88. All of the following are physical characteristics of real estate EXCEPT
  a. immobility.
  b. scarcity.
  c. indestructibility.
  d. nonhomogeneity.

89. Which of the following would NOT be permitted under the Federal Fair Housing Act?
  a. the USO in Chicago renting rooms only to service personnel
  b. an Arabian owner refusing to rent his home to a Jewish man
  c. the owner of a 20-unit residential apartment building renting only to African-American men
  d. an owner who lives on one side of a duplex refusing to rent to a family with children on the other side of the duplex

90. The words of conveyance in a deed appear in the
  a. heading.
  b. granting clause.
  c. alienation clause.
  d. purchase clause.

91. A purchaser contracts for a new home for $250,000 and, after making a 20% down payment, applies for a 30-year fixed-rate loan at the rate of 7.5%. At the settlement on April 10, the lender collects interest up to May 1. What is the interest charge to the buyer shown on the settlement statement?
  a. $1,250
  b. $416.60
  c. $833.33
  d. $875

92. Which of the following properties would likely merit the highest capitalization rate?
  a. a single-family residence
  b. a convenience store in an urban neighborhood
  c. a modern firehouse
  d. a strip mall with limited access to traffic

93. A tenant applicant confined to a wheelchair is interested in renting a townhome. A request is made to the landlord to allow the tenant to have an access ramp constructed. Which of the following is true in this situation?
  a. The tenant application must be rejected.
  b. The landlord must allow the tenant to make the modification at the tenant's expense.
  c. The landlord is required to fund modifications to the property to accommodate the access problem.
  d. The landlord may collect an additional deposit to assure compliance.

94. Which is NOT an exemption to the Federal Housing Act?
  a. An owner who occupies a one- to four-family dwelling may limit the rental of rooms or units.
  b. Housing may be limited for use by senior citizens if occupied by one person at least 55 years of age or older.
  c. a woman with three children
  d. Religious organizations may limit the occupancy of real estate that it owns to its own members if the units are not owned for business purposes.

95. A broker has a principal that he turns over to a salesperson. Which of the following statements is true regarding the fiduciary relationship?
  a. The broker still has full fiduciary responsibility to the principal.
  b. The salesperson has a fiduciary relationship to the principal because the broker relinquished the fiduciary responsibilities when he turned the principal over to the salesperson.
  c. The salesperson has the same fiduciary duties to the principal as the broker.
  d. both **a** and **c**

96. A clause in a mortgage or trust deed that declares the entire balance due and payable upon default is the
  a. defeasance clause.
  b. due-on-sale clause.
  c. acceleration clause.
  d. alienation clause.

97. The term *walk-through* refers to
  a. an appraiser's inspection of the interior of the subject property.
  b. empty office buildings where the vacancy rate in the community is high.
  c. a seller's check of the premises before an open house is held.
  d. the buyer's final inspection of the property to check its condition.

98. An article of personal property that is permanently attached and becomes part of the real estate is known as
  a. an emblement.
  b. an accretion.
  c. a chattel.
  d. a fixture.

99. A seller will list his property with agent Chad Newman and wants to net $58,000 after paying off his mortgage loan of $239,460, closing costs of $4,750, and a 5% commission to Chad. For how much must the property sell to accomplish the seller's goal?
  a. $318,115
  b. $302,210
  c. $317,320
  d. $325,000

100. A developer purchased 1,245 acres for a mixed use development that will be subdivided into both commercial and residential lots. Which method of legal description will best serve the needs of the developer?
  a. metes and bounds
  b. quantitative survey
  c. subdivision plat
  d. government survey

▶ Answers

1. **c.** Fair housing law does not require a lender to make a loan to an individual who does not meet credit standards.

2. **d.** The process of transfer of title and settlement of accounts takes place at the closing.

3. **a.** In the cost approach, the property's depreciated value is estimated.

4. **b.** Deed restrictions are private and non-governmental, set by previous owners of the property. They are enforced through neighbors' lawsuits, not by local building authorities.

5. **b.** The principal cannot empower the agent to do anything the principal cannot do. There is no guarantee that the principal has the necessary funds.

6. **b.** With a reverse mortgage, the homeowner receives a lump sum or monthly checks, and no repayment is made until the property is sold or the owner dies.

7. **d.** The Federal Housing Administration (FHA) loan is for owner occupancy only and insures lenders if a borrower defaults on the loan.

8. **b.** The right to exclude is one of the rights contained in the bundle of legal rights of ownership.

9. **c.** An oral lease for one year or less is enforceable and creates a tenancy at will.

10. **a.** Seller financing is often referred to as a purchase money mortgage.

11. **b.** The government issues flood hazard maps, and for mortgage loans within those areas, borrowers must carry flood insurance, which is available from the federal government.

12. **a.** Until it is accepted by a seller, the document remains simply a purchase offer.

13. **a.** An estate for years is one that has a definite termination date with no provision for an additional period of time.

14. **a.** Salespersons may receive compensation only from their principal broker. Gifts of merchandise, use of luxury cars, trips, and outings are also compensation and may only be given to a broker who disposes of them in accord with the company policy.

15. **c.** A lease defines the period of time during which the tenant has the right to occupy and enjoy a property. At the end of that period, the right reverts to the owner.

16. **c.** Under this covenant, the landlord guarantees that the tenant will not be evicted from the premises by any third party who may claim to have title to the property.

17. **a.** Only the operating expenses are used in the income approach to value. The operating expenses are subtracted from the effective income and divided by an appropriate capitalization rate to determine the appraiser's estimate of value. Debt service is the payment of a mortgage.

18. **d.** The Landlord Tenant Act in most states clearly establishes specific court procedures with strict time lines.

19. **a.** A defeasible/indefeasible fee is associated with a deed.

20. **b.** The term *alienation* means transfer of title. The lender reserves the right to call in the loan if the property is sold.

21. **d.** $5,000 + $93,000 = $98,000 total dollar expenses of closing. Convert 7% to a decimal and multiply: $125,000 × .07 = $8,750 commission; $125,000 − $98,000 − $8,750 = $18,250 net proceeds to seller.

22. **d.** The power of attorney authorizes the agent to perform certain acts in place of the principal.

23. **c.** The broker is responsible under the law and licensing regulations for the activities of any licensees affiliated with that firm.

24. **d.** Under most consumer protection laws, *caveat emptor* ("let the buyer beware") may not apply. Buyers should be strongly encouraged to hire professional inspectors as well as purchase home warranties or residential service contracts.

25. **c.** Regardless of an agency relationship, the agent must disclose all pertinent facts about a property or be charged with committing a fraud. The seller has the same obligation.

26. **c.** An appraisal is an estimate of market value through an analysis of data.

27. **b.** As customers, the Martins are entitled merely to fair and honest treatment. Chris is not acting in a fiduciary capacity.

28. **b.** Unless the buyer subsequently hires another buyer agent and purchases this property, the broker protection clause obligates the buyer to pay the broker's fee.

29. **a.** If a broker is handling both sides of a transaction, she may do so only as a transaction broker or by disclosing a "No Brokerage" relationship.

30. **d.** Alice's land serves Alex's need to cross the property for access to his property.

31. **a.** When a married couple buys any real estate as tenants by the entirety, neither can obtain a court order for partition.

32. **c.** Only a survey will show an encroachment.

33. **c.** A lead-based paint disclosure and the EPA pamphlet "Protecting Your Family" must be given to tenants of residential properties built prior to 1978.

34. **a.** A corporation is an artificial person and holds title in the name of its charter.

35. **b.** The agent's job is to show the client homes within his or her housing needs and ability to pay. Unless the client asks for a specific area, the agent should show representative homes in all areas that meets the client's needs and price range. The client, not the agent, should then decide on the area he or she wants to live.

36. **c.** The property manager typically is not involved in selling the property.

37. **c.** Mortgage brokers act as an intermediary between borrowers and lenders for a fee. They do not fund or services loans. Mortgage bankers fund loans in their name and often service the loans after closing.

38. **b.** The state becomes owner of a deceased person's property in the absence of a will or natural heirs, through the power of escheat.

39. **b.** Federal law requires that a lead-paint disclosure form be given to all tenants and buyers if the building was constructed before 1978.

40. **a.** $\$75,600 \div \$300 = \$252$; $\$252 \times \$0.55 = \$138.60$

41. **b.** Convert 6% to a decimal and multiply: $\$125,000 \times .06 = \$7,500$ total commission on sales price. Convert 50% to a decimal and multiply: $\$7,500 \times .50 = \$3,750$ total buyer's broker share.

42. **a.** The owner would save 40% of the total depreciation: $(\$15,000 + \$8,000 + \$7,500) \times .40 = \$12,200$.

43. **a.** In appraising residential real estate, the subject property is compared with similar properties that have sold recently.

44. b. There is a presumption that co-owners are tenants in common unless they are married to each other, in which case the presumption is that the property is held as community property.

45. a. The note contains the loan amount, interest rate, term of the loan, and monthly payments.

46. d. Interest is paid in arrears. The August payment included the interest for July. A banker's year is 360 days and a calendar year is 365 days (366 in a leap year): $187,523 × 6.75% = $12,657.80 interest for a year; $12,657.80 ÷ 360 = $35.16 interest per day; $35.16 × 21 days in August = $738.37 prorated interest due at closing for payoff.

47. c. When a borrower uses property to secure a loan while retaining the property's use and benefit, it is known as hypothecation.

48. d. Each state has a set of laws that define the distribution of real estate owned by someone who dies without leaving written instruction. If no heirs are located, the property reverts to the state.

49. b. An exculpatory clause acts as a non-recourse loan. The buyer is not personally responsible for the note.

50. c. Referral fees may be paid only to licensed brokers.

51. b. RESPA, the Real Estate Settlement Procedures Act, requires certain information be disclosed and documented for residential loans.

52. c. The Real Estate Settlement Procedures Act does not require a specific settlement location.

53. d. A general warranty deed contains covenants that warrant the new owner's undisturbed and clear title.

54. d. An interest that exists "so long as" a condition is met is a fee simple with a special limitation.

55. b. Calculate the annual interest of 8%, and then calculate the monthly interest charge: 8% = .08; $18,000 loan × .08 = $1,440 annual interest; $1,440 ÷ 12 months = $120 interest per month; $120 × 2 months = $240 interest owed for two months; $18,000 loan to be paid back + $240 interest = $18,240 total loan payoff.

56. a. A licensed salesperson sponsored by a broker is authorized to act on behalf of the broker who is the agent for all clients of the firm. The salesperson may bind the broker to certain specified contracts such as listing agreements and buyer representations.

57. b. The capitalization rate is an analysis of how much investors are willing to spend in a certain neighborhood in return for a certain amount of income.

58. d. The general agent is empowered to make binding decisions on behalf of the principal. Approving leases and property expenditures are among those activities.

59. d. 6% = .06; $340,000 loan amount × .06 interest = $20,400 interest for one year; $20,400 interest ÷ 12 months = $1,700 interest paid in first payment; $2,028 principal and interest payment − $1,700 interest = $328 principal paid; $340,000 loan − $328 principal paid = $339,672 loan balance after first payment.

60. c. Broker Peter Eklund has violated the fiduciary duty of confidentiality and put his client at a disadvantage in negotiating.

61. c. A percentage lease has a base rent plus a percentage (overage) of the gross sales after the retailer goes over a predetermined threshold in sales.

62. **d.** Net listings, in which the agent keeps any part of the sale price above a given amount, may subject a broker or associate licensee to license revocation or suspension.

63. **b.** The cost approach requires the building and land to be valued separately.

64. **b.** Mortgage insurance, which protects the lender from loss, should not be confused with mortgage life insurance, which pays off the loan in case of the borrower's death.

65. **b.** One-third of 15 is five years of depreciation, leaving ten years of remaining life; $\frac{2}{3} \times 15 = 10$.

66. **c.** A special assessment tax for a road is charged by the number of feet fronting the road.

67. **b.** The principle of highest and best use means that that value of the property will produce the greatest net return over a given period of time.

68. **d.** You should memorize the size of an acre, which some estimate at "somewhat more than 200 feet by 200 feet."

69. **b.** All cooperative sales fees are paid from the listing broker, who collects the listing fee from the seller and pays the selling broker who will disburse fees according to his or her company policy to individual agents.

70. **c.** 80% loan-to-value is based on the lesser of the appraised value or the sale price; $135,000 \times .80 = $108,000.

71. **b.** After disposing of the property, the seller may calculate losses and seek to recover compensatory damages from the defaulting buyer.

72. **c.** The appraiser subtracts the value of the fireplace from the sales price of the comparable house and adds the value of the garage that is found in the subject property: $198,000 − $3,000 + $12,000 = $207,000.

73. **d.** The word *severalty* comes from *sever* and implies that all other persons are severed, or cut off, from any share of ownership.

74. **b.** $57,300 ÷ $500 = $114.60, so use $115 (because the problem states "any portion thereof"); $115 × .50 = $57.50.

75. **b.** $180,000 × .9 = $162,000 maximum uninsured loan, so the buyer's entire loan of $145,000 can be figured by the described investor.

76. **b.** Chattel is an item of tangible personal property and is most appropriately transferred by a bill of sale. A chattel mortgage is a mortgage secured by personal property.

77. **c.** Assemblage is bringing together two or more properties to form an aggregate whole.

78. **c.** A court action brought against a party to a contract to force compliance with a legally binding contract is a suit for specific performance.

79. **a.** The general rule is that any offer or counteroffer may be withdrawn at any time before notice of its acceptance has been communicated to the other party.

80. **d.** With the information given, a garage is valued at $8,000. The subject property is never adjusted. House B would receive the deduction from value in order to make it as much like the subject property as possible.

81. **c.** There is no requirement for the broker to provide any office or workspace for the independent contractor.

82. **b.** The IRS's safe harbor guidelines for independent contractor status also require that the associate hold a real estate license and that a written contract exist.

83. **a.** The mortgage insurance premium (MIP) is the term used by FHA. Private mortgage insurance (PMI) is the term used in relationship to conventional loans.

84. **d.** An assignment is the transfer of the entire term of the lease. A sublet is the creation of a new lease.

85. **c.** Real estate must have four characteristics to be valuable: utility, transferability, scarcity, and demand.

86. **a.** The law does not require elevators or power lifts in residential real estate.

87. **a.** Unpaid, year-to-date property taxes are owed by the seller and are credited to the buyer who will be responsible for payment when taxes are due.

88. **b.** Scarcity is an *economic* characteristic of real estate.

89. **c.** The owner of more than four units cannot deny access to any member of a protected class as defined by federal fair housing laws.

90. **b.** The granting clause of a deed contains the words of conveyance, such as "[grantor] hereby grants . . ."

91. **d.** At closing, interest on new loans is collected in advance from the day of closing until the first of the next month. No payment is due until the month following and that payment includes the 30 days just earned; $(($250,000 \times .8 \times 0.075) \div 360) \times 21 \text{ days} = 875.

92. **d.** The strip mall would have the highest risk and thus bear the highest capitalization rate. The single-family residence could be appraised using the sales comparison approach.

93. **b.** So long as the tenant pays, there is no violation of building codes, and the tenant agrees to restore the property to its original condition, the landlord must approve the ramp.

94. **c.** The Fair Housing Amendments Act of 1988 prohibits discrimination based on familial status.

95. **d.** All salespersons have the same relationship with the principal as the broker has.

96. **c.** The acceleration clause gives the lender the right to call all sums owed to be immediately payable upon the occurrence of a specified event. The alienation clause and the due-on-sale clause are the same and provide that the balance of the loan may be due in full upon the sale of the collateral property.

97. **d.** The sales contract should contain a provision allowing the buyer a walk-through within 24 hours before closing.

98. **d.** Emblements are annual crops, accretion refers to land built up by soil deposits, and chattel is another word for personal property.

99. **a.** $58,000 net required + $239,460 loan payoff + $4,750 closing costs = $302,210 needed not counting the commission; $302,210 is 95% of the amount needed to include the 5% commission; $302,210 \div .95 = $318,115$ required sales price to accomplish the seller's goal.

100. **c.** A subdivided plat using lots and blocks is the simplest way to legally describe such a project.

▶ Scoring

Remember that this practice exam is not correlated exactly to your state's real estate sales exam. In general, to evaluate how you did on this second practice exam, find the number of questions you got right, and divide by 100 (the number of questions on this exam). This will give you your score as a percentage. Try to aim for 70% on this practice exam, or at least a higher score than you got on the previous practice exam.

Keep in mind that at this point, how you did on each of the basic areas tested by the exam is more important than your overall score. Use the following table to see where your strengths and weaknesses lie so that you can concentrate your efforts as you continue to prepare.

After working more on your problem areas, take the third practice exam in Chapter 8 to see how much you've improved. This will help you revise your study plan if need be. After your study plan is revised, turn again to the real estate refresher course and the real estate math review in Chapters 4 and 5, and to the real estate glossary in Chapter 6 to target areas that still need work.

EXAM 2 FOR REVIEW

Topic	Question Numbers
Financing	6, 7, 10, 19, 20, 37, 45, 47, 49, 51, 64, 83, 96
Settlement/Transfer of Property	2, 4, 11, 38, 46, 48, 52, 53, 66, 87, 90, 91, 97
Property Management	9, 13, 15, 16, 18, 33, 36, 39, 58, 61, 84, 86, 93
Property Valuations/Appraisal	3, 17, 26, 42, 43, 57, 63, 65, 67, 72, 77, 85, 92
Property Characteristics	8, 30, 31, 32, 34, 44, 54, 68, 73, 76, 88, 98, 100
Business Practices	1, 14, 23, 24, 25, 35, 50, 69, 81, 82, 89, 94,
Contracts/Agency Relationships	5, 12, 22, 27, 28, 29, 56, 60, 62, 71, 78, 79, 95
Mathematics	21, 40, 41, 55, 59, 70, 74, 75, 80, 99

CHAPTER

Real Estate Sales Exam 3

CHAPTER SUMMARY

This is the third of four practice exams in this book. Use this exam to identify which types of questions are still giving you problems.

YOU ARE NOW more familiar with these practice exams, and most likely, you feel more confident than you did at first. However, your practice test-taking experience will help you most if you have created a situation as close as possible to the real one.

For this exam, try to simulate real testing conditions. Find a quiet place where you will not be disturbed. Make sure you have two sharpened pencils and a good eraser. Be sure to leave enough time to complete the exam in one sitting. You should have plenty of time to answer all of the questions when you take the real exam, but you'll want to practice working quickly without rushing. Use a timer or a stopwatch and see if you can work through all the exam questions within two hours.

As before, the answer sheet follows this page, and the test is followed by the answer key and explanations. These explanations, along with the table at the end of this chapter, will help you see where you need further study.

► Real Estate Sales Exam 3 Answer Sheet

#	a	b	c	d
1.	a	b	c	d
2.	a	b	c	d
3.	a	b	c	d
4.	a	b	c	d
5.	a	b	c	d
6.	a	b	c	d
7.	a	b	c	d
8.	a	b	c	d
9.	a	b	c	d
10.	a	b	c	d
11.	a	b	c	d
12.	a	b	c	d
13.	a	b	c	d
14.	a	b	c	d
15.	a	b	c	d
16.	a	b	c	d
17.	a	b	c	d
18.	a	b	c	d
19.	a	b	c	d
20.	a	b	c	d
21.	a	b	c	d
22.	a	b	c	d
23.	a	b	c	d
24.	a	b	c	d
25.	a	b	c	d
26.	a	b	c	d
27.	a	b	c	d
28.	a	b	c	d
29.	a	b	c	d
30.	a	b	c	d
31.	a	b	c	d
32.	a	b	c	d
33.	a	b	c	d
34.	a	b	c	d
35.	a	b	c	d
36.	a	b	c	d
37.	a	b	c	d
38.	a	b	c	d
39.	a	b	c	d
40.	a	b	c	d
41.	a	b	c	d
42.	a	b	c	d
43.	a	b	c	d
44.	a	b	c	d
45.	a	b	c	d
46.	a	b	c	d
47.	a	b	c	d
48.	a	b	c	d
49.	a	b	c	d
50.	a	b	c	d
51.	a	b	c	d
52.	a	b	c	d
53.	a	b	c	d
54.	a	b	c	d
55.	a	b	c	d
56.	a	b	c	d
57.	a	b	c	d
58.	a	b	c	d
59.	a	b	c	d
60.	a	b	c	d
61.	a	b	c	d
62.	a	b	c	d
63.	a	b	c	d
64.	a	b	c	d
65.	a	b	c	d
66.	a	b	c	d
67.	a	b	c	d
68.	a	b	c	d
69.	a	b	c	d
70.	a	b	c	d
71.	a	b	c	d
72.	a	b	c	d
73.	a	b	c	d
74.	a	b	c	d
75.	a	b	c	d
76.	a	b	c	d
77.	a	b	c	d
78.	a	b	c	d
79.	a	b	c	d
80.	a	b	c	d
81.	a	b	c	d
82.	a	b	c	d
83.	a	b	c	d
84.	a	b	c	d
85.	a	b	c	d
86.	a	b	c	d
87.	a	b	c	d
88.	a	b	c	d
89.	a	b	c	d
90.	a	b	c	d
91.	a	b	c	d
92.	a	b	c	d
93.	a	b	c	d
94.	a	b	c	d
95.	a	b	c	d
96.	a	b	c	d
97.	a	b	c	d
98.	a	b	c	d
99.	a	b	c	d
100.	a	b	c	d

▶ Real Estate Sales Exam 3

1. Jeff and Alexandra Clancey have paid a total of $10,500 in mortgage interest and $1,500 in property taxes in this tax year. If they are in the 28% tax bracket, their tax savings is
  a. $12,000
  b. $1,000
  c. $294
  d. $3,360

2. An example of a seller's credit on a closing statement is
  a. a broker's commission.
  b. the contract sales price.
  c. the pay-off of a first mortgage.
  d. a transfer tax.

3. All the salespersons in Al's brokerage firm work as independent contractors. Their office most likely provides them with which of the following?
  a. access to the MLS
  b. health insurance
  c. income tax withholding
  d. paid vacations

4. The management agreement does all of the following EXCEPT
  a. identify the parties.
  b. authorize the manager to make personal deals resulting in outside compensation by suppliers.
  c. describe the manager's responsibilities and authorities.
  d. state the owner's overall goals for the property.

5. For appraising a 20-year-old single-family residence, the best data is the
  a. probable rental figure.
  b. recent sale prices of nearby houses.
  c. replacement cost.
  d. owner's original cost plus money spent on improvements.

6. Judith Munoz's stepmother is selling her home and the title insurance company has requested that Ms. Munoz release any interest she may have in the property. What will she be asked to sign?
  a. warranty deed
  b. quitclaim deed
  c. affidavit
  d. special warranty deed

7. The Bakers have a gross income of $60,000. The lender wants them to spend no more than 28% of their income on their housing expenses. A house they can buy for $240,000 has $2,400 in annual property taxes. Homeowners insurance would cost about $400 a year. At today's interest rates, monthly payments would be $6.65 per $1,000 borrowed on a 30-year mortgage. What is the smallest amount they can expect to spend for a cash down payment?
  a. $10,334
  b. $48,000
  c. $52,000
  d. $64,510

8. All are true about an appraisal EXCEPT
   a. it is the impartial third party who prepares the appraisal.
   b. the appraiser's service is performed for a fee.
   c. the appraiser does not have an agency relationship with the party for whom the appraisal is performed.
   d. an appraiser determines value.

9. Land consisting of a quarter section is sold for $1,850 per acre. The total sale price is
   a. $296,000
   b. $592,000
   c. $296,000
   d. $1,850,000

10. Two building owners in a large city plan to build a "bridge" between the buildings at the fifth-floor level above a city street. Which of the following is true?
   a. A lease for the airspace from the city must be obtained.
   b. A datum deed must be granted by the city.
   c. Nothing is necessary because no part of the land below is being used.
   d. A servient air easement from the city must be granted.

11. All are examples of involuntary conveyance of title EXCEPT
   a. adverse possession.
   b. condemnation through eminent domain.
   c. tax sale.
   d. dedication.

12. An option to purchase is
   a. a unilateral contract.
   b. a bilateral contract.
   c. an installment contract.
   d. enforceable by the optioner.

13. While Dana Nelson spends six months in Europe, she continues to pay rent to her landlord, but actually collects rent from her friend Tim Baylor, who is living there while she is gone. The situation is known as
   a. an assignment.
   b. a sublet.
   c. a lease option.
   d. a right of reverter.

14. If a principal terminates the listing agreement during the listing period, the broker may be able to do any of the following EXCEPT
   a. collect a commission for a transaction in process.
   b. recover marketing expenses.
   c. encourage termination of any contract in process.
   d. continue to cooperate with any subsequent listing broker.

15. Which of the following statements is NOT true?
   a. A VA loan is made by the Department of Veterans Affairs.
   b. The DVA or VA loan is designed to encourage lenders to make loans to qualified veterans.
   c. The DVA charges a funding fee based on a percentage of the loan amount.
   d. Depending on eligibility, a veteran may be able to borrow 100% of the purchase price up to four times his or her eligibility.

16. The most profitable way in which a particular property can be utilized is known as its
   a. plottage value.
   b. highest and best use.
   c. increasing return.
   d. principle of progression.

17. Which of the following would NOT be allowed under the Federal Fair Housing Act?
   a. the owner of a ten-unit apartment building renting to men only
   b. a landlord refusing to rent his double home in which he lives to a woman with three children
   c. an American Legion renting rooms only to members who belong to the American Legion
   d. housing limited to persons age 62 or older

18. The buyer gives the seller's agent a check for $5,000 to serve as earnest money accompanying a purchase offer. He asks that the agent not deposit the check for two weeks and also asks him not to tell the seller about this. When the agent presents the offer, he should
   a. say nothing to the seller but inform his supervising broker of the situation.
   b. say nothing to the buyer but tell the seller the exact status of the check.
   c. mention nothing about the check to anyone and wait to deposit it as requested.
   d. explain to the buyer that he has a fiduciary duty to inform the seller about the check.

19. No federal fair housing laws are violated if a landlord refuses to rent to
   a. people with children.
   b. Vietnamese.
   c. deaf persons.
   d. students.

20. A homeowner has a balance of $149,570.75 remaining on the mortgage. The interest rate is 9.5% and the monthly payment is $1,303.55. After the next two payments, the balance will be
   a. $149,451.30
   b. $148,267.20
   c. $149,330.91
   d. $149,570.75

21. Assuming the net operating income remains constant, if the capitalization rate increases, the present value of the property will
   a. increase.
   b. stay the same.
   c. decrease.
   d. increase at first and then decrease.

22. Which of the following would terminate a listing agreement?
   a. the death of the broker
   b. the retirement of the salesperson
   c. the receipt of an offer to purchase
   d. the expiration of the salesperson's license

23. An owner of a quadraplex will not rent to families with children under the age of 12. Which of the following statements is true?

   a. This is an obvious violation of fair housing law under familial status.

   b. This is an obvious violation of fair housing law under marital status.

   c. The owner lives in one of the units, which constitutes an exception to fair housing law.

   d. This is not a violation of fair housing law if the landlord specifies only children under 12.

24. A mini-ranch is being established on a newly acquired 25-acre parcel of land. The new owner plans to enclose the property with a split-rail fence. The rectangular lot has 1,000 feet of frontage on the state road. How many feet of fencing will be needed?

   a. 2,090 feet

   b. 4,178 feet

   c. 4,270 feet

   d. 4,595 feet

25. An investor requires a 12.5% cap rate. An apartment complex has an effective gross income of $755,500 and annual operating expenses of $318,000. What is the value of this property to this investor?

   a. $850,000

   b. $8,499,375

   c. $3,500,000

   d. $3,499,375

26. When negative amortization occurs, the

   a. monthly payment increases.

   b. term of the loan increases

   c. loan balance increases.

   d. term of the loan decreases.

27. All of the following are examples of a general lien EXCEPT

   a. a mortgage lien.

   b. federal income tax.

   c. state income tax.

   d. judgment.

28. Paul and John Mitchell are brothers who own a chain of auto shops. Paul Mitchell is also a real estate broker, and he's been authorized to find a buyer for their business. Paul has

   a. an ostensible agency.

   b. a designated agency.

   c. an agency by ratification.

   d. an agency coupled with an interest.

29. Using the cost approach to appraisal, the appraiser depreciated the property's cost to build because of several factors including its proximity to a nearby polluting factory. What type of depreciation is this?

   a. physical deterioration

   b. economic obsolescence

   c. physical obsolescence

   d. external obsolescence

30. Seventeen-year-old Louis Custer inherited a parcel of land from his grandfather and, soon after, signed a contract to sell it. This contract is therefore

   a. void.

   b. voidable by the buyer.

   c. binding on the buyer but voidable by the seller.

   d. binding on both parties.

31. Removal of encumbrances in order to provide free and clear title is the responsibility of
a. the title company.
b. the broker.
c. the seller.
d. the buyer.

32. Joanna Bruno bought a house for $120,000, putting 20% down and borrowing the rest with a conventional loan. At the end of the first year, her principal had been paid down by $480 and property values in the area had risen by 6%. Her equity at the end of that first year was
a. $7,200
b. $24,480
c. $31,680
d. $95,520

33. A tenant's lease has expired, but he continues to occupy the property without the landlord's consent. What type of tenancy exists?
a. none
b. tenancy at will
c. tenancy at sufferance
d. tenancy of termination

34. Soil that builds up gradually along a river bank is called
a. peat.
b. avulsion.
c. alluvion.
d. sod.

35. The person who receives real property through a will is known as a
a. devisee.
b. testator.
c. vendee.
d. legatee.

36. When a leased property is sold, the lease
a. has to be renewed.
b. is binding on the new owner.
c. creates a tenancy for month to month.
d. is considered void.

37. Transfer of title requires
a. the delivery and presence of grantee.
b. the acceptance and presence of grantee.
c. the delivery from the grantor.
d. both delivery and acceptance of the deed.

38. Under the Truth-in-Lending Law, Regulation Z, a buyer does NOT have the three-day right of rescission in which of the following cases?
a. a residential first mortgage to finance the acquisition of a home
b. a home improvement loan
c. a home equity line of credit
d. all residential loans when the home is security for the debt

39. Failure to comply with fair housing laws is
a. a civil violation.
b. a criminal violation.
c. grounds for disciplinary action against the licensee.
d. all of the above

40. A valid and enforceable real estate contract must contain at least which of the following?
a. an acknowledgement by a notary public
b. names of the parties' legal counsel
c. signature of the grantor and a legal description
d. a written offer and communication of acceptance

41. A property manager's compensation may be based on any of the following EXCEPT
   a. finder's fees from suppliers of goods and services.
   b. a flat fee.
   c. a percentage of gross income.
   d. a fee per unit.

42. Jerry Wright, the owner of a commercial building, estimates the depreciation of the physical plant at $15,000, the furniture and fixtures at $8,000, and the machinery at $7,500. If he is in the 40% bracket, his tax savings would be
   a. $12,200
   b. $30,500
   c. $18,300
   d. $1,220

43. When an appraiser deducts depreciation using the reproduction cost of a building, the depreciation represents
   a. costs to modernize property.
   b. loss of value due to any cause.
   c. lack of site improvements.
   d. amount of accrued depreciation.

44. The Millers put their house on the market, the Blacks made a written purchase offer, and the Millers accepted the offer in writing. When is the contract valid?
   a. immediately
   b. as soon as the signatures are notarized
   c. when the Blacks are notified of the acceptance
   d. when it is placed in the public records

45. John offers $100,000 for a home listed at $120,000. The seller counteroffers at $110,000. At this point,
   a. the original offer can still be valid.
   b. the owner must take the original offer if he wants to sell.
   c. the original offer is void.
   d. if the seller now chooses to take John's original offer of $110,000, John must go forward with the purchase.

46. What are some of the protected classes under fair housing law?
   a. race, color, national origin, and religion
   b. race, color, marital status, and religion
   c. race, age, national origin, religion, and sex
   d. familial status, handicapped, race, age

47. Personalty or chattels may include
   a. clothing, furniture, stocks, and bonds.
   b. cattle, horses, barns, and fences.
   c. fruit trees in an orchard.
   d. well water and flowing water in a stream.

48. Michael Brown refuses to sell his farm to the state, which needs it to complete the route for a new highway. The state may go to court and ask that his farm be condemned, allowing the state to purchase the land using its right of
   a. laches.
   b. adverse possession.
   c. easement by necessity.
   d. eminent domain.

49. In constructing her financial report, Noel Carpenter estimates that her real estate holdings have appreciated by 18% since purchase. If the original value was $585,000, what would her balance sheet show now?
   a. $690,300
   b. $585,000
   c. $479,700
   d. $526,500

50. The type of deed that provides the least protection is
   a. a special warranty.
   b. a quitclaim.
   c. a bargain and sale.
   d. a deed in trust.

51. When the Franks bought their first home, some of their costs included payment of points, establishment of an escrow account, premium for title insurance, and commission to their own buyers' agent. On that year's income tax return, they may deduct the
   a. points.
   b. title insurance.
   c. commission.
   d. escrowed amount.

52. Paul's storage building was built two feet over the property line between his property and his neighbor's property. This is an example of which of the following?
   a. an easement by prescription
   b. an easement by necessity
   c. an encroachment
   d. adverse possession

53. A salesperson is about to change firms. Should he contact all of his buyer clients and advise them that he will still represent them at his new firm?
   a. yes, because a listing is a personal service agreement and stays with the salesperson
   b. no, because the listing is with the broker
   c. yes, because the salesperson is the one the client looks to for representation
   d. no, because a listing cannot be terminated by a buyer

54. Conforming conventional loans funded by lenders are most often sold
   a. on the primary mortgage market.
   b. to Fannie Mae or Freddie Mac.
   c. on the private secondary mortgage market.
   d. at a discount rate to other lenders.

55. Which of the following is NOT necessary for a valid deed?
   a. competent grantor
   b. granting clause
   c. recording in public record
   d. signature of grantor

56. Which approach to value is best when appraising a six-unit apartment building?
   a. the sales approach to value
   b. the replacement cost
   c. the reproduction cost
   d. the income approach to value

57. What is the capitalization rate or rate of return on a property valued at $6,790,000 if the net operating income is $787,640?
   a. 11.6%
   b. 12.0%
   c. 10.6%
   d. 11.0%

58. The appraised value of a property is $325,000, assessed at 90% of its appraisal. If the tax rate is $2.90 per thousand of assessment, how much are the taxes for the first half of the year?
a. $471.25
b. $424.13
c. $942.50
d. $848.25

59. The best way to define market price is
a. the actual selling price of a property.
b. the most probable price a property should bring in a fair sale.
c. the price represents normal consideration for the property.
d. the price is not affected by unusual circumstances.

60. Which is NOT an example of a buyer's agency agreement?
a. an exclusive buyer agency
b. an open buyers' agency
c. an exclusive-agency buyer agency
d. a net buyer agency

61. Abe and Joel owned adjoining parcels of land. Abe's property had little road frontage that limited its value and Joel's property had ample road frontage but lacked depth. By offering the properties for sale as one parcel, the value was far more than either individually. What principle of value in appraisal applies here?
a. plottage
b. contribution
c. conformity
d. substitution

62. Antonio has a lease on a house for two years but must give a 30-day notice to terminate the lease or the lease will become a month-to-month lease. What type of lease is this?
a. gross lease
b. estate for years with a conversion to a periodic estate
c. periodic lease with a conversion to tenancy at will
d. tenancy at will

63. Mortgage loans described with an index, margin, and rate caps are
a. buydown mortgages.
b. adjustable-rate loans.
c. graduated payment loans.
d. growing equity loans.

64. A subdivider must place in the public records a map of the property known as a
a. plan.
b. zone.
c. plot.
d. plat.

65. Mary owned fee simple title to a lot next door to a church. She gave the lot to the church as a gift. However, she wanted to make sure it would always be used for church purposes. Her attorney prepared her deed to convey ownership of the lot to the church "so long as it is used for church purposes." The church owns a
a. fee simple estate.
b. fee simple determinable.
c. fee simple absolute.
d. fee simple defeasible.

66. A buyer offers, in writing, to pay $295,000 for a property. The buyer makes a down payment of 30% and finances the balance by obtaining a 30-year conventional loan. The factor for the PI payment is $7.34 per thousand. The lender opens an escrow account for payment of the annual property taxes of $3,000 and the property insurance premium of $600, collecting $\frac{1}{12}$ of those amounts with the monthly payment. What is the monthly PITI payment for this borrower?
- **a.** $1,515.71
- **b.** $1,815.71
- **c.** $2,798
- **d.** $2,498

67. A tenant paid rent of $500 due the first of the month and $500 security deposit. The property closes on September 15. How much money will the sellers owe the buyer at closing?
- **a.** $750
- **b.** $500
- **c.** $1,000
- **d.** $1,500

68. A seller accepted an offer to purchase her property, and both the buyer and seller signed a valid binding agreement. The sale is to be closed with an escrow agent in 45 days. What type of contract exists during the 45 days?
- **a.** fully executed
- **b.** contingent
- **c.** executory
- **d.** exclusive

69. Pat signed a five-year lease for a space in a shopping center for his candy store. His business failed, so he sublet the space to Neville for a flower shop. If Neville fails to pay the rent, the landlord
- **a.** has recourse against Pat.
- **b.** has recourse against Neville.
- **c.** has recourse against both Pat and Neville.
- **d.** may immediately evict Neville and sue both for damages.

70. A buyer is getting an 80% LTV mortgage loan on a house priced at $375,000. The payment will be based on an 8% interest rate for 30 years. The amortization factor is $7.34 per thousand. The lender will collect $864 per month to be escrowed for taxes and insurance. How much is the total monthly payment?
- **a.** $2,752.50
- **b.** $2,202
- **c.** $3,066
- **d.** $3,616.50

71. A broker presents a purchase offer to his seller who refuses to accept the offer because the prospects are Mexican. The broker should
- **a.** obey the client's instruction and return the offer to the prospect.
- **b.** explain to the seller that his refusal to accept or negotiate violates fair housing law because of the prospect's national origin.
- **c.** take only non-Mexican offers to the seller.
- **d.** show the buyers other properties.

72. Tony and Teresa opted for a 100% loan and will pay only interest for ten years when the entire loan balance will be due and payable. What type of loan is this?
a. variable rate
b. partially amortized
c. straight or term
d. balloon

73. Both buyer and seller must consent to the agent's role in the transaction so that they know
a. who is responsible for the commission.
b. whether they need a lawyer.
c. whom to ask about hidden defects.
d. whether their disclosures will be held in confidence.

74. Riparian rights refers to all EXCEPT
a. rivers.
b. streams.
c. waterways.
d. oceans.

75. The Simons have defaulted on their loan payments and are behind in paying the rest of their bills, so their home is being sold in a foreclosure auction. Of the many liens against it, which will have first claim on the proceeds of the sale?
a. the first mortgage recorded
b. unpaid real estate taxes
c. mechanic's lien
d. home equity loan

76. A shoe store in the town mall pays a base rent each month plus additional rent based on the amount of business it does. It is operating under a
a. ground lease.
b. percentage lease.
c. net lease.
d. holdover lease.

77. Commercial building site value is commonly quoted to a buyer by price per
a. square foot.
b. front foot.
c. acre.
d. parcel or tract.

78. Prices are likely to rise when there is a
a. buyer's market.
b. seller's market.
c. thin market.
d. broad market.

79. Regarding real property, which of the following statements is true?
a. Emblements are considered as fixtures because they are attached to the land.
b. Trade fixtures attached to the building are always the landlord's property.
c. Air rights can be granted separately by deed.
d. Mineral rights always run with the land.

80. Which of the following statements is true of a land contract?
a. The buyer is given the right to possess.
b. The seller has a lien on the title.
c. The buyer has legal title to the property.
d. The seller cannot provide any of the financing.

81. The Sinclairs needed two different loans to buy their first home. The loan that will have first claim on the value of the house in case of fore-closure is the one that was first
   a. negotiated.
   b. signed.
   c. recorded.
   d. satisfied.

82. Easements, encroachments, and licenses are examples of
   a. water rights.
   b. types of estates.
   c. encumbrances.
   d. government powers.

83. When tenant Heather Grayson opened her ice cream shop in the mall, she installed counters and special freezers. When Heather closes the shop, can she remove them?
   a. It depends on whether her lease specifically states that she can.
   b. No, because as a tenant, she gives up the right of possession.
   c. Yes, she can if she repairs any damage caused by their removal.
   d. No, because as fixtures, they have become part of the real estate.

84. Dennis Sorensen is buying land on which he plans to build a cabin. He wants 200 feet in road frontage and a lot 500 feet deep. If the asking price is $9,000 an acre for the land, how much will Dennis pay for his lot?
   a. $10,000.49
   b. $20,661.15
   c. $22,956.37
   d. $24,104.03

85. Which clause, if included in a mortgage, allows a lien recorded subsequent in time to have a superior position to the mortgage that was recorded prior in time?
   a. a release clause
   b. a subordination clause
   c. a cognovit clause
   d. a superior clause

86. Which approach to value will an appraiser likely use to estimate the value of a custom-built home on a 200-acre farm that includes an indoor tennis court and swimming pool?
   a. sales comparison
   b. cost
   c. market data
   d. capitalization

87. A seller has $5,000 closing costs, a $93,000 loan balance, and pays 7% commission on a $125,000 sale. What are his net proceeds from the sale?
   a. $81,490
   b. $43,510
   c. $23,250
   d. $18,250

88. Under the Equal Credit Opportunity Act (ECOA), a lender does NOT have to offer a loan to a
   a. recipient of public assistance with poor credit history.
   b. recipient of Social Security.
   c. recipient of food stamps.
   d. 90-year-old man looking for a 30-year mortgage.

89. Sisters Anna Lee and Vera Lee are buying a rental property together. If either one should die, they want the survivor to receive the other's share of ownership. Under what form of ownership will they take title at closing?
   a. tenants in common
   b. survivor rights title
   c. joint tenancy
   d. tenancy in severalty

90. According to the federal fair housing laws, all these practices are illegal EXCEPT
   a. blockbusting.
   b. steering.
   c. redlining.
   d. appraising.

91. With an amortized loan, each month
   a. the amount of principal and interest in each payment remains the same.
   b. the interest and principal payments each increase.
   c. the interest portion decreases and the principal portion increases.
   d. the interest portion increases and the principal portion decreases.

92. The purpose of the Real Estate Settlement Procedures Act is to
   a. determine the total move-in cost to the buyer.
   b. provide an itemized account of all closing costs for the buyer and the seller.
   c. provide an estimate of the seller's net proceeds.
   d. help the escrow agent explain the settlement process to the parties to the transaction.

93. Nell Woodhouse wants to buy a certain condo in Florida. In order to pay for the unit, the furniture, and all the appliances, she needs a
   a. package mortgage.
   b. blanket mortgage.
   c. wraparound mortgage.
   d. buydown mortgage.

94. A property manager may legally attract prospective tenants to a building by doing all of the following EXCEPT
   a. offering generous concessions.
   b. removing troublesome tenants.
   c. undertaking an extensive remodeling effort.
   d. paying referral fees to salespersons.

95. The lender's right to call in the loan in case of default and put the secured property up for sale is based on the mortgage document's
   a. alienation clause.
   b. acceleration clause.
   c. defeasance clause.
   d. equity of redemption.

96. In order to appraise property valued over $1,000,000 in a federally related transaction, the person performing the appraisal would need to be
   a. state-certified.
   b. federally licensed.
   c. certified by the bank.
   d. approved by the government.

97. Nancy Tomsic's tenants all had several months remaining on their leases when she sold her six-unit apartment building to Chuck Dwight. Tenants in this situation typically

   a. must renegotiate their leases with the new landlord.

   b. can be required to leave with one month's notice.

   c. lose their leases when the new owner takes possession.

   d. need do nothing and may remain until the end of their leases.

98. Henry Benton hires Brittany Crandall, a property manager, to lease a house that he owns. Henry is Brittany's

   a. customer.

   b. client.

   c. fiduciary.

   d. subagent.

99. The owner of a large apartment complex plans to create a section specifically for families with children. Other sections are to be designated as adult only. Which of the following is true?

   a. This is a good marketing plan and will appeal to consumers.

   b. This violates fair housing law under marital status.

   c. This violates fair housing law under familial status.

   d. This is not a violation of fair housing law if the plan is disclosed properly in all advertising and in the lease contract.

100. The statute of frauds requires that

   a. real estate brokers answer buyers' and sellers' questions honestly.

   b. the seller of real estate provide a written disclosure about the condition of the property.

   c. certain contracts, including those for the sale of real estate, must be in writing to be enforceable.

   d. a mortgage borrower has three days in which to cancel the loan.

▶ Answers

1. d. The taxpayer is permitted to deduct $12,000 from earned income. At the 28% tax rate, the savings would be $3,360; ($10,500 + $1,500) × .28 = $3,360.

2. b. A credit represents an amount of money that is to be received by a party at settlement.

3. a. An independent contractor can receive nothing that resembles an employee benefit.

4. b. The manager must avoid conflicts of interest by refusing to accept gratuities from suppliers.

5. b. How much buyers have paid for similar nearby properties is the best guide to market value.

6. b. A quitclaim deed releases any interest the grantor may have in a property and does not include any warranty of title.

7. d. The Bakers' monthly gross income is $5,000 ($60,000 ÷ 12). The lender allows them a monthly mortgage payment no higher than 28% of $5,000 = $1,400. From that $1,400, a month's property taxes must be subtracted ($2,400 ÷ 12 = $200) and a month's home-owner insurance premium ($400 ÷ 12 = $33.33). That leaves $1,167 to pay for the mortgage itself, principal, and interest. At $6.65 per thousand dollars, $1,167 will pay for $175.49, or $175,490 borrowed on a mortgage ($1,167 ÷ $6.65 = $175.49). If they buy for $240,000 and borrow $175,490, the Bakers will need $64,510 as a cash down payment ($240,000 − $175,490).

8. d. An appraiser does not determine value but rather provides an estimate of value.

9. a. A quarter section contains 160 acres (160 × $1,850 = $296,000).

10. a. Air rights are part of the real property owned by the city and may be leased or purchased. In most cases of this type, the air rights are leased.

11. d. Dedication is the giving of land to a municipality for public use.

12. a. An option to purchase is enforced by one party (unilateral contract)—the optionee, the buyer.

13. b. With a sublet, Dana remains responsible for the rent.

14. c. The agent is prohibited from interfering with any transactions that originated during the relationship.

15. a. The Department of Veterans Affairs does not make or fund loans. It is strictly a guarantee program benefiting eligible, qualified veterans.

16. b. Analyzing a parcel's highest and best use (in terms of money) is a standard part of the appraisal process.

17. a. The Federal Fair Housing Act prohibits discrimination based on gender.

18. d. The seller has a right to full information before making a decision about the offer. The buyer has a right to honest and straightforward treatment, which includes notice that his instructions will not be obeyed.

19. d. Occupation and source of income are not protected classes under federal laws.

20. c. $149,570.75 × .095 ÷ 12 = $1,184.10 month interest; $1,303.55 − $1,184.10 = $119.45 principal; $149,570.75 − $119.45 = $149,451.30; $149,451.30 × .095 ÷ 12 = $1,183.16 month interest; $1,303.55 − $1,183.16 = $120.39 principal; $149,451.30 − $120.39 = $149,330.91.

21. c. The greater the cap rate, the lower the value.

22. a. The death of either party will cancel the listing.

23. c. This exception applies to an owner when he or she resides in a one- to four-family residential dwelling and does not use the services of a real estate broker or use discriminatory advertising.

24. b. (25 acres × 43,560 square feet per acre) ÷ 1,000 front feet = 1,089 feet deep; (1,000 feet × 2 sides) + (1,089 feet × 2 sides) = 4,178 feet.

25. c. $755,500 effective gross income – $318,000 expenses = $437,500 net operating income; $437,500 ÷ 12.5% cap rate = $3,500,000 indicated value.

26. c. In a negative amortized loan, the payments do not cover the principal amount of the loan, thereby increasing the balance of the loan after each payment.

27. a. A mortgage lien is an example of a specific lien.

28. d. Paul is not only an agent, but also has an interest (part ownership) in the property, and should disclose this to potential buyers.

29. d. External obsolescence is caused by factors not on the subject property but that affect the desirability or use of the property and, thus, the value of the property.

30. c. A contract entered into with a minor, a person under 18 years of age, is voidable by the minor.

31. c. It is the seller's responsibility to deliver title to the buyer free and clear of any encumbrances.

32. c. Her equity is the present market value of her home, minus the amount of debt remaining on it. Present market value is $127,200 ($120,000 × 106%). Remaining debt is $95,520 ($120,000 × 80%, reduced by $480). Thus, her present equity is $31,680 ($127,200 – $95,520).

33. c. A tenancy at sufferance exists when a tenant who rightfully possessed the property at one time continues in possession after all rights have expired and without the landlord's consent.

34. c. Alluvion (or alluvium) is the soil that is deposited by the action of a flowing stream.

35. a. The transfer of real property through a will is known as a devise.

36. b. A lease is valid for the entire term and is binding on future owners.

37. d. Ownership is not considered "transferred" until the deed is actually delivered and accepted by the grantee.

38. a. The three-day right of rescission does not apply to a residential first mortgage loan to finance the initial purchase or construction of a dwelling.

39. d. If you fail to comply with fair housing laws, it is considered both a criminal and a civil violation and is grounds for disciplinary action against the licensee.

40. d. For a contract to be valid, it must be in writing and accepted by the offeree who must deliver acceptance to the offeror at which time the contract becomes effective.

41. a. A property manager may not solicit or accept gratuities from suppliers of goods or services.

42. a. The owner would save 40% of the total depreciation; ($15,000 + $8,000 + $7,500) × .40 = $12,200.

43. b. In an appraisal, depreciation is a loss of value in property because of any cause.

44. c. Acceptance of an offer must be communicated to the offeror.

45. **c.** Once there is a counteroffer, the original offer is void.

46. **a.** The protected classes under federal fair housing law are color, race, religion, national origin, sex, familial status, and handicapped.

47. **a.** Chattels and personalty are personal property, as opposed to real property, and are moveable.

48. **d.** The government's right of eminent domain is enforced through condemnation.

49. **a.** The property today is valued at 118% of purchase price: $585,000 × 1.18 = $690,300.

50. **b.** A quitclaim deed is the weakest type of deed for a grantee to receive because no warranty of good title is given by the grantor.

51. **a.** Points paid for a purchase money mortgage on one's own home are immediately deductible as prepaid interest.

52. **c.** An unauthorized intrusion of an improvement onto another's property is an encroachment.

53. **b.** Listings are with the broker, not the salesperson. Unless a contractual agreement exists to the contrary, the salesperson may not interfere with any legal relationship the broker may have with a client.

54. **b.** Conforming loans conform to Fannie Mae/Freddie Mac uniform standards.

55. **c.** While it is wise to record a deed to give public notice of ownership, recording is not required for the validity of a deed.

56. **d.** The income approach to value is used for valuation of income-producing properties.

57. **a.** The formula to determine cap rate is NOI ÷ Value = Cap Rate: $787,640 ÷ $6,790,000 = .116, or 11.6%.

58. **b.** $325,000 × 9% × .5 (half-year) = $424.13

59. **a.** Market price is what a property actually sells for—its sale price.

60. **d.** There are three basic types of buyer agency agreements: exclusive buyer agency, open buyers' agency, and exclusive-agency buyer agency.

61. **a.** Plottage value is the increased usability and value that results when two or more parcels are combined into a larger parcel. It is also called assemblage.

62. **b.** An estate for years is a lease for a definite period of time, and a periodic, or period-to-period, estate requires notification to terminate by either the landlord or the tenant.

63. **b.** The index is an economic indicator to which the loan regularly adjusts, and the margin is a percentage added to the index and is the rate charged to the borrower. Caps limit the highest rate that may be charged.

64. **d.** The subdivision map, which shows lots, blocks, streets, and the like, is known as a plat. It is filed in a plat book, open to the public.

65. **b.** Feasible title with a special limitation is called fee simple determinable.

66. **b.** $295,000 × .7 = $206,500 loan; 206.5 × 7.34 = $1,515.71 principal and interest; ($3,000 + $600) ÷ 12 = $300 taxes and insurance; $1,515.71 + $300 = $1,815.71 PITI.

67. **a.** The security deposit transfers to the new owner: $500 plus $\frac{1}{2}$ month's rent ($250) = $750.

68. **c.** An executory contract is one in which the parties must perform certain requirements to fulfill their respective obligations. An executed or fully executed contract is one in which the parties have completely fulfilled all promises and agreements and nothing remains to be done.

69. a. The original lessee remains responsible for the lease upon subletting the property. In an assignment of lease, the new tenant is responsible to pay the rent directly to the landlord; however, the original lessee may remain liable.

70. c. 80% = .80; $375,000 sales price × .80 = $300,000 loan amount. The formula for principal and interest (PI) is loan ÷ 1,000 × factor = PI; $300,000 ÷ 1,000 × 7.34 = $2,202 PI payment; $2,202 + $864 taxes and insurance (TI) = $3,066 PITI payment.

71. b. Federal fair housing law prohibits discrimination based on the country of ones origin, such as Mexico, Canada, China, or any other country.

72. c. An interest-only loan is a straight-term loan with the entire loan due at the maturity date; partially amortized loans pay principal and interest with a balloon payment with the remaining loan balance due at the maturity date.

73. d. The question of confidential information is the main reason for all the new state laws on agency disclosure.

74. d. Littoral rights include oceans.

75. b. Whether entered in the public records or not, real estate property taxes automatically take priority over all other liens.

76. b. The store will pay as additional rent a percentage of its receipts each month.

77. a. In putting the high cost of commercial land in perspective, sellers and brokers commonly quote the price per square foot to compare property costs for buyers.

78. b. In a seller's market, buyers are competing for the few homes on the market and are likely to offer more for them.

79. c. Even though air rights are considered part of the real property, they can be conveyed separately by deed.

80. a. The buyer may take possession of the property, but legal title remains with the owner until the terms of the purchase are met.

81. c. Liens generally take priority from the order in which they were entered in the public records.

82. c. Anything such as a mortgage, tax or judgment lien, an easement, or a restriction on the use of the land is considered an encumbrance.

83. c. Trade fixtures, installed for use in a trade or business, may be removed by the tenant prior to the expiration of the lease if the premises are returned to their original condition.

84. b. The lot will measure 200' by 500', or 100,000 square feet in all (200' × 500'). An acre contains 43,560 square feet, so the lot contains 2.2957 acres (100,000 ÷ 43,560). At $9,000 per acre, the total cost is $20,661.15 (2.2957 × $9,000).

85. b. A subordination clause allows a subsequent mortgage to be placed ahead of the existing mortgage and would generally also have an escalation clause that would increase the interest rate caused by the increased risk.

86. b. Most residential appraisals are based on the sales comparison approach, but in this case, it is unlikely that such comparables exist. The cost approach is the appropriate choice.

87. d. $5,000 + $93,000 = $98,000 total dollar expenses of closing. Convert 7% to a decimal and multiply; $125,000 × .07 = $8,750 commission; $125,000 − $98,000 − $8,750 = $18,250 net proceeds to seller; 206,500 × (7.34 ÷ 1,000) = $1,515.71 principal and interest; ($3,000 + $600) ÷ 12 = $300 taxes and insurance; $1,515.71 + $300 = $1,815.71 PITI.

88. **a.** The ECOA prevents lenders from prohibiting loans based on age.

89. **c.** The basic idea of joint tenancy is unity of ownership. The death of one member of the unit does not destroy the unit and survivors own the total property.

90. **d.** Appraising a property is not an illegal act so long as you are not discriminating under fair housing laws.

91. **c.** As the debt is paid down, the amount of interest due each month becomes smaller, and more of the payment is available to be applied to the principal.

92. **b.** RESPA requires an itemized accounting of all settlement charges to protect consumers from overcharges, hidden costs, and kickbacks.

93. **a.** A package mortgage covers both real and personal property.

94. **d.** It is illegal to pay referral fees to anyone except a principal broker.

95. **b.** The acceleration clause allows the lender to declare the whole debt immediately due and payable in case of default.

96. **a.** Under FIRREA, appraisers need to be certified by the state to perform an appraisal as part of a federally related transaction when the property value exceeds $1,000,000.

97. **d.** A lease survives the sale, and the new landlord is in exactly the same position with tenants as the old one was.

98. **b.** The person who retains an agent is usually known as the client.

99. **c.** Familial status protects families or any person who has legal custody of a child under the age of 18.

100. **c.** Every state has adopted the statute of frauds, which requires offers, acceptances, land contracts, and other real estate documents to be in writing to be enforceable.

Scoring

Again, evaluate how you did on this practice exam by finding the number of questions you got right, disregarding, for the moment, the ones you got wrong or skipped.

If you didn't score as high as you would like, ask yourself the following: Did I run out of time before I could answer all the questions? Did I go back and change my answers from right to wrong? Did I get flustered and sit staring at a difficult question for what seemed like hours? If you had any of these problems, be sure to go over the LearningExpress Test Preparation System in Chapter 2 to review how best to avoid them.

You probably have seen improvement between your first two practice exam scores and this one; but if you didn't improve as much as you'd like, following are some options:

If you scored below your personal goal, you should seriously consider whether you're ready for the exam at this time. A good idea would be to take some brush-up courses in the areas you feel less sure about. If you don't have time for a course, you might try private tutoring.

If your score was close to your personal goal, you need to work as hard as you can to improve your skills. Go back to your real estate license course textbooks to review the knowledge you need to do well on the exam. If math is your problem area, check out the Learning-Express book *Practical Math Success in 20 Minutes a Day*. Also, reread and pay close attention to the information in Chapter 4, "Real Estate Refresher Course"; Chapter 5, "Real Estate Math Review"; and Chapter 6, "Real Estate Glossary." It might be helpful, as well, to ask friends and family to make up mock test questions and quiz you on them.

If you scored well above your personal goal, that's great! You may have an excellent chance of passing your license exam. Don't lose your edge, though; keep studying right up to the day before the exam.

Now, revise your study schedule according to the time you have left, emphasizing those parts that gave you the most trouble this time. Use the following table to see where you need more work, so that you can concentrate your preparation efforts. After working more on the subject areas that give you problems, take the fourth practice exam in Chapter 9 to see how much you've improved.

EXAM 3 FOR REVIEW

Topic	Question Numbers
Financing	7, 15, 20, 26, 54, 63, 66, 72, 81, 85, 91, 93, 95
Settlement/Transfer of Property	2, 6, 9, 11, 31, 35, 37, 50, 51, 55, 67, 89, 92
Property Management	4, 13, 19, 33, 36, 41, 62, 69, 76, 83, 94, 97, 98
Property Valuations/Appraisal	5, 8, 16, 21, 29, 43, 56, 59, 61, 77, 78, 86, 96
Property Characteristics	10, 24, 27, 34, 47, 48, 52, 64, 65, 74, 75, 79, 82
Business Practices	3, 17, 18, 23, 38, 39, 46, 53, 71, 88, 90, 99
Contracts/Agency Relationships	12, 14, 22, 28, 30, 40, 44, 45, 60, 68, 73, 80, 100
Mathematics	1, 25, 32, 42, 49, 57, 58, 70, 84, 87

9 ▶ Real Estate Sales Exam 4

CHAPTER SUMMARY

This is the last of the practice exams in this book, but it is not designed to be any harder than the other three. It is simply another representation of what you might expect for your state's exam. Just as when you take the real exam, there shouldn't be anything here to surprise you. In fact, you probably already know what's in a lot of it! That will be the case with the real exam, too.

FOR THIS EXAM, pull together all the tips you've been practicing since the first practice exam. Give yourself the time and the space to work. Because you won't be taking the real exam in your living room, you might take this one in an unfamiliar location such as a library. Make sure you have plenty of time to complete the exam in one sitting. In addition, use what you've learned from reading the answer explanations on previous practice exams. Remember the types of questions that caused problems for you in the past, and when you are unsure, try to consider how those answers were explained.

After you've taken this written exam, you should try the computer-based practice questions using the CD-ROM at the back of this book. That way, you'll get familiar with taking exams on a computer.

Once again, use the answer explanations at the end of the exam to understand questions you may have missed.

▶ Real Estate Sales Exam 4 Answer Sheet

#	a	b	c	d
1.	ⓐ	ⓑ	ⓒ	ⓓ
2.	ⓐ	ⓑ	ⓒ	ⓓ
3.	ⓐ	ⓑ	ⓒ	ⓓ
4.	ⓐ	ⓑ	ⓒ	ⓓ
5.	ⓐ	ⓑ	ⓒ	ⓓ
6.	ⓐ	ⓑ	ⓒ	ⓓ
7.	ⓐ	ⓑ	ⓒ	ⓓ
8.	ⓐ	ⓑ	ⓒ	ⓓ
9.	ⓐ	ⓑ	ⓒ	ⓓ
10.	ⓐ	ⓑ	ⓒ	ⓓ
11.	ⓐ	ⓑ	ⓒ	ⓓ
12.	ⓐ	ⓑ	ⓒ	ⓓ
13.	ⓐ	ⓑ	ⓒ	ⓓ
14.	ⓐ	ⓑ	ⓒ	ⓓ
15.	ⓐ	ⓑ	ⓒ	ⓓ
16.	ⓐ	ⓑ	ⓒ	ⓓ
17.	ⓐ	ⓑ	ⓒ	ⓓ
18.	ⓐ	ⓑ	ⓒ	ⓓ
19.	ⓐ	ⓑ	ⓒ	ⓓ
20.	ⓐ	ⓑ	ⓒ	ⓓ
21.	ⓐ	ⓑ	ⓒ	ⓓ
22.	ⓐ	ⓑ	ⓒ	ⓓ
23.	ⓐ	ⓑ	ⓒ	ⓓ
24.	ⓐ	ⓑ	ⓒ	ⓓ
25.	ⓐ	ⓑ	ⓒ	ⓓ
26.	ⓐ	ⓑ	ⓒ	ⓓ
27.	ⓐ	ⓑ	ⓒ	ⓓ
28.	ⓐ	ⓑ	ⓒ	ⓓ
29.	ⓐ	ⓑ	ⓒ	ⓓ
30.	ⓐ	ⓑ	ⓒ	ⓓ
31.	ⓐ	ⓑ	ⓒ	ⓓ
32.	ⓐ	ⓑ	ⓒ	ⓓ
33.	ⓐ	ⓑ	ⓒ	ⓓ
34.	ⓐ	ⓑ	ⓒ	ⓓ
35.	ⓐ	ⓑ	ⓒ	ⓓ

#	a	b	c	d
36.	ⓐ	ⓑ	ⓒ	ⓓ
37.	ⓐ	ⓑ	ⓒ	ⓓ
38.	ⓐ	ⓑ	ⓒ	ⓓ
39.	ⓐ	ⓑ	ⓒ	ⓓ
40.	ⓐ	ⓑ	ⓒ	ⓓ
41.	ⓐ	ⓑ	ⓒ	ⓓ
42.	ⓐ	ⓑ	ⓒ	ⓓ
43.	ⓐ	ⓑ	ⓒ	ⓓ
44.	ⓐ	ⓑ	ⓒ	ⓓ
45.	ⓐ	ⓑ	ⓒ	ⓓ
46.	ⓐ	ⓑ	ⓒ	ⓓ
47.	ⓐ	ⓑ	ⓒ	ⓓ
48.	ⓐ	ⓑ	ⓒ	ⓓ
49.	ⓐ	ⓑ	ⓒ	ⓓ
50.	ⓐ	ⓑ	ⓒ	ⓓ
51.	ⓐ	ⓑ	ⓒ	ⓓ
52.	ⓐ	ⓑ	ⓒ	ⓓ
53.	ⓐ	ⓑ	ⓒ	ⓓ
54.	ⓐ	ⓑ	ⓒ	ⓓ
55.	ⓐ	ⓑ	ⓒ	ⓓ
56.	ⓐ	ⓑ	ⓒ	ⓓ
57.	ⓐ	ⓑ	ⓒ	ⓓ
58.	ⓐ	ⓑ	ⓒ	ⓓ
59.	ⓐ	ⓑ	ⓒ	ⓓ
60.	ⓐ	ⓑ	ⓒ	ⓓ
61.	ⓐ	ⓑ	ⓒ	ⓓ
62.	ⓐ	ⓑ	ⓒ	ⓓ
63.	ⓐ	ⓑ	ⓒ	ⓓ
64.	ⓐ	ⓑ	ⓒ	ⓓ
65.	ⓐ	ⓑ	ⓒ	ⓓ
66.	ⓐ	ⓑ	ⓒ	ⓓ
67.	ⓐ	ⓑ	ⓒ	ⓓ
68.	ⓐ	ⓑ	ⓒ	ⓓ
69.	ⓐ	ⓑ	ⓒ	ⓓ
70.	ⓐ	ⓑ	ⓒ	ⓓ

#	a	b	c	d
71.	ⓐ	ⓑ	ⓒ	ⓓ
72.	ⓐ	ⓑ	ⓒ	ⓓ
73.	ⓐ	ⓑ	ⓒ	ⓓ
74.	ⓐ	ⓑ	ⓒ	ⓓ
75.	ⓐ	ⓑ	ⓒ	ⓓ
76.	ⓐ	ⓑ	ⓒ	ⓓ
77.	ⓐ	ⓑ	ⓒ	ⓓ
78.	ⓐ	ⓑ	ⓒ	ⓓ
79.	ⓐ	ⓑ	ⓒ	ⓓ
80.	ⓐ	ⓑ	ⓒ	ⓓ
81.	ⓐ	ⓑ	ⓒ	ⓓ
82.	ⓐ	ⓑ	ⓒ	ⓓ
83.	ⓐ	ⓑ	ⓒ	ⓓ
84.	ⓐ	ⓑ	ⓒ	ⓓ
85.	ⓐ	ⓑ	ⓒ	ⓓ
86.	ⓐ	ⓑ	ⓒ	ⓓ
87.	ⓐ	ⓑ	ⓒ	ⓓ
88.	ⓐ	ⓑ	ⓒ	ⓓ
89.	ⓐ	ⓑ	ⓒ	ⓓ
90.	ⓐ	ⓑ	ⓒ	ⓓ
91.	ⓐ	ⓑ	ⓒ	ⓓ
92.	ⓐ	ⓑ	ⓒ	ⓓ
93.	ⓐ	ⓑ	ⓒ	ⓓ
94.	ⓐ	ⓑ	ⓒ	ⓓ
95.	ⓐ	ⓑ	ⓒ	ⓓ
96.	ⓐ	ⓑ	ⓒ	ⓓ
97.	ⓐ	ⓑ	ⓒ	ⓓ
98.	ⓐ	ⓑ	ⓒ	ⓓ
99.	ⓐ	ⓑ	ⓒ	ⓓ
100.	ⓐ	ⓑ	ⓒ	ⓓ

▶ Real Estate Sales Exam 4

1. An individual may acquire ownership of real property by which of the following methods?
   a. escheat
   b. eminent domain
   c. devise
   d. subrogation

2. The area of a lot that measures 850' × 850' is approximately how many square yards?
   a. 80,278
   b. 240,833
   c. 26,759
   d. 722,500

3. The Franks receive two offers on their condo, which is listed for $140,000. Anne Hill offers to pay $138,000 cash for the unit. Bob Stone offers $141,000, putting 20% down, if the Franks will pay three points to Stone's lender for the mortgage loan the buyers need. What is the difference between the two offers?
   a. $384
   b. $3,000
   c. $2,000
   d. $1,128

4. Irene Shapiro will qualify for a mortgage loan of $350,000 if she can get an interest rate of 5.75%. The lender has quoted a rate of 6.25% but agreed that she could get the desired rate if she pays discount points equal to one point per .25% of interest rate reduction. How much will Irene pay in points?
   a. $3,500
   b. $7,000
   c. $8,750
   d. $2,187

5. Sue Addison owns an apartment building that was constructed in 1965. According to federal law, which of the following must be attached to the leases Sue prepares for prospective tenants?
   a. a report of the building's radon level
   b. a lead-based paint disclosure statement
   c. an illustration of the building's location relative to electromagnetic fields (EMFs)
   d. any known instances of groundwater contamination in the building's water supply

6. A borrower can expect to pay a mortgage insurance premium (MIP) for
   a. an 80% LTV conventional loan.
   b. a VA loan.
   c. a graduated payment loan.
   d. an FHA 203(b) loan.

7. A property is valued at $850,000 by an appraiser and generates an annual net income of $144,500. What capitalization rate percentage did the appraiser use in determining value?
   a. 11.5%
   b. 13%
   c. 14.45%
   d. 17%

8. If a property generates a negative cash flow, in order to be an attractive investment to a prospective purchaser,
   a. there must be a substantial down payment.
   b. there must be a large depreciable base.
   c. there must be a substantial increase in property value.
   d. there must be little deferred maintenance.

9. Which of the following is NOT a physical characteristic of land?
   a. improvements
   b. nonhomogeniety
   c. immobility
   d. indestructibility

10. Who will fund a primary loan?
   a. a mortgage broker
   b. a mortgage banker
   c. both **a** and **b**
   d. neither **a** nor **b**

11. A comprehensive buyer representation agreement would address the
   a. buyer's desired property description.
   b. duties of the agent, termination date, and compensation agreement.
   c. agent's contact information.
   d. family contact names and numbers.

12. To qualify for innocent landowner status, a purchaser under federal law must have the property environmentally inspected
   a. prior to taking title.
   b. within 30 days of ownership.
   c. in the first year of ownership.
   d. when economically feasible.

13. Which of the following investment opportunities would involve the greatest risk even though it would likely produce the highest rate of return?
   a. before construction is started
   b. during construction
   c. after construction
   d. upon occupancy by anchor tenants

14. A 3,500-square-foot house in a neighborhood of 2,000 to 2,700 square foot houses is of less value per foot because of the appraisal principle of
   a. substitution.
   b. assemblage.
   c. conformity and contribution.
   d. increasing and diminishing returns.

15. An appraiser may consider which of the following depreciation factors in the cost approach to appraisal?
   a. a nearby noisy factory
   b. the ethnic makeup of the area
   c. familial status
   d. square footage of the land

16. Which is true of owner's title insurance?
   a. It guarantees ownership in perpetuity.
   b. It is transferable to the next property owner.
   c. It will reimburse for title losses up to the face amount of the policy.
   d. It protects the lender against loss of lien rights.

17. The owner of Highland Apartments has determined that his vacancy rate is less than 5%. What, if any, action should he take?
   a. He should spend less money on advertising.
   b. He should renovate the lobby.
   c. He should survey his market to determine if the rents should be increased.
   d. He should do nothing.

18. The closed sales price of an income property divided by its gross monthly rent equals the
  a. estimated market value.
  b. capitalization rate.
  c. gross income multiplier.
  d. gross rent multiplier.

19. An abstract of title provides which of the following?
  a. insures ownership in perpetuity
  b. pays owner for full or partial title loss
  c. insures against unrecorded documents, such as unpaid previous property taxes
  d. a history of documents in public records that affect title to the property

20. In order to appraise property valued over $1,000,000 in a federally related transaction, the person performing the appraisal would need to be
  a. state-certified.
  b. federally licensed.
  c. certified by the bank.
  d. approved by the government.

21. George bought a condominium that included appliances and furnishings. His mortgage loan covered the condo and the personal property. What type of mortgage loan is this?
  a. package mortgage
  b. blanket mortgage
  c. participation mortgage
  d. fixture mortgage

22. A real estate agent stated in his advertising, "Condo with fabulous city view will appreciate greatly within one year!" This is an example of
  a. professional marketing.
  b. representing the seller.
  c. puffing.
  d. stating obvious facts.

23. Of the following, the most important factor that a lender will consider would be
  a. the borrower's investments.
  b. the borrower's marital status.
  c. payment history of previous car loans.
  d. payment history of previous home loans.

24. The house on Summit Street is up for sale because last year a suicide took place in an upstairs bedroom. In real estate circles, the house is now considered
  a. latently defective.
  b. environmentally unsound.
  c. functionally obsolescent.
  d. stigmatized.

25. Marian Snyder recently acquired a property and is required to provide access ramps, Braille markings, lowered water fountains, and other accommodations for handicapped persons. What federal law requires this?
  a. Fair Housing Law
  b. Americans with Disabilities Act
  c. Handicapped Use Act
  d. Open and Accessible Properties Law

26. How many square feet are in a half-acre parcel?
- **a.** 43,560
- **b.** 2,780
- **c.** 20,001
- **d.** 21,780

27. A property manager should NOT consider which of the following when selecting a tenant?
- **a.** the tenant's ability to pay
- **b.** space requirements of the tenant
- **c.** compatibility of the tenant's business with other tenants' businesses
- **d.** the gender of the tenant

28. A licensed real estate agent who is also a REALTOR® is bound to a higher standard of ethics. If there is a conflict between the National Association of REALTORS® Code of Ethics and state law, the agent should
- **a.** follow the Code of Ethics to avoid an ethics violation.
- **b.** ignore the state law because it is unethical.
- **c.** follow the state law.
- **d.** inform the NAR that it is in violation of the state law.

29. A landlord's duties under a residential lease agreement include the requirements that the landlord
- **a.** make all repairs to the property specified by the tenant.
- **b.** meet the legal requirements to protect the safety and health of the tenant.
- **c.** meet only the lease requirements for repairs.
- **d.** maintain the property in the same condition as at the initial time of tenant occupancy.

30. In the cost approach to appraisal, depreciation is deemed to be curable if it may be
- **a.** repaired or remedied at a reasonable cost.
- **b.** an income tax deduction.
- **c.** cured by value adjustment.
- **d.** cured by extension of the economic life of the property.

31. The right that a power company acquires in order to lay a service line across a customer's property is called
- **a.** an easement in gross.
- **b.** a license.
- **c.** a condemnation.
- **d.** a restrictive covenant.

32. Reconciliation is
- **a.** used to determine reproduction cost of a building.
- **b.** loss of value.
- **c.** an element of value.
- **d.** analyzing the three estimates of value in the appraisal process to arrive at an estimate of market value for the property.

33. The Truth in Lending Act is implemented by the
- **a.** Department of Housing and Urban Development (HUD), Regulation X.
- **b.** Federal Trade Commission (FTC), Regulation B.
- **c.** Department of Justice (DOJ).
- **d.** Federal Reserve Board, Regulation Z.

34. A metes and bounds survey begins at the point of beginning and ends at the
- **a.** point of beginning.
- **b.** endpoint.
- **c.** monument.
- **d.** last benchmark.

35. An odorless substance created by decaying radioactive materials in the soil is known as
  a. urea formaldehyde.
  b. radon gas.
  c. carbon monoxide.
  d. polychlorinated biphenyl.

36. A zoning commission may grant a variance to property use when which of the following exists?
  a. over-budget development costs to a subdivider
  b. environmental concerns as to use
  c. alternative building sites that increase owner's costs
  d. limitation of feasible building sites because of land contours

37. For there to be a valid right to purchase or terminate, an option contract must contain
  a. notice to terminate.
  b. at least seven days to back out of the agreement.
  c. dollar consideration.
  d. a right of recission.

38. Which form or action of discrimination was NOT in violation of the Federal Fair Housing Act when established in 1968?
  a. gender
  b. religion
  c. color
  d. national origin

39. If a seller's agent shares his or her commission with a buyer's agent,
  a. this is not necessarily an indication of agency representation.
  b. the seller's agent may advise the seller of this cooperation.
  c. the buyer's agent does not have to disclose this to the buyer.
  d. the seller agent may deduct that amount from the total he or she pays his or her agent.

40. The form of ownership that would give an investor the greatest flexibility when selling his or her interest would be
  a. a general partnership.
  b. ownership in severalty.
  c. joint tenancy.
  d. a limited partnership.

41. The most accurate way to uniquely locate and bound a parcel of real property is to use
  a. a topographical map.
  b. latitude and longitude bearings.
  c. the assessor parcel number.
  d. a metes and bounds survey.

42. Which of the following deeds provides the purchaser with the least protection in regards to covenants and/or warranties given by the seller?
  a. trustee's
  b. special warranty
  c. general warranty
  d. quitclaim

43. When money is escrowed each month to cover annual payments of insurance and taxes, the mortgage is called
   a. a blanket mortgage.
   b. a budget mortgage.
   c. a graduated payment mortgage.
   d. a growing equity mortgage.

44. The term that describes the percentage of the appraised value of a property that a lender will finance is called
   a. loan-to-value ratio.
   b. owner's equity.
   c. certificate of reasonable value.
   d. capital investment.

45. Jill Adams, a property owner, just received a bill from her local taxing authority in the amount of $2,040. Property taxes in this jurisdiction are based on 80% of assessed value and the rate is $1.50 per hundred. What value has the assessor placed on Jill's property?
   a. $136,000
   b. $170,000
   c. $163,200
   d. $190,000

46. Commercial banks prefer to make short-term loans like construction loans and 90-day business loans. The reason for their preference is
   a. the source of their funds is primarily from CDs (Certificates of Deposit).
   b. the source of their funds is primarily from savings accounts.
   c. the source of their funds is primarily from checking accounts.
   d. the source of their funds is primarily from issuing bonds.

47. Upon the buyer signing the sales agreement, a licensee is obligated to give a copy to the
   a. buyer upon request.
   b. buyer by law.
   c. buyer after the seller signs.
   d. the lender.

48. At what point is transfer of ownership by deed completed?
   a. The deed is signed by a competent grantor.
   b. The deed is signed by a competent grantor and delivered to and accepted by the grantee or his or her agent.
   c. The deed is signed by a competent grantor and grantee.
   d. The deed is given to the grantee.

49. A buyer wants to purchase a home. However, he has his present home to sell. The best way to write the contract of sale would be to
   a. wait until his present home sells.
   b. include a sale-of-existing-home contingency.
   c. use an option agreement.
   d. include an addendum.

50. If a contract for real estate is vague in its basic terms, a court would hold that it is
   a. binding on the offeror.
   b. unenforceable.
   c. valid against all parties.
   d. invalid until rewritten by an attorney.

51. Market data approach appraising may require adjustments of sold comparables by an appraiser for all of the following EXCEPT
  a. sale date of comparable.
  b. replacement cost of structure.
  c. financing made available by seller.
  d. lot size and location.

52. Samantha Mulder goes to a bank and borrows money for the purchase of her first home, thereby becoming a
  a. mortgagor.
  b. mortgagee.
  c. lienor.
  d. lienee.

53. Broker Donna Williams received a buyer referral from an out-of-state broker and agreed to pay him a 20% referral fee from her total commission when the transaction closes. Donna sold the buyer a property for $895,000 and received a commission as selling broker for 2.5%. How much does Donna owe the referring broker?
  a. $1,790
  b. $2,237.50
  c. $4,475
  d. $4,237.50

54. An accrued charge on a closing statement is paid
  a. in advance.
  b. in arrears.
  c. always by the buyer.
  d. always by the seller.

55. What is the square footage of a living room measuring 30 feet by 23 feet?
  a. 960
  b. 690
  c. 609
  d. 906

56. What did the 1972 amendment add to the Federal Fair Housing Act of 1968?
  a. qualifications as to the age of children in certain housing facilities
  b. landlords making reasonable property alterations for handicapped tenants
  c. operation of an adults-only apartment complex
  d. display of equal housing poster in broker's place of business

57. A property manager must have which type of contract with the owner?
  a. a listing agreement
  b. a management agreement
  c. a lease agreement
  d. a multi-peril agreement

58. The vendee has
  a. equitable title in the property.
  b. an obligation to sell the property.
  c. temporary title to the property.
  d. no obligation to the seller.

59. The Federal Reserve Board's Regulation B implements which of the following?
  a. Home Mortgage Disclosure Act
  b. FACT Act
  c. Equal Credit Opportunity Act
  d. Community Reinvestment Act

60. An appraiser estimates annual rental collections on an investment property of $99,000. The vacancy factor is 5% and operating expenses run 30% of gross income. A similar investment should generate a return on investment of 15%. Using the income approach to value, what is the market value of this property?
  a. $462,000
  b. $627,000
  c. $429,000
  d. $660,000

61. A property management agreement creates what type of agency?
  a. special agency
  b. universal agency
  c. general agency
  d. limited agency

62. Earnest money is entered on a closing statement as a
  a. credit to the seller.
  b. charge to the buyer.
  c. debit to the seller.
  d. credit to the buyer.

63. Failure to act timely to have a court enforce deed restrictions may result in the violations being allowed because of the legal concept called
  a. non-conforming use.
  b. laches.
  c. constructive notice.
  d. injunction.

64. A landlord NOT offering as many properties to an Asian family as were offered to others is an example of
  a. channeling prospects.
  b. redlining.
  c. malice before the fact.
  d. less favorable treatment.

65. Which of the following phrases is NOT discriminatory in an advertisement to lease a nonexempt 100-unit apartment complex under the current Federal Fair Housing Act?
  a. no handicapped alterations will be made
  b. adults only, no children
  c. no smoking on premises
  d. females only

66. In which real estate closing must a HUD Uniform Settlement Statement be used?
  a. cash transaction on the sale of a single-family dwelling
  b. commercial sale funded by a federally chartered bank
  c. one- to four-family home with federal related loan
  d. agricultural vacant land purchased with a federally backed loan

67. Which of the following statements concerning an easement is true?
  a. An easement is always appurtenant.
  b. An easement is an estate at sufferance.
  c. An easement can be created only by a deed.
  d. An easement appurtenant runs with the land.

68. When a buyer makes an offer and a seller changes a few of the terms before he or she signs and returns it, that is a
 a. rejection.
 b. conditional acceptance.
 c. conditional rejection.
 d. counteroffer.

69. An agent with Broker A has a purchase offer for a property listed with an agent associated with Broker B. The buyer's agent should
 a. present the offer to the seller as quickly as possible to best serve her buyer.
 b. present the offer to the agent of Broker B as soon as possible to be presented to the seller.
 c. call the office of Broker B and tell them she has an offer for their client.
 d. take the offer to her broker, Broker A, to be presented to the seller.

70. Duane Temme did not have an official deed to 582 acres of land, but was granted title to the property because he has lived on the land for more than 15 years. The previous owner of record could not be located. By what legal means did Ms. Temme acquire title?
 a. estoppel
 b. adverse possession
 c. sheriff's affidavit
 d. escheat

71. Which of the following would NOT affect realty value?
 a. permitted uses by city zoning ordinances
 b. number of real estate brokers in the area
 c. marketable and/or indefeasible title of a property
 d. demand for property by qualified buyers

72. If real estate property taxes are paid in arrears, what would the seller be debited on a September 14 closing with annual taxes of $2,700? (Use statutory method, taxes accrue from January 1 through closing date, seller responsible for day of closing.)
 a. $1,880
 b. $1,902
 c. $1,905
 d. $1,913

73. John Fitzpatrick holds $800 in security deposits from the six tenants in his apartment building when he sells the building to Helen Baker. The tenants can expect a return of their security deposits from
 a. John at closing.
 b. Helen upon termination of the lease.
 c. the person who conducted the closing.
 d. John upon completion of the tenancy.

74. An income approach appraisal would include which of the following information?
 a. annual net operating income generated
 b. sold comparables within the same market area
 c. replacement cost of structure and site improvements
 d. building value based on cost per square foot

75. Which method of foreclosure is used in a deed of trust mortgage lien?
 a. nonjudicial power of sale
 b. judicial court ordered sale
 c. sheriff's sale at the courthouse
 d. deed in lieu of accepted by lender

76. The entity that loses ownership through a deed of trust mortgage foreclosure is the
   a. lender.
   b. beneficiary.
   c. mortgagee.
   d. mortgagor.

77. The four unities required for the creation of a joint tenancy are
   a. time, title, consideration, and interest.
   b. competent parties, title, possession, and interest.
   c. time, title, legal purpose, and possession.
   d. time, title, possession, and interest.

78. During negotiations, the parties to a contract agreed to attach a document to the contract to fully express the terms of the agreement. What is this attached document called?
   a. amendment
   b. codicil
   c. addendum
   d. exhibit

79. A property manager should do all of the following EXCEPT
   a. screen prospective tenants for the HIV/AIDS virus for the protection of the other tenants.
   b. show available rental units to prospective tenants.
   c. produce the highest possible profit for the owner.
   d. execute leases.

80. When a property owner leases his or her property, at the end of the lease, he or she has
   a. a reversionary interest in the property.
   b. a remainderman interest in the property.
   c. 30 days to terminate the lease.
   d. a possessory right to the property.

81. Office space rents for $700 per month. The tenant has a three-year lease. Your commission is 7% of the gross lease; what is your fee?
   a. $1,764
   b. $1,674
   c. $490
   d. $1,470

82. Which fee does NOT have to be disclosed in a lender's advertisement when the actual note interest rate is mentioned?
   a. required down payment
   b. appraisal fee
   c. number of payments over loan term
   d. monthly payment amount

83. An owner who transfers real property through a will is known as the
   a. testator.
   b. legatee.
   c. devisee.
   d. beneficiary.

84. An apartment unit rents for $500 per month the first year and $550 per month the second year. How much total rent will this tenant pay during his two-year lease?
   a. $16,200
   b. $6,600
   c. $12,600
   d. $6,000

85. What are fiduciary duties?
   a. duties owed by all real estate licensees to sellers
   b. duties of performance owed by clients in all contractual agreements
   c. duties of agents to principals
   d. duties regarding monetary obligations

86. Under Regulation Z, the right of rescission does NOT apply to
   a. home equity loans.
   b. owner-occupied residential first mortgages.
   c. refinancing a home.
   d. both a and c

87. In comparing a competitive market analysis to a comparative market analysis, what is the differing factor?
   a. sold comparables used
   b. amenity differences between the comparables
   c. adjustments for time of sale, such as location and property condition
   d. properties currently for sale in the same market area

88. Fines for noncompliance under Regulation Z are imposed by which jurisdiction?
   a. municipal court
   b. county court
   c. state attorney general's office
   d. Federal Reserve

89. Simon Hersch, a salesperson associated with broker Bob King, lists a house for sale for $620,000, with 5% commission due at closing. Three weeks later, the owner accepts an offer for $595,000, brought in by Simon. Bob's practice is that 45% of commissions go to the brokerage and the rest to the salesperson. How much will Simon make on the sale?
   a. $17,050
   b. $32,725
   c. $16,362.50
   d. $13,387.50

90. Ownership of real property includes the land, the improvements, and certain rights often referred to as the "bundle of rights." Which of the following is NOT included in these rights?
   a. exclusion
   b. enjoyment
   c. disposition
   d. encumbrance

91. A salesperson has earned $120,000 in gross commissions this year. If the average commission is 2.6% per transaction, and the salesperson receives 60% of the commission from each transaction, approximately how much sales volume has that salesperson settled this year?
   a. $7,200,007.69
   b. $4,615,380.05
   c. $7,692,307.69
   d. $8,000,000

92. Gina Prince, the buyer, has entered into a contract to purchase a house owned by Oscar LaClare. During the period of time of this executory contract, which of the following statements is true?
   a. Gina has equitable title to the property.
   b. Oscar has equitable title to the property.
   c. Gina has an escrow interest in the property.
   d. Oscar has equitable title to the property, and Gina has an escrow interest in the property.

93. Laura Murphy is buying a new home for $193,000. She makes a $40,000 down payment and finances the balance with a 7.5% 30-year conventional loan. The factor for repayment is $7 per thousand. After making the first payment, what is the remaining balance on Laura's loan?
   a. $153,135.25
   b. $152,808.75
   c. $152,635.25
   d. $152,885.25

94. Which of the following would be classified as "limited" common elements in a condominium development?
   a. elevators
   b. hallways
   c. assigned parking places
   d. limited access gates

95. The legal right by which the state may acquire property to widen a state highway is
   a. escheat.
   b. eminent domain.
   c. enterprise zoning.
   d. enabling legislation.

96. A borrower must pay $5,600 for points on a $140,000 loan. How many points is the lender charging for this loan?
   a. 2.5
   b. 4
   c. 4.5
   d. 5

97. In determining the value of an income property, the appraiser will use the net operating income of $56,792 and a capitalization rate of 11.5%. What is the indicated value (rounded to the nearest dollar)?
   a. $653,108
   b. $650,000
   c. $493,843
   d. $553,843

98. If a bilateral contract is signed,
   a. either party may back out prior to closing.
   b. both parties are legally obligated to perform.
   c. the seller can be forced to perform on the agreement.
   d. the buyer can be forced to perform on the agreement.

99. In the reconciliation of an appraisal on a home in a large subdivision, the appraiser's decision of value would rely most on which appraisal approach?

a. cost

b. market data

c. income

d. reproduction

100. A residential broker usually relies on which form of valuation to assist a seller in setting the listing price?

a. *ad valorem* tax assessment

b. fee appraisal prepared by a licensed appraiser

c. cost approach analysis

d. competitive market analysis

► Answers

1. c. A devise is the transfer of property under a will. The person who signs the will is the testator or devisor, and the person receiving the property according to the will is the devisee.

2. a. 850' times 850' divided by 9 is just less than 80,278 square yards.

3. a. Bob will get a mortgage for $112,800 ($141,000 × 80%). Three points will cost $3,384 ($112,800 × .03). The Franks will end up with $141,000 less $3,384, or $137,616. This is $384 less than Anne Hill's all cash offer ($138,000 − $137,616).

4. b. 6.25% − 5.75% = .50% reduction needed; .50% ÷ .25% per discount point = 2 discount points must be paid. A discount point is equal to 1% of the loan amount: 2% = .02; $350,000 × .02 = $7,000 must be paid in discount points.

5. b. Federal law requires that a lead-paint disclosure form be given to all tenants and buyers if the building was constructed before 1978.

6. d. The premium paid to purchase mortgage insurance provided by FHA is referred to as MIP, or mortgage insurance premium.

7. d. Capitalization rate for annual rate of return on investment is computed by dividing a property's annual net income by the property value. This math problem is solved by dividing $144,500 (net operating income) by $850,000 (property value), which equals a capitalization rate of 17%.

8. c. A negative cash flow can be offset by a substantial increase in property value. Even in ownership of a personal residence where there is a negative cash flow, the house could be a good investment if it is sold at a substantial gain over the original purchase price.

9. a. Improvements are human-made additions and are an economic characteristic of real estate. Nonhomogeniety means there are no two parcels of real estate exactly alike. Immobility means that the land cannot be moved, and indestructibility means that the land cannot be destroyed.

10. b. The mortgage banker is an intermediary between the primary and secondary markets and may make direct loans. A mortgage broker operates only in the primary market and brokers the loan.

11. b. A buyer's representation agreement should be a specific outline of what is expected of the broker and of the buyer.

12. a. Under federal law, to qualify as an innocent landowner, a purchaser must have the property professionally inspected for environmental hazards prior to taking ownership. If the property is not inspected prior to ownership, the owner is responsible for all previous environmental hazards.

13. a. There is very little security in an investment before construction is started; therefore, to attract an investor, the developer must offer the greatest return.

14. d. Improvements eventually reach a point at which they no longer result in an increase in value. In the case of a larger home in an area with smaller homes, the law of diminishing returns applies. In the case of a small home in an area with much larger homes, the law of increasing returns will apply.

15. a. External or economic depreciation is something outside the property that may adversely affect the value of the property.

16. c. Buyer's title insurance covers monetary losses due to a covered loss of title up to the face amount of the policy. It does not guarantee ownership, nor is it transferable.

17. c. A 5% vacancy rate is considered normal; anything lower means rents are too low.

18. d. The gross rent multiplier is a number derived from a sold comparable to determine the value of an income property being appraised. The gross rent multiplier is multiplied by object property monthly rent to determine its current market value.

19. d. An abstract of title is a history of a property's legal records prepared by an abstracter. There is no insurance for loss of money or possession if title problems occur in the future.

20. a. Under FIRREA, appraisers need to be certified by the state to perform an appraisal as part of a federally related transaction when the property value exceeds $1,000,000.

21. a. A blanket mortgage covers more than one parcel of real estate and more than one lender funds a participation mortgage. A package mortgage includes both real and personal property.

22. c. Puffing is exaggeration or using superlatives rather than stating facts. Promising future profits is misrepresentation.

23. d. The real estate lender will be greatly concerned with how a prospective borrower has performed on previous real estate loans.

24. d. State laws and court decisions vary on whether potential buyers are entitled to notification of past murders, suicides, and other "stigmas."

25. b. The ADA provides that persons with disabilities have full and equal access to services and facilities of public property.

26. d. An acre (43,560 sq. ft.) ÷ 2 = 21,780 sq. ft.

27. d. Under the Fair Housing Act, the federal law prohibits discrimination in housing based on gender.

28. c. Always follow the statutory law when there is conflict with the code of any private or trade organization.

29. b. A landlord of residential property is obligated to protect the tenant's safety and health during the term of the lease, according to local and state laws. The lease cannot be in conflict with these requirements.

30. a. Incurable depreciation includes items that cost more to remedy than is economically feasible or that exist outside the property and cannot be changed.

31. a. If a power company wants to lay a service line across customer properties and has to acquire an irrevocable right to do so, that right would be called an easement in gross.

32. d. Reconciliation is the art of analyzing and effectively weighing the findings from the three approaches to value.

33. d. The Federal Consumer Credit Protection Act includes the TILA. HUD's Regulation X regulates the Real Estate Settlement Procedures Act.

34. a. A metes and bounds survey begins at the point of beginning and ends at the point of beginning in order to describe the entire tract.

35. b. Radon gas is a naturally occurring gas that may cause deadly health hazards in high concentrations inside a structure.

36. d. A variance is a change in zoning requirements to lessen restrictions when building site hardships occur, such as limited building sites.

37. c. The lack of dollar consideration may invalidate an option. The courts want "something at risk" for the right to purchase/terminate at a later time.

38. a. Discrimination based on a person's gender was added to fair housing laws through the Housing and Community Development Act of 1974.

39. a. The mere payment of a fee does not indicate an agency relationship.

40. b. Ownership in severalty, that is, severed from anyone else's interest, would give the individual owner complete freedom to dispose of the property.

41. d. A metes and bounds survey is the most accurate way to locate and bound a parcel of real property.

42. d. A quitclaim deed grants no covenants or warranties from the seller to the buyer. If the seller has no ownership rights, then the buyer will not acquire any title; also, the buyer will not have any claim against the seller.

43. b. A budget mortgage is a mortgage wherein the lender will escrow money from the borrower's monthly payment to pay annual taxes and insurance.

44. a. The lender will divide the loan amount by the appraised value (or purchase price, whichever is lower). This is called the loan-to-value ratio. If a property is appraised at $100,000 and the lender will lend $90,000, this would be a 90% loan to value.

45. b. $2,040 \div 1.5 \times 100 \div .8 = \$170,000$

46. c. Because a bank's funds are by definition short term, that is, from checking accounts also known as "demand deposits," the banks prefer to make short-term loans.

47. b. Immediately upon the buyer making the offer by signing the agreement of sale, a licensed real estate agent is obligated by law to voluntarily give a copy of that agreement of sale to that buyer.

48. b. Only the grantor is required to sign the deed, which must be delivered to and accepted by the grantee. It may also be accepted by the grantee's appointed representative.

49. b. A contingency creates an additional condition that must be satisfied before an agreement is fully enforceable.

50. b. Contracts must be in writing and contain all of the basic elements to be legally enforceable.

51. b. Sales date, seller financing, lot size, and location of a property are adjustments to sold comparables an appraiser must consider in determining market value of an object property. Replacement cost of a structure is used to determine value in a cost approach appraisal.

52. a. The borrower mortgages the property, giving the lender a claim against the real estate. As the one who does the mortgaging, she is the mortgagor.

53. c. 2.5% = .025; $895,000 \times .025 = \$22,375$ Donna's total commission; 20% = .20; $\$22,375 \times .20 = \$4,475$ referral fee.

54. b. Accrued means owed but not paid; therefore, an account is paid after charges were made, such as real estate property taxes or credit cards.

55. b. Square footage is calculated as length times width: ($30 \times 23 = 690$).

56. d. In making the public more aware of federal fair housing laws, Congress requires all brokers to display the HUD Equal Housing poster in their place of business.

57. b. A management agreement is between the owner of income property and a management firm or individual property manager that outlines the scope of the manager's authority.

58. a. Equitable title is an interest in *acquiring* legal title. Legal title will not be obtained until the buyer has actually purchased the property.

59. c. ECOA passed in 1974 and amended in 1976 protects against discrimination in lending.

60. c. The formula for the income approach is NOI divided by cap rate = value: $99,000 × .95 = $94,050 net income; $99,000 × .3 = $29,700 operating expense; $94,050 − $29,700 = $64,350 NOI; $64,350 ÷ .15 = $429,000.

61. c. General agency gives the property manager, the agent, rights to act on behalf of the owner, the principal, to conduct the business of income producing property. This may include signing leases, handling monies, signing maintenance contracts, and any other functions granted by the property management agreement.

62. d. Earnest money is used to partially satisfy the transaction sales price on behalf of the buyer; therefore, it would be a credit to the buyer on the closing statement.

63. b. Laches is a legal tenet to set a statute of limitations on court-ordered removal of a deed restriction violation. A property owner's failure to act timely may result in a loss of court-ordered action to correct a deed restriction violation.

64. d. Not offering as many choices is considered less favorable treatment. It is also discrimination based on race, but that choice was not given in the question.

65. c. Smoking rights are not protected under fair housing laws. Landlords may enforce no smoking as a lease provision.

66. c. The Real Estate Settlement and Procedures Act requires the use of the HUD closing statement on all federal related one- to four-family home loans.

67. d. An easement appurtenant runs with the land, which means that if the property is transferred, the easement goes with it to the new owner.

68. d. If an offer is changed at all, it becomes a rejection combined with a new offer. The offeree is not obligated to accept this new offer.

69. b. The buyer's agent should notify the seller's agent (listing agent for Broker B) that she has an offer from her buyer and deliver it for presentation to the seller.

70. b. Title to property may be acquired by adverse possession, which means that a person by means of open, notorious, hostile, and continuous possession for a statutorily number of years may be granted ownership.

71. b. The number of realty brokers in a market area has no effect on property market value, because the market is sensitive to the economic theory of supply and demand. However, agency contracts that brokers have with their clients demand that the brokers obtain the best price for their clients.

72. c. $2,700 divided by 360 days equals $7.50 per day, times 254 days equals $1,905 debit to the seller. January 1 through September 14 equals 254 days (statutory method).

73. b. The new landlord is responsible for the return of the security deposits, which should have been credited to her when the sale was settled.

74. a. Annual net operating income results after operating expenses are deducted from gross income. Annual net operating income divided by appraiser capitalization rate equals property value.

75. a. A deed of trust mortgage permits the trustee/fiduciary to sell the property at public auction to protect the lender's/beneficiary's lien position without a judicial court hearing.

76. d. The mortgagor (borrower) who deeds the property into trust for the mortgagee (lender) will lose ownership through foreclosure.

77. d. The four unities required for the creation of a joint tenancy are time, title, possession, and interest.

78. c. An addition to a contract to complete the agreement is an addendum. After the parties have entered into contract and desire to change some part of the contract, an amendment is used.

79. a. People with HIV/AIDS are members of a protected class (disability) and cannot be discriminated against.

80. a. A lease is a temporary condition. Ownership remains with the owner. Revert means to "bounce back" to the owner.

81. a. $700 per month × 12 (1 year) = $8,400 × 3 (3-year lease) = $25,200 × 7% = $1,764.

82. b. A lender-required appraisal fee is not disclosed in advertising under Regulation Z, because it is not a component in computing loan annual percentage rate.

83. a. A person who wills his or her property upon death to an heir is called the testator, or will maker. The legatee, devisee, and beneficiary are parties that receive property both real and personal through a will.

84. c. $6,000 for first year (500 × 12); $6,600 for second year (550 × 12); that totals $12,600 for two years.

85. c. The relationship of trust and loyalty exists between agents and principals or clients. Fiduciary duties require that an agent representing a client be obedient and loyal, make full disclosure of all material facts, maintain confidentiality, account for all monies, and perform competently.

86. b. The right of rescission does not apply to owner-occupied residential first mortgage loans, but it does apply to refinancing a home mortgage and to a home equity loan.

87. d. A competitive market analysis includes both sold comparables and the sales price of current properties on the market to determine value. A comparative market analysis evaluates only sold comparables in property valuation, which results in a competitive market analysis being more informative as to value of the object property.

88. d. Regulation Z, which is part of the Truth-in-Lending Act, is under the supervision of the Federal Reserve, which would impose fines for noncompliance.

89. c. Total commission is $29,750 (5% of sale price $595,000). Simon receives $16,362.50 (55% of $29,750).

90. d. An encumbrance is a claim or lien attached to the property. The bundle of rights include possession, control, enjoyment, exclusion, and disposition.

91. c. $120,000 ÷ .60 ÷ .026 is approximately $7,692,307.69.

92. a. The interest held by a buyer under a sales contract, installment contract, or contract for deed gives the purchaser the right to obtain absolute ownership from the legal title holder at a specified time under certain conditions.

93. d. 153 × 7 = $1,071 PI; $153,000 × .075 ÷ 12 is $956.25 interest; $1,071 − $956.25 = $114.75 principal; $153,000 − $114.75 = $152,885.25 remaining balance.

94. **c.** Assigned parking spaces are limited to specific unit owners, whereas the other items are unlimited in their use and are available to all unit owners.

95. **b.** Eminent domain is the power by which the federal government, the state, or other political entity may take private property for necessary public use with just compensation to the private owner.

96. **b.** Divide the dollar amount of the discount points by the loan amount: $5,600 ÷ $140,000 = .04, or 4 points.

97. **c.** Net operating income ÷ capitalization rate = value; 11.5% = .115; $56,792 ÷ .115 = $493,843.47, which is rounded to $493,843.

98. **b.** A bilateral contract is one in which both parties make promises and are charged with performance of the agreement.

99. **b.** Market data approach appraisal reveals the current trend in market sales, which reflects parties attitudes toward real estate value.

100. **d.** A competitive market analysis is the least expensive method of determining value for a seller with much greater accuracy than tax assessor value. This value information is commonly available through broker networking systems, such as a multiple-listing service.

▶ Scoring

Once again, in order to evaluate how you did on this last practice exam, find the number of questions you got right. Take a look at the following table to see what problem areas remain.

The key to success in almost any pursuit is to prepare for all you're worth. By taking the practice exams in this book, you have made yourself better pre-pared than other people who will be taking the exam with you. You have diagnosed where your strengths and weaknesses lie and learned how to deal with the various kinds of questions that will appear on the test. So go into the exam with confidence, knowing that you are ready and equipped to do your best.

EXAM 4 FOR REVIEW	
Topic	**Question Numbers**
Financing	3, 6, 10, 21, 23, 33, 43, 44, 46, 52, 59, 86, 93
Settlement/Transfer of Property	1, 16, 19, 42, 48, 54, 62, 66, 70, 72, 75, 76, 83
Property Management	8, 13, 17, 25, 27, 29, 57, 61, 73, 79, 81, 84, 94
Property Valuations/Appraisal	7, 14, 18, 20, 30, 32, 51, 71, 74, 87, 97, 99, 100
Property Characteristics	9, 12, 31, 34, 35, 36, 40, 41, 63, 67, 77, 90, 95
Business Practices	5, 15, 22, 24, 28, 38, 56, 64, 65, 69, 82, 88,
Contracts/Agency Relationships	11, 37, 39, 47, 49, 50, 58, 68, 78, 80, 85, 92, 98
Mathematics	2, 4, 26, 45, 53, 55, 60, 89, 91, 96

How to Use ▶
the CD-ROM ▶

SO YOU THINK you are ready for your exam? Here's a great way to build confidence and *know* you are ready: Use LearningExpress's Real Estate Licensing Tester AutoExam CD-ROM software developed by PEARSoft Corporation of Wellesley, Massachusetts. The disk, included inside the back cover of this book, can be used with any PC running Windows 95/98/ME/NT/2000/XP. (Sorry, it doesn't work with Macintosh.) The following description represents a typical "walk through" the software.

To install the program:

1. Insert the CD-ROM into your CD-ROM drive. The CD should run automatically. If it does not, proceed to Step 2.
2. From Windows, select **Start**, then choose **Run**.
3. Type D:\Setup
4. Click **OK**.

The screens that follow will walk you through the installation procedure.

From the Main Menu, select **Take Exams**. (After you have taken at least one exam, use **Review Exam Results** to see your scores.)

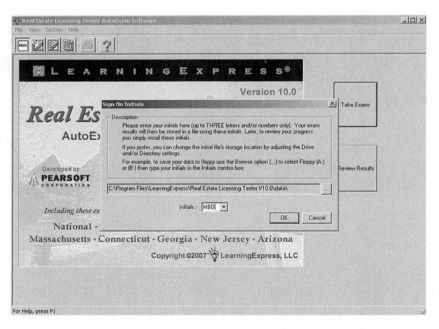

Now enter your initials. This allows you to record your progress and review your performance for as many simulated exams as you would like. Notice that you can also change the drive and/or folder where your exam results are stored. If you want to save to a floppy drive, for instance, click on the **Browse** button and then choose the letter of your floppy drive.

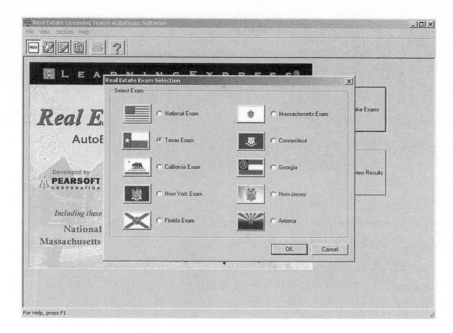

Now, because this CD-ROM supports ten different real estate exams, you need to select your exam of interest. Let's try Texas, as shown above.

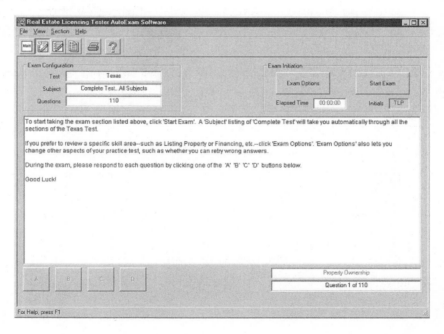

Now you are in the **Take Exams** section, as shown above. You can choose **Start Exam** to start taking your test, or **Exam Options.** The next screenshot shows you what your **Exam Options** are.

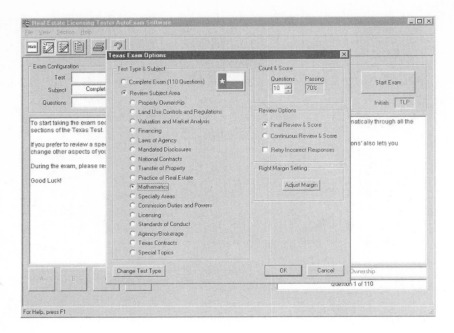

Choosing **Exam Options** gives you plenty of options to help you fine-tune your rough spots. How about a little math to warm up? Click **Review Subject Area**, and then the **Mathematics** option. Choose the number of questions you want to review right now. On the right, you can choose whether to wait until you have finished to see how you did (**Final Review & Score**) or have the computer tell you after each question, whether your answer is right (**Continuous Review & Score**). Choose **Retry Incorrect Responses** to get a second chance at questions you answered incorrectly. (This option works best with **Review Subject Area** rather than **Complete Exam.**) If you have chosen the wrong exam, you can click **Change Test Type** to go back and choose your exam. When you finish choosing your options, click **OK**. Then click the **Start Exam** button on the main exam screen. Your screen will look like the one shown next.

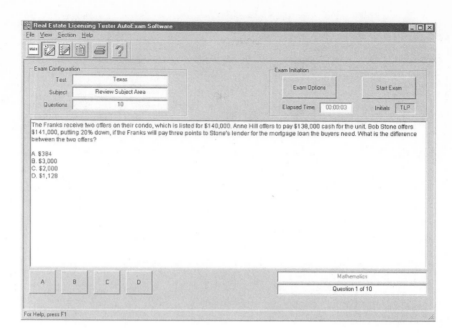

Questions come up one at a time, just as they will on the real exam, and you click on A, B, C, or D to answer.

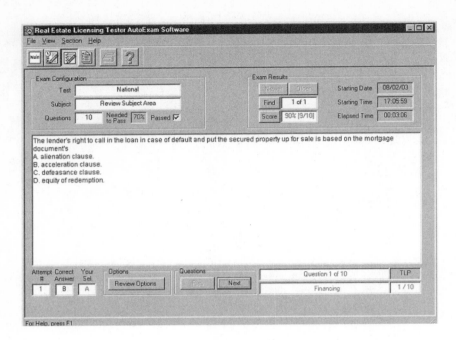

When you have finished your exam or subject area, you will have the option of switching to **Review Exams**. (If you don't want to review your results now, you can always do it later by clicking on the **Review Exams Section** button on the toolbar.) When you use **Review Results**, you will see your score and whether you passed. The questions come up one at a time. Under **Review Options**, you can choose whether to look at all the questions or just the ones you missed. You can also choose whether you want an explanation of the correct answer displayed automatically under the question.

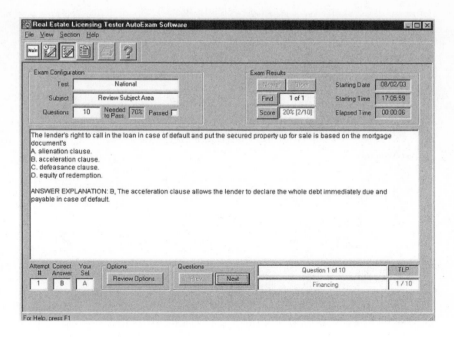

When you are in the **Review Results** section, click on the **Find** button to look at all the exams you have taken.

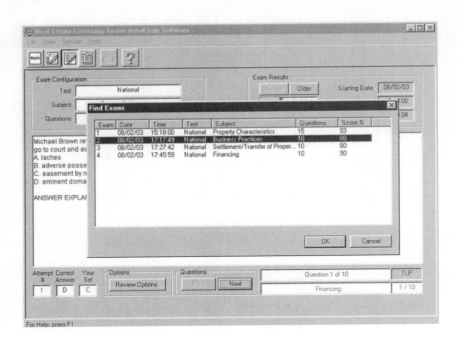

By default, your exam results are listed from newest to oldest, but you can sort them by any of the headings. For instance, if you want to see your results arranged by score, you can click on the **Score %** heading. To go to a particular exam you have taken, double-click on it.

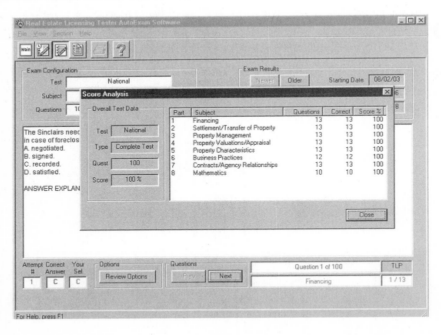

In the **Review Results** section, if you click on the **Score %** button, you will get a breakdown of your score on the exam you're currently reviewing. This section shows you how you did on each of the subject areas on the exam. Once again, you can sort the subject areas by any of the column headings. For instance, if you click on the

Score % heading, the program will order the subject areas from your highest percentage score to your lowest. You can see which areas are your strong and weak points, so you will know what to review.

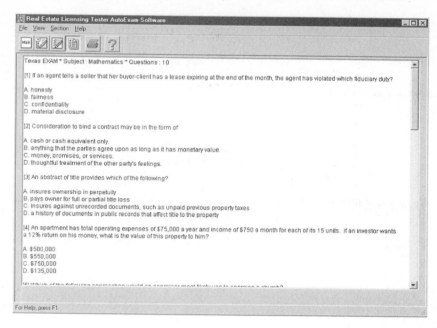

What's that? No time to work at the computer? Click the **Print Exams** menu bar button and you will have a full-screen review of an exam that you can print out, as shown above. Then take it with you.

For technical support, call 800-295-9556.

NOTES

NOTES